The
Ransom
of the Soul

The
Ransom
of the Soul

AFTERLIFE AND WEALTH IN
EARLY WESTERN CHRISTIANITY

Peter Brown

 Harvard University Press

Cambridge, Massachusetts
London, England

First Harvard University Press paperback edition, 2018
Second printing

LIBRARY OF CONGRESS CATALOGING-IN-PUBLICATION DATA
Brown, Peter, 1935–
The ransom of the soul: afterlife and wealth in early
western Christianity / Peter Brown
pages cm
Includes bibliographical references and index.
ISBN: 978-0-674-96758-8 (hardcover : alk. paper)
ISBN: 978-0-674-98397-7 (pbk.)
1. Future life—Christianity—History of doctrines—Early church,
ca. 30–600.   2. Wealth—Religious aspects—Christianity—History of
doctrines—Early church, ca. 30–600.   I. Title.
BT821.3.B76 2015
270.2—dc23
2014037508

For Betsy

Contents

Preface

IN THIS BOOK I wish to approach a fragment of the deep past of
Christianity. This is the belief that was held, both in Jewish
and in Christian circles, that heaven and earth could be joined
by money. I will concentrate particularly on the manner in
which the imagined joining of heaven and earth through
money was held to affect the fate of the soul in the afterlife. I
will deal with the Christianity of the Latin world, between
around 250 and around 650 AD—that is, in the transitional period between the end of the ancient world and the beginning of
the Middle Ages in Western Europe. I will attempt to show
how the social and economic context of the Christian Church
in Western Europe changed in the course of this period, and
how these changes were reflected in changes in Christian
representations of the other world and in the religious practices
connected with the death and afterlife of Christian believers.

But this book is not only about death and the soul. It is also
about the manner in which the other world was believed to

impinge on this world—how the other world was brought into this world, through accounts of dreams and visions, through constant preaching and meditation on the theme of the Last Judgment, through miracles connected with the tombs of long-dead saints, and, increasingly, through the proliferation of churches and monasteries whose primary function was to offer prayer on behalf of the dead.

It might help readers to know, at the outset, what this book offers, and where it steps aside from many traditions of scholarship from which I have decided to part company. In the first place, it is a book that sees the formation of Christian views of the afterlife in terms of a perpetual argument among Christians themselves. This emphasis on constant argument is different from treatments that are content to summarize the development of a Christian doctrine of the afterlife as if it were the unfolding of a single master narrative.

In many traditional histories of the Catholic Church, the master narrative emphasizes the slow blossoming through the ages of notions inherited from the very beginnings of Christianity. In Protestant circles, by contrast, the master narrative takes the form of plotting, through the centuries, the loss of some original, reputedly more Christian, vision of death and the afterlife. Either way, these traditions of scholarship tend to tell the reader *what* happened, not *why* it happened. Many narratives of these changes are written like an exercise in painting by numbers, in which different blocks in a landscape are filled in, one by one, with the appropriate, numbered colors. In the same way, successive Christian representations of the afterlife are recounted in due order, century by century. The result is a thor-

oughly reliable account of the various phases of Christian belief on this topic. We move from the mighty eschatological
hopes for a new heaven and a new earth that were characteristic of the early church to a sense of the drawn-out and painful
journey of the individual soul that is associated with the emergence of the medieval Catholic doctrine of purgatory. But we
end with a somewhat flat and tensionless picture that conveys
little sense of the shifts and struggles within the Christian communities that caused certain notions of the afterlife to emerge
with unusual urgency at certain times, for reasons that were
never exclusively theological.

In this sense, the present book continues the approach I
adopted when writing my larger book, *"Through the Eye of a
Needle": Wealth, the Fall of Rome, and the Making of Christianity
in the West, 350–550 AD* (Princeton University Press, 2012). That
also was a book about continuous arguments. In it, I dealt with
the issue of the use of wealth in the Christian churches. I attempted to show how arguments about wealth and poverty in
Christianity are not timeless matters. They emerged from the
specific, concrete circumstances of the Christian communities
of the Latin West in differing regions and at different times. I
emphasized that, in order to understand the urgency with which
many of these arguments were pursued, the historian of the
Christian Church has to take into account the social and economic history of the period. This concern for a precise context
also led me to point out that many scholarly views of the social
and economic texture of late Roman and early medieval society, though frequently repeated in standard accounts of the
period, are out of date. The revision of these views directly

affects our judgment on Christian debates on wealth and poverty and on the manner in which the Christian churches accumulated and used their wealth in this period.

In many ways, this book adopts the same approach—applied this time to debates about the afterlife in Western Christianity. But this is as far as the resemblance goes. Readers should know that this book is by no means a "spin-off" of *Through the Eye of a Needle.*" For the relation between wealth and the afterlife involves issues of the religious imagination that I felt I did not need to address when writing *"Through the Eye of a Needle."* At that time, wealth, poverty, and the arguments concerning both, as they existed in this world, held my attention. Now I am concerned with the other world. It is the relation between society and the religious imagination, as it played upon the theme of the afterlife, that is central to my argument.

In now focusing on these issues, I have returned to work in which I was engaged in the late 1990s. In a series of articles and lectures that were published between 1997 and 2000, I dealt with the manner in which changing views of the afterlife (which included the emergence of a notion of purgatory) reflected the cultural, religious, and social changes that characterized the transition from late antiquity to the early Middle Ages. These changes led to the emergence of notions of the afterlife (and, consequently, of the individual) that made the Christianity of Western Europe significantly different from that of its Eastern Christian neighbors—in Byzantium and in the Middle East—and from Islam.

By choosing to approach the history of Christian notions of the afterlife in this manner—in terms of the arguments they provoked and of the social and religious pressures that brought these notions to the forefront—I realize that I have ventured, once again, into challenging territory. I have had to learn to weave into the standard narratives of Christian views of the afterlife a sense of the social context and the social implications of these views. As difficult as it was to determine the cause and nature of the changes in notions of the afterlife in this period, I felt I also needed to determine the *pace* of these changes— when did they happen, how fast did they happen, to what extent did they represent breaks in the continuity of a religious system, and to what extent were they continuous with previous conglomerates of notions, whether Christian or non-Christian? Altogether, I learned the hard way, by constant reference to major works on the history of early Christianity, that the issue of the pace of change in a religious community—and especially of a community as fluid as the emergent Christianity of the late antique period—is the one aspect of Christian history that is most challenging to the historian. And yet it is the aspect that is most often taken for granted by the majority of modern scholars.

However, the issue of the pace of change in the religious imagination is crucial. It is difficult enough for secular historians of Rome and of the world after Rome to measure the pace of change in well-known institutions and social structures. For some scholars the pace of change in the later empire seems to have been vertiginous. Others do not accept this view. Historians continue to disagree as to whether the fall of Rome marked a drastic rupture in the flow of Western history, or whether this fall was only one transformation among many—and not the most disastrous one at that. Their disagreement shows how difficult it is to measure the pace of change in a complex society. To put it briefly: Is the pace of change in the last centuries of Rome to be measured only by a brisk series of dates—by the reigns of emperors, the dates of battles, and the course of well-known barbarian invasions? Or are these dates no more than so many whitecaps on the surface of a wider ocean whose tides run at a different speed from that of the more obvious political and military events—sometimes faster, sometimes much slower?

When it comes to the imaginative structures of religious communities such as the Christian Church, it has proved even more difficult than it has been for secular historians to establish a pace of change and to isolate moments of definitive transformation or rupture. What I myself have learned, when writing this book, is that some of the most decisive changes in the Christian imagination cannot be linked in any direct way to the brisk pace of history as it is conventionally related in textbooks of the history of the fall of Rome and the beginning of the Middle Ages. Grand events, such as the conversion of Constantine, did not necessarily affect the views of the afterlife of the Christians whom we first meet, in Chapter 1, assembled at the graves of their loved ones. No sense of growing insecurity in the Roman Empire of the late fourth and early fifth centuries can, of itself, explain the lucubrations of Augustine on the tenacity of sin. No shock of barbarian invasion can account for the emergence of a fear of hell and of the demonic forces that lie in wait for the soul at the moment of death. These dark imaginings defy our attempts to link them to known political and social crises. They gathered momentum generations before the fall of the empire in the West, and they did so in some of the most sheltered and prosperous provinces of the Roman world. In the same way, no brutal rupture between a Roman order and a new, "barbarian" age—such as we are often tempted to imagine—can explain the differences between an Augustine and a Gregory of Tours.

Yet there is change, and it is the business of the historian to dig deeper to look for the roots of these changes in phenomena that are not always those privileged by conventional narratives of the period. This is what I have attempted to do here. Whether such an approach proves helpful to those who wish to understand the manner in which Christians and their notions of the afterlife changed over time in the days before and after Rome is for the reader to judge.

But first things first. In order to set the scene for my account, I begin at the end of my story: with a sketch of the afterlife as this was imagined by a leading Christian of the late seventh century AD—Bishop Julian of Toledo, writing in 688 AD. How much Julian's notions of the afterlife represented a change since early Christian times can be measured by his encounter, through the books in his library, with the very different Christianity of a leading Christian from more than four centuries prior—with Cyprian, bishop of Carthage from 248 to 258 AD. It is to this contrast between two ages—between the third and the seventh century—that we now turn.

Chronology

The
Ransom
of the Soul

The Latin West: 250–650 AD.

Introduction

As I made plain in my Preface, this book grew out of three public lectures. Because the content of the lectures was limited, I expand upon them here by providing a brief introduction to the big picture—to the principal outlines of the development of Latin Christian views of the afterlife between 200 and 700 AD.

For the sake of brevity, I will compare two ages—the world of the early church in the late second and third centuries and the early medieval world of the seventh century: in other words, the beginning and the end point of our story. Only when this comparison is made—when we are sure of what these two worlds (separated by almost half a millennium) have in common and what they do *not* share—can we fully explore the implications of the changes that led from the one to the other. I have been encouraged to adopt this approach by a little-read text from the seventh century that I first read in the mid-1990s. It is the

Prognosticon of Bishop Julian of Toledo. The text has fascinated me ever since I read it. It struck me as a poignant document.

Julian of Toledo, 688 AD

In 688 AD, Bishop Julian of Toledo, the capital of the Visigothic kingdom of Spain, and Bishop Idalius of Barcelona were quietly reading in a library. Idalius was an ill man, tormented by gout. Now that Toledo had emptied out as the king and his army left for their springtime campaign, Julian set to work among his books to put together an anthology of the great writers of the Latin Church with which to comfort his sick friend at the approach of death.

Julian called his anthology a *Prognosticon futuri saeculi—A Medical Report on the Future World.*[1] The collection was supposed to have the certainty of a doctor's prognosis. It presented the future of the soul, stage by stage, from the moment of death, through an afterlife in a disembodied state, to the final, glorious remaking of all creation (that included the rejoining of body and soul) at the time of the Resurrection and the Last Judgment.

The book became a best seller in medieval times.[2] This is not surprising. Julian's *Prognosticon* introduced the reader to what Claude Carozzi, his best exponent, has called a "universe of certitudes" on death and the fate of the soul.[3] It claimed to have behind it the weight of over four centuries of Christian thought. The bishop of Toledo had worked his way along the shelves of his capacious library to make extracts on the subject of death and the afterlife from every Christian author that he could find, from the great Bishop Cyprian of Carthage in the mid-third century to Pope Gregory the Great at the end of the sixth century. It is an anthology that spans almost the entire length of the four centuries that we will study.

The *Prognosticon* is precious to us because it gives us nothing less than a panorama of Christian views of the afterlife as they were held at the very end of an ancient Christianity, on the threshold of the Middle Ages. Little did Julian know that he himself lived at the end of an age. Only a generation later, the Visigothic kingdom would be swept away by Arab invaders from the distant East, and Toledo would become, for many centuries, a Muslim city.

This poignancy is not all that there is to Julian's *Prognosticon*. What I had not realized at the time that I first read it was that the *Prognosticon* offers more than a precious summary of beliefs about the afterlife in Julian's own times. It also gives the reader an opportunity to do something that historians seldom have the chance to do—to read over the shoulder of an ancient author as he reads texts that we ourselves have read. What did Julian make of the early Christian works from which he made his extracts? In what way did what he saw in them differ from what we, as historians of the early church, might see in the same texts?

This historical approach, of course, reflects modern methods. Julian was little aware of the gulf of time between himself and the earlier texts that he had copied out. He was convinced that the anthology that he had composed for his friend represented a timeless and unbroken tradition. He grouped extracts from all periods around each aspect of the afterlife. He showed no sense that these extracts might reflect Christianities of very different ages. Why should he have? He was not a modern historian of religion. He had an urgent task. He was a Christian bishop compiling a manual—almost a scientific manual—of eternal verities with which to help his friend pass through death.

But once modern historians come to place theses extracts in their chronological order, they realize that they speak from very different periods of Christianity. Each of these periods was characterized by a different worldview. We (as historians) could have told Julian that, had he met many of the early Christian authors whom he cites in his anthology, they might have struck him, despite their common Christianity, as strange, almost Jurassic creatures from a world very different from his own times; and these early Christian authors, in turn, would have felt the same about him.

So let us look at the extracts in Julian's *Prognosticon* from the earliest Christian authors known to him. We will see what he saw in them. We will also see what he probably did not know as we do—the exact historical context of these extracts and the worldview that each of them reflected.

Martyrdom in Carthage, 250 AD

In the first place, we are looking at an attitude toward death and the afterlife that was very different from that of Julian. The earliest writer that he extracted was Cyprian, bishop of Carthage from 248 to 258 AD. Cyprian was a dominant figure in the creation of a Christian view of the afterlife. He had the added authority that he himself had ended his life as a martyr. Julian copied out whole pages of Cyprian's tract *On Mortality* and his *Exhortation to Martyrdom addressed to Fortunatus*.[4] In these tracts, Cyprian stared through death. He presented death as a mere moment to be "got through"—*expuncta*.[5] The death of the martyr was the happiest of all, because, for the martyr, death and entry into heaven were instantaneous: "What a high honor it is, what a feeling of security, to exit from here in joy, to go forth covered with glory . . . To close in a moment the eyes by which human beings and the world are seen, and to open these same eyes instantly to see God and Christ." For a martyr, there was no "afterlife," only the instant presence of God. Julian may have felt a twinge of strangeness as he read these words of Cyprian. He was careful to add immediately (from the writings of Augustine) that not only martyrs, but all saints, would reach heaven in this instantaneous manner.[6]

But Cyprian was not like Julian, and not even like Augustine. The martyrs of his own time held the center of his attention. Only the martyrs were certain to enter directly into the presence of God. The entire balance of his view of the afterlife was tilted toward the martyrs.[7] The incandescent pages from the works of Cyprian that Julian had copied out to comfort his friend belonged, in fact, to a very distant Christianity, dominated by the notion of martyrdom. Let us explore for a moment this alien world.

Cyprian was no bishop of seventh-century Spain. He was the leader of a tiny religious group—probably no more than 2,500 (at most one-thirtieth of the population of Carthage). Many members of his congregation did, indeed, face death through execution as martyrs—as "witnesses"—to the Christian faith. They also faced a plague that raged in Carthage at that time. It was to brace such persons that Cyprian wrote.

They needed bracing. It would be wrong to think of the Christians of Carthage as a solid body of embattled saints, facing an unremittingly hostile world and fully prepared to die for their beliefs. As Éric Rebillard has made clear in his brilliant recent book, most early Christians in Carthage, as elsewhere, did not spend their whole time being early Christians. They had many identities. They maintained all manner of connections with a pagan society that, for most of the time, took little notice of them as Christians. Many of them did not think that being a Christian was a full-time and irrevocable identity. They joined the church easily. But when they realized that commitment to Christianity clashed with other, stronger loyalties they lapsed just as easily. For this reason, the invocation of the deaths of the martyrs by Cyprian was not the expression of a monolithic Christian community. Rather, the ideal of the death of the martyrs and the notion of their instant entry into heaven was brought forward to challenge a potentially indifferent Christian congregation. Cyprian's assertions were all the more dramatic because he was not certain that they would be heard.[8]

The need to persuade average Christians to live up to their faith ensured that, in the Carthage of Cyprian as elsewhere, the issue of the deaths of the martyrs riveted the attention of contemporaries (pagans as well as Christians). It did so in a manner that overshadowed all other Christian ruminations on the afterlife. Normal death was of little interest; martyrdom was special. Martyrdom was "a death for God, new and extraordinary."[9]

It stood for Christianity at its most extreme and at its most authentic.

For non-Christians it stood for Christianity at its most flamboyant. We must remember that to suffer martyrdom was not simply to fall victim with Christian fortitude and Christian patience to a judicial sentence carried out in relative obscurity. This is too tame a modern image, derived from a modern penal system. Public trials and public executions were part of the life of every Roman city. As a result, martyrdoms were remembered by Christians as high and terrible events, acted out in public, in law courts and amphitheaters, for all to see.[10]

Yet, what for Christians such as Cyprian was an "extraordinary" death struck the average pagan as abnormal. Christians were seen by pagans as suicidal exhibitionists. As the Emperor Marcus Aurelius (161–180) wrote in his *Meditations:* a wise man could decide to leave the world through suicide. But to court death out of a mere spirit of opposition "as is the case with the Christians" was a form of "stage heroics" that repelled him. The phrase "as . . . with the Christians" may have been added by a later copyist.[11] But the copyist got the point. Some deaths (and not only the deaths of Christians) were public theater of the most obtrusive and unwelcome sort.

We should always remember that, for the average pagan, Christian martyrs were not a unique phenomenon. They fitted all too easily into a long line of gore-soaked and crazed figures. Gladiators played with death in the arena. Their blood and mangled corpses were associated with uncanny powers.[12] Maverick philosophers also courted death by going out of their way to insult the powerful. The craziest of these, the philosopher

Peregrinus, had even toyed for a time with Christianity. He gained great prestige among Christians as a potential martyr. He ended his life, in 165 AD, by committing suicide through burning himself near the crowds assembled at Olympia for the Olympic Games.[13] The deaths of Christian martyrs did not necessarily impress outsiders. Rather, these deaths struck them as bizarre and disturbing. But pagans and Christians had one thing in common: heroic or pathological, the grisly, fully public deaths of the Christian martyrs held their attention, at the expense of more ordinary deaths.

The Resting of the Soul

Behind Christian elevation of the martyrs there lay a view of the afterlife, which, had he followed it in all its ramifications (as a modern religious historian must do), would have struck Julian, in seventh-century Toledo, as belonging to a very different world from his own. The sonorous phrases of Cyprian seemed to Julian to be part of an unbroken Christian tradition. But, in reality, Cyprian belonged to a very different world with very different views on the nature of the soul and of the afterlife.

We can appreciate this if we go back for a further half-century, to the very beginning of the third century AD. Here we will meet the indefatigable Christian author Tertullian of Carthage (ca.160–ca.240). Cyprian marked the furthest reach of Julian's vision of the early church. While Julian mined the works of Cyprian, Tertullian was not included in the *Prognosticon*. In the seventh century, Tertullian only lurked in the shadows of orthodox Catholicism as Julian knew it. He had been condemned as a heretic. But this had not been the case in the age of Cyprian. The copious and vigorously argued works of Tertullian deeply influenced the Latin Christianity of Cyprian's time and for several generations afterward. Cyprian referred to him as "the Master."

For Tertullian, the average Christian soul was a strangely subdued thing. As with Cyprian, the dim souls of the many were of little interest to him compared with the souls of the martyrs. But this was not all. The trajectory of the individual soul after death was not important to him. The notion of the afterlife was dwarfed, in Tertullian's thought, by the idea of the transformation of the entire universe associated with the Christian doctrine of the Resurrection. It was thought that this mighty transformation was about to happen. Tertullian imagined it to be so majestic, so radical, and so total as to make the interval between death and the Resurrection of the dead seem short and empty of significance.

This view of Tertullian should not be confused with the tradition of "Christian mortalism" that has survived in some circles up to today. In "Christian mortalism," the soul of the dead person is believed to be unconscious—as good as dead—until awakened again at the Resurrection and the Last Judgment. For Tertullian, the souls of the departed never lapsed into total unconsciousness. Rather, they lived a suspended, interim existence, waiting for the next great act in the drama of God's salvation to begin: the glory that would be bestowed on them at the Resurrection and after the Last Judgment.[14] To put it briefly, for Tertullian (and for many others), thought of the Big Future (the Future with a capital F) associated with the Resurrection and the Last Judgment left little room for thought on the little future (the future with a lowercase f): the future of the individual soul after death.

This attitude was widespread among Christians of the late second and early third centuries. It blocked certain imaginative options when Christians thought of death. The most notable and challenging of these blocks to the imagination was the Christian denial of the outright immortality of the soul. Many Christian thinkers thought that to speak of the soul as immortal gave too much autonomy to it. No soul could claim to go directly to heaven merely on the strength of being a soul, as pagan philosophers were believed to have said. Rather, Christian apologists insisted, against their pagan opponents, the soul itself was dependent for its very existence on the will of God. Its reward would come from God's mighty hand and in God's good time. Christians died for the Resurrection, not for the immortality of their souls.

Here we have entered truly strange territory that Julian of Toledo would barely have recognized as Christian. But the fact remains that Latin Christians in the days of Tertullian were not encouraged to believe that they would go instantly to heaven as disembodied souls (as most Christians tend to believe nowadays), far from it. In contrast, the leading pagans of the time took the ascent of the soul to heaven for granted. They believed that the souls of the great and of their own beloved (parents, wives, and children) would ascend instantly to the stars. Like tongues of flame, they returned to their natural home among the burning clusters of the Milky Way. Those who had high souls were expected to go at once to such high places.[15] On the issue of the immortality of the soul, the Christians of the age of Tertullian were the odd men out.

Tertullian (and many other leading Christians of his time) regarded belief in the immortality of the soul not only as arrogant but as trivial. The Resurrection was the center of gravity of their thought. They argued forcibly that it was not enough for the soul merely to escape from the body. Rather than fly straight to heaven, Christian souls marked time. They waited for something better—for the Big Future of the Resurrection. God would do nothing less than re-create the entire universe for their benefit. In a gesture of supreme power that defied both common sense and the most advanced findings of ancient science, God would re-create each human body, joining body and soul in an unimaginably glorious "interweave."[16] Only then would the Big Future come true. The reintegration of all creation, of all society, and of every human body was regarded by Christians as a far greater thing than was the ethereal flight of the soul to the stars. Confronted by pagan critics, Christian intellectuals (such as Tertullian) held out with seemingly crazed intensity for more—far more—than the mere immortality of the soul.

Hence for Tertullian there is a sense of time in the afterlife that would have struck Julian and his contemporaries as alien. We are dealing with a world of waiting souls. The mighty transformation, in which body and soul would be reunited and in which the tired earth itself would be turned into paradise, was worth waiting for. In the tradition represented by Tertullian and continued for many generations after him, Christian souls were expected to wait until they were reunited with their bodies. Only then could they be thought to enjoy the fullness of God's new creation. Only the souls of the martyrs escaped this shadowy time of waiting. They passed directly into paradise, for they had already become "friends of God." They could enter the blazing inner chamber of God's palace. They were "received" into His presence. They were kissed and embraced by Christ, their emperor, as privileged persons were kissed and embraced by the emperor on earth.[17]

But the martyrs formed an elite. Other souls (even the souls of the righteous) had to settle down to a little future characterized by a period of waiting. This time of waiting was by no means bleak. It was thought of as a time of rest in a secure and shaded place. The notion of repose and refreshment—of *refrigerium*—was the center of gravity of this view of the afterlife. In Christian belief and in Christian art, the notion of the refreshment of souls was conjured up through images that had always meant much to persons of the ancient Mediterranean and the Middle East. Good souls enjoyed what Tertullian called a *refrigerium interim*— a refreshing period of rest in the other world, as delightful as the taste of cool water and of food shared, in shady bowers, with boon companions.

We must remember that, in a society that placed a high value on leisure as a privilege of the elite, there was nothing wrong with waiting. The souls of the righteous enjoyed this leisure— vast leisure, such as ancient intellectuals regarded as the sine qua non for all creative thought. They could settle down to begin to understand the immensity of the change that still lay ahead of them—in the Big Future of the Resurrection. Even for the greatest souls, it took time "to become acclimatized to God."[18]

They did not ask for more. Modern persons find this notion of the afterlife puzzlingly incomplete—as would Julian of Toledo. Indeed, compared with earlier Christians, Julian is a modern man. But this is because, even in the third century, the views held with such fervor by Tertullian were becoming a little out of date. A high-pitched, Platonic notion of the soul as an utterly spiritual substance, entitled to the immediate enjoyment of the vision of God, had begun to spread in Christian circles at the expense of earlier notions of the waiting of souls. Heaven was the true "fatherland" of the soul. The idea that the souls of good Christians did not make their way instantly to heaven struck later Christians as almost a denial of Christianity itself.[19]

As we know, a view of the soul as immediately bound for heaven after death won out in Latin Christianity. This victory has placed a glass wall between ourselves and the fierce hopes of a more ancient Christianity. The notion that all souls should, as it were, mark time before entering heaven—that they should wait until God had brought about a mighty transformation of the universe as a whole—was lost in Western Christianity. It would have struck a seventh-century Christian such as Julian of Toledo as a voice from an alien world.

The Other World of Julian of Toledo

Having explored the worlds of Cyprian and Tertullian, we can now compare these worlds with that of Julian. In order to do this, let us imagine how a Tertullian or a Cyprian might have reacted to the panorama of the afterlife propounded by Julian.

What aspects of this panorama would have struck them as strange?

Put very briefly: In the writings of Cyprian (and even more so of Tertullian), the epic grandeur of the notion of the creation of a new heaven and a new earth combined with an emphasis on the utterly unique deaths of the martyrs to drain the color from average souls. There was little room left in the early Christian imagination for an interest in individual destinies and for the emergence of individual profiles among the departed. Too short an interval of time stretched between death and the glory of the Resurrection.

By contrast, for Julian of Toledo, the distance between death and Resurrection had become longer. There was time for the trajectory of each soul to be charged with individual drama and interest. An entire history of the soul after death was spread out in all its richness. The afterlife of the average Christian was not reduced to a passing moment between death and the vast upheaval of the Resurrection.

There was, of course, much in the *Prognosticon* that was directly continuous with the ancient Christianity of a Cyprian or a Tertullian. The mighty transformations associated with the Resurrection and the Last Judgment still stood on Julian's horizon. They were still there—as immense and as awesome as the Himalayas. But, by Julian's time, the humble foothills of that mighty range had become more clearly visible. The "little future" of the world between death and the Resurrection was now examined as minutely as was the "Big Future" of the end of time. Julian and Idalius wanted to know exactly what their souls would be like in that intermediate period.[20]

Indeed, the *Prognosticon* could be called a futurology of the Christian soul. The two bishops wanted to know every detail of that future. This future was no mere time of waiting. It stretched out before Julian and Idalius as an exciting landscape that might include any number of uncharted perils. Death was only the beginning of a journey. A note of tense excitement accompanied the departure of every soul into the other world at the moment of death. The deaths of great saints, or of great sinners, had come to be associated with vivid tales of near-death experiences and of deathbed encounters with angels and demons. Julian knew these tales and took them seriously.[21] Above all, unlike Cyprian, Julian was concerned with the death and afterlife of average Christians, not the unique deaths of the martyrs.

So let us look for a moment at Julian's view of the fate of the soul of every Christian after death. Three features stand out in this view. First and foremost, in Julian's imaginative world, souls no longer marked time. Each soul (provided that it was not cast into hell) moved toward heaven at a different pace. Some souls were a lot slower than others. Rather than a vast waiting room (as it was for Tertullian), the Christian other world had become like a present-day city marathon. Long lines of stragglers trailed behind the tight group of frontrunners. Second, for each of the stragglers—the nonsaints—the journey was tinged with uncertainty: which way would the soul turn as it entered this unknown world—to heaven or to hell? What otherworldly beings—angels or demons—would the soul encounter?[22] Last but not least, Julian was convinced that a purifying fire awaited some souls, through which they had to pass, each at its own speed.[23] (This was the *purgatorius ignis* that would later develop into the full-blown purgatory of the medieval and modern Catholic Church).

As a pious bishop, Idalius might still hope to wake up *statim*—at once—to see the face of Christ, as Cyprian had said that the martyrs would do. But his friend Julian's *Prognosticon* spelled out a wide range of other eventualities for less perfect souls. For each soul now had a story of its own. This was because departed souls were thought to have brought their entire lives with them into the other world. Each was marked, for good or ill, by its own, irrevocable individuality, for which it had to give account in detail (often to forbidding angelic or demonic figures). The ease with which each soul reached heaven depended on this individuality—on a complex alloy of virtues and vices, sins and merits, that had accrued in the course of a lifetime.

It was this growing attention to the destinies of individual souls in terms of the precise admixture of their sins and merits that made the world of Julian of Toledo so very different from that of Cyprian of Carthage. We have moved from an early Christianity where the unique deaths of the martyrs and the gigantic tremor of the Resurrection held the center of attention to a world where (to adopt the modern axiom) it took all sorts to make a Christian other world.

The Twilight Zone and the Ransom of the Soul

This overall development has been the subject of many excellent handbooks on Christian eschatology on which I have drawn continually and with gratitude.[24] It is the purpose of this book to take the developments that these handbooks have described and to place them against the backdrop of a changing society. As I made plain in the Preface, this will be a "why" book, not a "what" book. It will not be content simply to describe the development of Christian notions of the afterlife. It will attempt to determine why certain notions and practices emerged, why some were widely adopted and others stirred up vigorous debate, even opposition, in differing regions and in differing situations. For it is only by trying to combine the two aspects of Christian experience—the religious and the social—that we can do justice to the centuries-long process of change by which the distinctive, massive early Christian representation of the other world became the finely differentiated story of the journey of innumerable souls, the details of which Julian of Toledo had assembled for his sick friend, as he worked in his library in 688 AD.

So let us end this Introduction by following one basic theme for which changes took place over time within the churches. These changes were particularly visible. We will concentrate on one issue only: What could the living do for the dead, and what were the social repercussions of their efforts?

This is so basic a question that we frequently forget to ask it. Let me suggest that that there was something in the nature of Christian representations of the other world that seemed always to draw the living and the dead together. There was the nagging sense that both living and dead were, in some way or other, indeterminate, incomplete creatures. Each side—the living and the dead—was believed somehow to need the other. The dead, in particular, needed the living. This was true, in differing ways, of almost every religion of the ancient Mediterranean. But,

in the Christian case, the relation between the living and the
dead came to be presented, with marked emphasis, as a relation
of sin and intercession. A large number of the dead (the saints
excluded) were seen as incomplete beings because of their sins.
The living were seen to be capable of aiding the dead precisely
because they also shared with the dead a fundamental incompleteness that was increasingly ascribed to sin. It was the sense
of a shared incompleteness that gave such imaginative power to
the notion of intercession in the Christian churches of this time.

In differing forms, this was true of every stage of Christianity between the days of Cyprian and the time of Julian of
Toledo. Indeed, if we look closely at the differing models of the
Christian afterlife, we are struck by one feature that they all had
in common: In the overall picture of the other world, there was
always a "twilight zone."

This was true even in the stark world of Tertullian. Somehow,
between the blazing white of the martyrs and the jet black of
the vast majority of "impious" pagans (nonpersons destined to
hell, over whose fate Christian writers of the age of the martyrs
shed few tears and spilled little ink) there existed the great, tran-
quil number of those of the *interim*—of waiting Christian souls
who enjoyed the *refrigerium* of the other world. The waiting creatures in Tertullian's vision of the other world could not be called
"sinners" in the strict sense. But they were incomplete. They did
not suffer. They did not hope for promotion to some higher state
(in the way that, at a later time, Catholic souls hoped to exit in
due course from purgatory). For them, that promotion would
come in its own good time—at the Resurrection. But there was,
nonetheless, an unfinished quality about them, a straining for-

ward, that brought them closer to the living than to the glorious martyrs who already lived securely in paradise. The austere Tertullian found nothing strange in a husband making annual offerings at the Eucharist for the spirit of his departed wife. She may not have been a sinner. But she was still marking time, and, in that sense, she was closer to her former, still living spouse than she was to the awesomely complete, unshaken martyrs.

In later centuries, the twilight zone between the blaze of the saints and the still impenetrable darkness of the impious became ever wider. It took on the features of an entire world. This was the other world inhabited by the souls of average Christians—by the stragglers in the marathon, as it were, who were neither great saints nor hardened sinners. These souls made up the majority of the church. They were the souls of the unheroic everyday Christians in an established church that no longer produced the blinding, unique figures of the martyrs, but that had room for any number of sinners.

Latin writers closer in time to Julian of Toledo than were Tertullian and Cyprian came to peer into the twilight world of average Christians in the afterlife with ever-closer attention. The most notable of these was Pope Gregory the Great (590–604), whose works provided Julian of Toledo with a large proportion of his extracts. Gregory was convinced that Christians could make out, through dreams and visions, the principal features of the dark land beyond the grave. It was as if the afterlife was already bathed in the soft half-light of the dawn of the end of time. Gregory included many of these visions of the afterlife in his famous *Dialogues,* which appeared in 594. He did so because he wished to warn average believers of what lay ahead of them after death. He also did so in order to commend those Christian practices—intercessory prayer and, most especially, the celebration of the Eucharist—that might tip the balance between heaven and hell for the souls of the departed.[25] It was in these grey zones that the dead and the living could be imagined to meet. The blank wall between the living and the dead might be penetrated (indeed, might almost be rendered porous) by actions performed by the living.

The sense that the living could do something about the dead gave a much-needed sense of agency to the average believer. But it is here—in the vital link between the living and the dead— that one can sense the silent pressure of an entire society. The coming chapters will follow the working of this pressure. Wealth came to play a role in linking the living to the dead. We will end our story (close to the days of Julian of Toledo) with a virtual arms race of pious practices by which the wealthy—and that far wider group who wished to imitate the wealthy—sought to protect, nourish, and eventually bring home to heaven their own souls and the souls of the deceased.

This development was already evident in the late fourth and early fifth centuries. It is revealed by the precautions taken by the rich to secure privileged burial for their loved ones beside the shrines of the martyrs (which we will touch on in Chapter 2). Throughout the fifth and sixth centuries, the churches increasingly became places where the rich members in the Christian communities of the West were able to flex the muscles of their social power. They did so mainly through donations designed to protect their souls and those of their relatives and loved ones. But it was also in the churches that a remarkable succession of bishops and Christian writers attempted to hold the rich to account against the backdrop of an afterlife that was portrayed by them in ever-more vivid and menacing colors (as we will see in Chapters 4 and 5). We end, in the time of Julian of Toledo (in the Epilogue), with the landscape of Western Europe dotted with funerary churches and monasteries, each intensely committed to prayer for the souls of the departed.

In the grand monastic foundations of the seventh century, the ancient affirmation of the bonds between the living and the dead reached a crescendo. The memory of the far-from-perfect dead (kings and queens, noblemen and their wives, and political bishops) was preserved in magnificently endowed institutions. These monasteries and convents were treated as powerhouses of prayer on behalf of the souls of the departed. In abbeys, convents, and in great churches, the privileged dead—in effect, the very wealthy or the very holy—lay in chapels where their tombs would be bathed in the perpetual light of perfumed candles. The ever-burning lights around the tomb were believed to reflect, on a dark earth, the unending blaze of glory enjoyed or soon to be enjoyed (so it was hoped) by the dead person in paradise.[26]

It was in these ways that money—often big money—had come to speak in the churches of Western Europe. The development was summed up in one phrase, taken from the book of *Proverbs* (13:8):

> *Redemptio animae viri divitiae eius.*
> The ransom of the soul of a man is his wealth.

Associated with the supreme wisdom of King Solomon, the phrase was popular among the well-to-do of the seventh century AD.[27]

Like so many gnomic phrases taken from the Hebrew Bible, it had changed its meaning over the ages. To the blasé author of the book of *Proverbs,* in the third century BC, the phrase meant no more than that a rich man could use his wealth to save his skin, as a poor man could not.

By the beginning of the Middle Ages, however, the *anima*— the soul—had come to be thought of as the lonely Christian soul, which hung tremulously between heaven and hell, in sore need of the comfort that only the gifts of the living could provide. Such was the view of Bishop Leodegar of Autun, as he drew up his will in 675–676, only four years before his brutal assassination in 679. He did so "remembering the warning of the Wisdom [of Solomon]: *The ransom of the soul of a man is his wealth.*" And, "Out of love of God and for the remission of sins," Leodegar donated to the church of Saint Nazarius (the cathedral church of Autun) a sizeable tract of land—some four fully equipped villas—to maintain a poor house for forty paupers at the gate of the cathedral.[28] This expensive foundation was an appropriately lavish "ransom" for the soul of a powerful political bishop.

Apart from the will of Leodegar and a few other examples, the dramatic phrase "the ransom of the soul" occurs surprisingly seldom as a formula in donations at this time. It would only come into its own in the next century.[29] But I have chosen this phrase as the title of this book because of the epic quality of the *pro redemptione* formula. It was a formula heavy with echoes of the ransom of captives associated with the Redemption—of the ultimate ransom of all humanity by Christ himself. The formula emphasized that there was more than life beyond the grave. There were ransoms to be paid. There were links, vivid links, to be forged and maintained between the living and the dead. Those links enabled the living to intervene (in some way or other) to touch the souls of the departed after death. Belief in the existence of such links enabled the rich to care for their dead with ever-more demonstrative splendor.

Altogether, it was the presence of increasing wealth within the Christian churches that ensured that Christian notions of the afterlife did not remain airy speculations. An entire Christian society found itself engaged in unremitting debate about the relation between money and the grave. At times, the deployment of wealth "for the ransom of the soul" led to stunning feats of generosity to the poor. It also led to spectacular achievements in art and architecture. One thinks of the great sarcophagi in milk-white marble that were gathered in or near so many early Christian shrines in an attempt to allow the dead to lie ever closer to the saints or of the shimmering gold mosaics, the brilliant greens, the blood-red poppies, and the star-studded skies that brought a touch of paradise to the tombs of the great in mausoleums and in funerary chapels. There would have been less beauty in the late antique world if there had been less concern for the link between this world and the next that was established at the grave.

Every now and then, of course, novel deployments of wealth (if excessive or imprudently displayed) rattled contemporaries. They prompted stormy debates as to the proper use of wealth in society in general and for the care of the dead in particular. Throughout the centuries, these debates kept alive the fundamental question, the basic conundrum of how, indeed, if at all, heaven and earth, living and dead, could be joined by human agency and hence, inevitably, by money.

We should not underestimate the long-term effects of these drawn-out arguments. Without the twilight zones that hinted at the possibility of some role for the living in the life of souls beyond the grave, and, one suspects, without the wealth that enabled the more fortunate among the living to render the frail bond between the living and the dead concrete, visible, and, indeed at times stunningly beautiful, there would have been less incentive for Latin Christians to envision, with such imaginative daring, entire worlds beyond the grave. A very different constellation of representations and expectations concerning the afterlife might have settled in across the Latin West. It would have been closer, perhaps, to what we find in rabbinic Judaism, in Islam, and in many regions of the Christian East, where lucubrations on the intermediate state of the soul—the little future of the soul—were less prominent than in the Latin world and where the Resurrection and the Last Judgment retained, to the full, their ancient majesty.[30] Indeed, by the time of Julian of Toledo, the representation of the other world current in the Christian West had come to look very different from that of its neighbors: Eastern Christian, Jewish, and Muslim. How had this come about? In order to understand this, we should go back to the beginning. We now turn to the issue of religious giving in the Christian churches and its relation to the memory of the dead in the second and third century AD.

1

Memory of the Dead in
Early Christianity

"Treasure in Heaven"

When Latin Christians of late antiquity thought of religious giving, they went back to what for them was the beginning— to the words of Jesus. The words of Jesus to the Rich Young Man encapsulated the whole notion of the transfer of "treasure" from earth to heaven: "And Jesus said to him, 'If you would be perfect, go, sell what you possess and give to the poor, and you will have treasure in heaven.'"[1] Jesus repeated this challenge to his disciples: "Sell your possessions and give alms; provide yourselves with purses that do not grow old, with a treasure in the heavens that does not fail, where no thief approaches and no moth destroys."[2]

This notion was also current in Jewish circles. In the Jerusalem Talmud of the late fourth century, there is a story about

King Monobazos, the Jewish king of Adiabene on the Euphrates. He was said to have spent his fortune on providing food for the poor in Jerusalem. His infuriated relatives accused him of living up to his name, which was derived from the word *bazaz*—"to plunder." Monobazos was plundering the earthly inheritance of his family. He answered them at length: "My fathers laid up treasure for below, but I have laid up treasures for above. They laid up treasures in a place over which the hand of man may prevail: I in a place over which no hand can prevail . . . My fathers laid up treasures for others, I for myself. [For] my fathers laid up treasures useful in this world, I for the world to come."[3]

The commands of Jesus and the story of King Monobazos urged or described heroic acts of renunciation and generosity. By the third century AD, however, in both Judaism and Christianity, the gesture of giving had become miniaturized, as it were. One did not have to perform feats of heroic self-sacrifice or charity to place treasure in heaven. Small gifts would do. But the notion of the transfer of "treasure" to heaven by acts of mercy retained its otherworldly shimmer. Cyprian, for instance, treated the steady, low-profile flow of alms to the poor as a form of "thesaurization" in heaven on the same footing as the renunciation of all wealth that Jesus had urged on the Rich Young Man.[4]

In Christian circles, the notion of "treasure" placed in heaven through almsgiving colored perceptions of other sayings of Jesus. For instance, Jesus had also told the story of the Unjust Steward. This steward had used his tricky financial dealings to make friends, so that those who were obliged to him might take him into their houses once he had been dismissed from his job. Jesus concluded: "And I tell you, make friends for yourselves by means of unrighteous mammon, so that when it fails they may receive you into the eternal habitations."[5] Christians of this period took this to mean that those who received money from believers (whether the recipients were holy persons, clergymen, or the poor) would welcome these believers into their dwelling places in heaven. Indeed, believers could even build their own mansions using the funds that they transferred to heaven through acts of charity on earth. Heaven was not only a place of great treasure houses, it included prime real estate in a state of continuous construction due to the good deeds performed on earth by means of common, coarse money.

This notion was summed up in a delightful story told in the *Dialogues* of Gregory the Great, which were written in 594:

There was a pious cobbler, Deusdedit, in Rome (so Gregory tells us). Every Saturday he took a portion of his week's earnings to the courtyard of the shrine of Saint Peter at Rome. With these he gave alms to the poor who assembled at the shrine. The result of the cobbler's charity was revealed in a vision to a pious person. The vision was of a house being built in heaven. But this happened only on Saturdays. For Saturday was the day on which Deusdedit went to Saint Peter's to give alms to the poor. The house was the cobbler's "mansion" in heaven, built by the "treasure" that he had transferred to heaven every Saturday through his gifts to the poor.[6] A similar vision revealed that these mansions were treasure houses in themselves. They were built with bricks of pure gold.[7]

Gregory stood at the end of many centuries of Christian giving inspired by the notion of the transfer of treasure to heaven through almsgiving. Gregory's stories circulated largely unchanged and unchallenged for a further thousand years. But, when one turns to present-day scholarship on this theme, we find that the idea of "treasure in heaven" is surrounded by a loud silence. Neither in the Catholic *Dictionnaire de la Spiritualité* nor in the Protestant *Theologische Realenzyklopedie* is there an entry on *trésor* or on *Schatz*. Nor can such an article be found in the *Oxford Dictionary of the Jewish Religion*. Indeed, it is only recently (in 2013) that the lucid and refreshingly uncensorious study of Gary Anderson, *Charity: The Place of the Poor in the Biblical Tradition*, has offered a satisfactory analysis of the relation between almsgiving and the accumulation of "treasure in heaven" in the Old Testament, in later Judaism, and in early Christianity.[8]

Even the few articles devoted to the theme of "treasure in heaven" have approached it with ill-disguised embarrassment. In one such study, Klaus Koch insisted that, when Jesus spoke of "treasure in heaven," he must have meant something very different from the meanings that came to be attached to it in later centuries. Belief in the direct accumulation of treasure in heaven through almsgiving on earth (which was illustrated so vividly by the stories of Gregory the Great) was dismissed by Koch: It was "*für den Protestanten eine abscheuliche Vorstellung*"—"a notion abhorrent to any Protestant."[9]

Modern Catholic authors have been no less reserved when confronted with this notion. A large grave inscription erected over the tomb of the famous bishop of Arles, Hilary (430–449), declared that the bishop, through his renunciation of wealth, had "bought up heaven with earthly gifts."[10] There is no hint of embarrassment in those proud lines. Not so with their modern interpreters. The editors of a 2001 catalog of the early Christian monuments of Arles suggested, somewhat timidly, that such a phrase might strike a modern person as "a formula which certain of us . . . would no doubt have found somewhat abrupt or heretical!"[11] It is the same in Jewish circles. Faced by the tale of King Monobazos, even the great Jewish scholar Ephraim Urbach felt ill at ease. He confessed that it was difficult to see, in Monobazos's "prolonged and monotonous explanation . . . traces of a more refined doctrine . . . [some] sublimation of the materialistic simile of collecting treasures above through squandering them below."[12]

Altogether, we are dealing with a notion that causes acute embarrassment to modern persons. Such embarrassment is calculated to make the historian of religion sit up and take notice. Why is it that a way of speaking of the relation between heaven and earth that late antique and medieval Christians took for granted seems so very alien to us? Perhaps it is we who are strange. Why is it that we have such inhibitions in approaching the subject of the joining of God and gold?

Faced by the need to explain modern inhibitions, the religious historian is well advised to turn to modern anthropologists. Their work reminds us that we, as modern persons, are out of step with past ages. They have pointed out that our particular notion of exchange is the product of the commercial revolution of modern times. As the anthropologist John Parry makes clear: "As economic transactions become increasingly differentiated from other types of social relationship, the transactions appropriate to each become ever more polarized in terms of their symbolism and ideology . . . Western ideology has so emphasized the distinctiveness of the two cycles [religious relations with heaven and commercial transactions on earth] that it is then unable to imagine the mechanisms by which they are joined."[13] Nowadays, the thought of such a joining of religion and commerce strikes us as something more than a harmless exercise of the imagination. Rather, it has the quality of a joke in bad taste.

Modern anthropologists have done well to explain part of our inhibitions when confronted with the images in which early Christian and medieval giving practices were saturated. But these inhibitions are not solely a modern phenomenon. As Marcel Hénaff has shown in his brilliant and extensive meditation *The Price of Truth: Gift, Money, and Philosophy*, ancient philosophers, from Socrates onward, made a clear distinction between ordinary exchanges for ordinary goods and the existence of goods so precious and so nourishing to the mind and soul (such as their own teachings) that they would be tarnished and diminished by being connected in any way with mere money.[14]

Early Christians were well aware of this tradition. They appealed to it relentlessly when attacking the rituals of their rivals—pagan and Jewish sacrifice, for instance, in which large outlays were involved.[15] But they retained the great images of the transfer of treasure from earth to heaven and of the preparation of heavenly mansions through regular almsgiving. These were much more to them than "mere" metaphors. To adapt the title of a modern book on the role of metaphor in structuring social cognition, these were "metaphors to live by."[16] The constant use of the metaphor of "treasure in heaven" charged the circulation of money, on all levels within the churches, with a touch of the glory of heaven.

The notion of placing "treasure in heaven" through alms-giving remained a "metaphor to live by" for Jews and Christians because, in the words of Gary Anderson in his book *Charity*, the act of almsgiving "allowed the individual to enact the miracle of God's grace" on earth. Even a small gift to the destitute mirrored the mercy of God to a human race that was as totally dependent on Him for its survival as beggars were dependent on the rich for alms. Almsgiving triggered the ultimate hope of a world ruled by a Creator who would reward mercy with mercy.[17]

Furthermore, on a more subliminal level, the notion of treasure in heaven gripped the imagination because it seemed to join apparent incommensurables. To transfer money to heaven was not simply to store it there. It was to bring together two zones of the imagination that common sense held apart. In an almost magical imaginative implosion, the untarnished and eternal heavens were joined to earth through "unrighteous mammon"— through wealth that was traditionally associated with all that was most transient and, indeed, with all that was most sinister, on earth—all too heavy with associations of violence and deceit and, even when honestly come by, still smelling of the grave. If the brutal antithesis between heaven and earth, pure spirit and dull matter, could be overcome in this way, then all other divisions might be healed.

Not the least of these divisions was the gulf between rich and poor. In the Christian imagination, the joining of heaven and earth was refracted (in miniature, as it were) through the joining of two persons (or groups of persons) in incommensurable social situations—the rich and the poor—through the gift of alms. Hence we should not imagine that the relation between rich and poor in Christian circles was governed only by compassion and by a sense of social justice. Christians could be compassionate. Their reading of the Hebrew scriptures (the Old Testament) kept them fully aware of the passionate concern for social justice of the prophets of ancient Israel. But both Jewish and Christian giving to the poor always involved something more than that. Almsgiving was not only a matter of "horizontal" outreach to the poor within society. It evoked a symbolically charged "vertical" relationship. It tingled with the sense that almsgiving created a bridge over a chasm that was as vertiginous as that which separated earth from heaven, and human beings from God.

For, like God, the poor were very distant. Like God, the poor were silent. Like God, the poor could all too easily be forgotten by the proud and the wealthy. Hence there was an imaginative weight, for early Christian readers, in the seemingly matter-of-fact reminder of Saint Paul in his Letter to the Galatians "that we should remember the poor." For by remembering the poor, pious believers (Jewish and Christian alike) took on something of the vast and loving memory of God. God never forgot the poor, while human beings—whether because they were proud or simply because they were too busy—found the poor to be, alas, eminently forgettable.[18]

In this way, "to remember the poor" was seen as a joining of opposites that echoed, in society itself, the paradoxical joining of heaven and earth, of base money and eternity, and of God with humanity. Without such perilously anomalous bridges (each of which flouted human common sense), the universe itself would fall apart. The rich would forget the poor. The living would forget the dead. And God would forget them all.

Rich and Poor in the Church—Rome, 140 AD

One should add that the transfer of treasure from earth to heaven through almsgiving was not the only great image with which Jews and Christians sought to bridge the many chasms that played a vivid role in their imaginative world. Other images addressed the same problem—how to join the seemingly unjoinable. In order to appreciate this, let us turn for a moment to the parable of Hermas, a Christian prophet who was active in Rome sometime around 140 AD. Walking in his farm outside Rome, Hermas noticed a vine trained over an elm tree. The vine was fruitful. The elm tree was dead. He noted: "I am thinking about the elm and the vine, that they are excellently suited to each other . . . This vine bears fruit, but the elm is an unfruitful stock. Yet this vine, except it climbs up the elm cannot bear fruit. The rich man has much wealth, but in the things of the Lord he is poor, being distracted by his riches. But the poor man, being supplied by the rich, makes intercession for him."[19]

The rabbis faced a similar juxtaposition of potentially irreconcilable groups within the Jewish community. These antithetical groups were not simply the rich and the poor. Talmudic scholars were also contrasted with the ignorant common people—the *ammei ha-aretz*. A vivid rabbinic saying resembles the parable of Hermas. It spoke of the fruitful and the unfruitful parts of the vine so as to show that each contrasted group in the Jewish community (though poles apart in many ways) was dependent upon the other: "This people is like unto a vine; its branches are the wealthy, its clusters are the scholars, its leaves are the common people . . . Let the clusters pray for the leaves, for were it not for the leaves, the clusters could not exist."[20]

In both cases, the image of the vine was used to conjure up an ideal of organic, almost subliminal, symbiotic unity. Matter and spirit, fruitful vine and mere unfruitful wood, earthly treasure and heaven (all of them normally considered to be antithetical and mutually exclusive) could be seen to flow into each other. At stake in the Christian communities in Rome, as with their Jewish neighbors, was not simply how to care for the poor but how to maintain solidarity in a community in which the poor represented one pole alone (but a highly charged pole) in a culturally and socially differentiated group.

This preoccupation with solidarity, and with the overcoming of potential cleavages, fitted very well with what little we know of the social composition of the Christian communities in Rome that Hermas had addressed. In the second and third centuries AD, most Christians were not rich. Most thought of themselves as *mediocres*—as respectable, middling persons, such as had always found a social niche for themselves in large cities like Rome and Carthage. Their charity was not spectacular. It was low profile and effectively limited to fellow Christians. There was little or no outreach to the pagan poor. Rather, the average "poor" person in the Christian communities was a fellow believer down on his or her luck.

For this reason, we should be distrustful of the high-pitched language of Christian writers and preachers of this and later times. They wished to present Christian giving as the joining of mighty opposites. Their language drew a notional crevasse between rich and poor across what was, in reality, a socially low-profile and relatively unstratified community. What mattered for such authors was not to feed the masses but to conjure up imagined antitheses within the Christian community that only Christian charity and Christian prayer could overcome.[21]

It is important, however, to realize that the maintenance of a sense of solidarity in the Christian communities involved far more than the circulation of money. Ritual practices that combined almsgiving with intense prayer on behalf of fellow Christians (whether living or dead) played an even more central role in maintaining solidarity among Christians than did charity to the poor alone.

The crucial issue was how best to express solidarity with the dead. In this, the practice of intercessory prayer was decisive. Prayer was thought to bridge the most poignant of all crevasses—the ultimate, chill chasm between the living and the dead. What was distinctive in Jewish and Christian circles was the manner in which relations with the dead echoed closely the metaphors associated with the notion of "treasure in heaven" accumulated through alms to the poor.

Almsgiving to the poor became an irremovable part of the celebration of Christian funerals and memorial meals. And it did so, in no small part, because the state of the physically dead echoed with chill precision the state of the socially dead. Both the dead and the poor were creatures reduced to ultimate helplessness. Both depended on the generosity of others. Both cried out to be remembered in a world that could all too easily have forgotten them. But to forget either the dead or the poor was doubly abhorrent to religious groups, such as Jews and Christians, whose worst fear was that their God might forget them.[22] Let us now see how these powerful imaginative tensions worked out in practice for Christians of the late third century AD.

Dining at the *Triclia* at San Sebastiano, 250–300 AD

Circa 250 to 300 AD, Christians who walked out from Rome along the Appian Way to what are now the well-known catacombs of San Sebastiano would have made their way to a walled enclosure standing in the midst of ancient tombs. The enclosure was lined with benches and protected by a loggia. It boasted a well and a little kitchen. It was one of the many *tricliae* that offered banqueting facilities to those who wished to celebrate their loved ones by funerary meals in proximity to their tombs. In the homely words of Richard Krautheimer, this third-century *triclia*—discovered in 1915–1916 beneath the fourth-century basilica built at what is now called San Sebastiano—"was like any tavern on the green."[23] It was in this unprepossessing building, like any other *triclia*, that Christians met to celebrate with a meal in the proximity of their dead. The meal was called a *refrigerium*, a feast of refreshment and good cheer. It was thought to mirror the rest that the departed soul was believed to have come to enjoy.[24]

In the word *refrigerium* alone we are introduced to a very ancient Christianity, such as we have conjured up through the writings of Cyprian and, above all, of Tertullian. For many believers, this was still a Christianity of waiting souls. There was no doubt that the souls for whom the *refrigerium* meal was celebrated did not wait in despair, or even with impatience. They relaxed, and they did so with an exquisite sense of relief. They were, at last, released from the sufferings of this world. We can see what this meant in the remarkable prison diary of the African martyr Perpetua. While awaiting death in Carthage, in 203 AD, the martyr Perpetua experienced two dreams about her brother Dinocrates. Dinocrates had died young through a terrible cancer of the face. Her first vision of him was grim: Ill-dressed, his face marred by a great scar, he was straining in vain to reach the edge of a cistern of cool water. In the second dream, Perpetua saw Dinocrates at last at peace: "And Dinocrates drew near the water and began to drink from it. Having drunk his fill, he went further in from the water, and began to play as a little child would do, rejoicing."[25] Whether this *refrigerium* was imagined as a state of waiting or as a final rest in heaven, this was how one would wish to think of one's beloved at rest in the other world.

Many of those who celebrated a *refrigerium* of this kind recorded the meal and the prayers that accompanied it in graffiti written on the painted walls of the enclosure. Around 330 of these graffiti have survived.[26] For a historian of the Christian Church, it is a moving experience to come across these scribbled phrases. In a Christianity that we know of largely from assertive written works (such as those of Cyprian) and from dramatic and grisly accounts of the deaths of the martyrs, we come, at last, to an oasis of peace. Great happenings seem far away. Here we can listen to quiet voices—to ordinary Christian men and women of the generation before Constantine practicing their religion at the graves of their heroes and of their relatives.

Memory of the Dead and Memory by the Dead

What is it that we hear? What we hear above all is a tenacious
work of memory. Not only do the living remember the dead,
that was normal practice shared by Christians with pagans. What
is distinctive about these Christian graffiti is that they reveal that
the living prayed intently to be remembered *by* the dead.[27] The
first evidences of the cult of Peter and Paul (who were believed
to have lain for some time beside this humble banqueting space)
take the form of prayers that ask for us to be remembered:

> *Petre et Paule, in mente habetote.*
> Peter and Paul, have [us] in mind
> Holy Spirits, hold in your mind.[28]

But these prayers were not addressed to the great martyrs
alone. They were also made to the ordinary dead as they enjoyed
their *refrigerium*. The tombs of Peter and Paul formed the principal focus of the graffiti on the walls of the *tricliae* at San Sebastiano. But even there, dead relatives and fellow believers were
asked to pray for the living. Elsewhere, requests to the dead for
their prayers were often written poignantly close to the grave,
on the fresh plaster that surrounded the small marble plaque that
bore the name of the deceased.[29] The request to the dead for their
prayers runs as a refrain through the Christian inscriptions:

> *Ianuaria, bene refrigera et roga pro nos.*[30]
> Januaria, take your rest well, and ask for us.

But what exactly was it to "ask," and, especially, to "hold in
the mind"? Here, I think, we are dealing with notions of the

working of memory that are different from our own. For early Christians, as for many other ancient persons, memory was far more than a passive storage space. It implied an act of will. In the ancient world, memory was the tool of social cohesion par excellence. Patrons held clients to them by remembering and rewarding their services. In return, clients were careful to remember their patrons, even to the extent of solemnly celebrating their birthdays.[31]

Altogether, there was an element of militancy in the use of memory in the late antique world. To "remember," to "hold in the mind," was not to store away a fact: It was to assert a bond; it was to be loyal and to pay attention to somebody. Memory was as much a gift to the potentially forgotten dead in the other world as almsgiving was a gift to the all-too-easily forgotten poor in this world. In the same way, "forgetfulness" was nothing as innocent as mere absence of mind. To forget was an aggressive act. It was an act of social excision that severed links that had previously been established by an equally purposive act of memory.

In practice, to remember was to intercede. Peter and Paul were held to further the prayers of human petitioners by presenting these prayers to the memory of God. The prayers recorded in the graffiti were frequently characterized by this double appeal to memory—they asked for the petitioner to be remembered by the holy dead who, in turn, had the power to mobilize the memory of God: "Peter and Paul *apetite pro Dativu in perpetuum*, pray perpetually for Dativus."[32]

It is important to recapture the intensity with which the Christians who wrote these graffiti linked memory with

intercession. As Claudia Rapp has shown, belief in the power
of intercessory prayer accounts for much of the authority of
Christian bishops and of Christian holy men and women
throughout the late antique period. She has rightly urged us to
take account of the dense network of relations between believers established through belief in the power of prayer.[33] As
Augustine remarked in passing in the *City of God*, the phrase
"*Memor mei esto*"—"be mindful of me"—had become almost a
colloquialism: It was the conventional phrase with which
Christians took leave of pious fellow Christians.[34] In the Christian imagination, the silent flow of intercessory prayer wrapped
even the most low-profile Christian community in a perpetual
flicker of divine power.

Tertullian had written proudly, in his *Apology*, of the power
of prayer among the Christians: "We gather in an assembly . . .
and, as if we had formed a military unit, we force our way up to
God by prayer. This power—this *vis*—is pleasing to God."[35] The
vis orationis—"the power of prayer"—was central, also, to the
imaginative world of those who wrote the graffiti at San Sebastiano. But what did this power of prayer achieve?

Not all of these prayers were prayers for the souls of the departed. Many were frankly directed toward earthly benefits and
to protection in this world. One group asked for a safe sea voyage:
"that they should sail well through the power of prayer."[36] But,
whatever the objects of the prayers, the principal aim of intercession of all kinds was to hold together entities that common
sense treated as incommensurable. Antithetical worlds were
joined through intercessory prayer. The flexing of the muscles
of memory joined the dead to the living and God to human-

kind in an intense bond. The afterlife was very real to those who wrote these inscriptions. But (to use a spatial image) it did not hover high above them. It was next door. And it was kept close by prayer.

Rich and Poor: Heaven and Earth, 250–650 AD

One cannot but think that, in these Christian communities, there was a congruence between the sense of almost symbiotic bonds between the living and the dead and the bonds between each other that these groups imagined in their own society. The dead were thought to be as close to the living as the living were expected to be as close to each other. We are looking at relations between the living and the dead that reflected a view of the Christian community as a place where social boundaries were relaxed, both in this world and in the next. The other world, like the Christian community, was seen as a place of ease. Pagan burial imagery featured bucolic landscapes and peaceful gardens. Christians picked up this imagery with enthusiasm. It did justice to their own notion of the relaxed and joyful state of the souls of the departed. This bucolic art also echoed a similar sense of relaxation among the living. It summed up a countercultural longing for a religious community that avoided, as much as possible, the blatant hierarchies and abrasive differences in wealth and status that characterized the dark "world" outside the church.[37]

The fact that, by 300 AD, many Christians were already wealthy, cultivated, and even powerful, did not contradict this representation. Rather, it caused well-to-do Christians to work even harder in their imaginations to overcome divisions of which they were only too well aware. A pastoral imagery expressed to perfection the "deep humane dreams" that haunted well-to-do believers of the late third century—dreams of the relaxation of hierarchy in a privileged, secluded place.[38]

Hence there is a paradox that cannot but strike the historian. We end with two significantly different views of the little banqueting space in the tombs beside the modern church of San Sebastiano. In many ways, what we see (and rightly value) is an intimate and cheerful group, rooted in a long Roman tradition of sociability. Like the similar meetings of the *collegia* (the voluntary associations that proliferated in the Rome of the second and third centuries AD), there is an agreeably homegrown quality about such meetings. In the words of Eberhard Bruck, discussing the *collegia: "Sie haben das Parfüm von Chianti und Salami"* ("they have about them the reassuring smell of chianti and salami").[39] But this cheerfulness cannot be taken for granted. For, if we look at this group another way, we see that the imaginative world of its members was riven with notional crevasses. These seemingly cozy Christian communities saw themselves as struggling, through an intense work of intercessory prayer and almsgiving, to join a series of mighty incommensurables—God and man, heaven and earth, rich and poor, living and dead.

No small part of the theme of the following chapters will be the manner in which these notional crevasses widened under the pressure of new circumstances. The gap between rich and poor became sharper and more contested. After the conversion of Constantine, and most notably in the late fourth century, truly rich members of the Roman upper class joined what had hitherto been a distinctly low-profile institution—a church of the *mediocres* in the true Roman sense of the term. The *triclia* and its inscriptions were covered over by a gigantic shrine of the apostles. This shrine became a fashionable burial place. By the end of the fourth century, its apse was lined, on the outside, by the large family mausoleums of minor senators and public servants.[40] The martyrs themselves became that much more distant. The apostles Peter and Paul were declared to have "penetrated the ethereal depths of the sky." This language echoed just those pagan notions of apotheosis through ascent to the Milky Way of which Christian theologians of an earlier time had disapproved.[41]

The language of prayer itself lost some of its intimacy. It became insensibly hardened by osmosis with the forms of the ruler-subject and patron-client relationships that prevailed in the hierarchical society of the fourth century AD. The saints were no longer seen as partners in prayer. They became *patroni*—"patron saints"—in the late Roman sense. They stood as intercessors between the average believers and God, much as great noblemen, as patrons and protectors, represented their submissive clients at the court of the emperor.[42]

Furthermore, the impact of the entry of the rich into the church was heightened by the rapid emergence, at the same time, of the poor as objects of greater public interest. Having hitherto been largely invisible in Roman society at large, the poor became charged figures in the social imagination. After the conversion of Constantine in 312, the poor now flooded the churches. They needed charity on a far greater scale than previously. They were largely anonymous and very different from the brothers and sisters down on their luck whose care had made the workings of Christian charity in the third century so effective because it was so much more "homey" and manageable.

As a result, the "vertical" aspect of almsgiving—that stressed the stark drop between God and humanity, rich and poor—gained ever-greater prominence. The anonymous poor who had come to crowd around the churches were "others," and no longer "brothers," and it became more difficult to see almsgiving as a gesture of solidarity, as had been the case when the poor were known fellow believers. Rather, it became easier to see almsgiving as a purely expiatory action that involved little or no bonding with the poor themselves. Acts of mercy to the faceless poor simply mirrored (and so could be thought, on some level, to provoke) the acts of mercy by which a distant God cancelled the sins of the almsgiver.

Dead and living also drifted apart. By the end of the fourth century, bishops such as Augustine came to regard with increasing suspicion views of the afterlife that seemed to present the dead as hovering in too comfortable a manner around the living. Notions of the easy flow between the living and the dead in dreams and visions came under suspicion. At the same time, bishops also challenged burial customs (such as feasting at the grave—and especially at the graves of the martyrs) that assumed too cozy a relationship between the living and the dead. For these customs seemed to them to make the fate of the soul after death more predictable than it was in reality, and to make the initiatives of the living appear more effective beyond the grave than they—the bishops—considered to be theologically correct. Only certain forms of remembering the dead—notably almsgiving, prayers, and the celebration of the Eucharist—were deemed to be of any use to the souls of the deceased in the other world. A jolly party at their grave was not enough to nourish them. But nor (as we will see) was a special tomb sufficient to protect them.

Finally, the gradual penetration of Latin theology by Platonic ideas that stressed the immediate ascent to heaven of the disembodied soul sharpened the sense that some Christian souls were more clearly bound for heaven than were the souls of average believers. By the 380s, if not earlier, inscriptions at Christian graves all over Roman Italy declared that the souls of the departed had already reached the starry heavens associated with pagan notions of apotheosis. Those who were praised in this flamboyant manner were not martyrs. They were simply Christians whose high birth alone encouraged the living to ascribe a high destiny to them.

"Let no one think that sublime souls go down beneath the shades" was said of a Christian wunderkind in Bolsena.[43] Tertullian, by contrast, would have been quite content to urge the young man to wait in "the shades" until God had finished His mighty business with the universe. But the members of the Christian aristocracy of fourth-century Rome were not prepared to mark time in this manner. For example, Proiecta was the daughter of a major official. Her spectacular silver wedding casket can still be seen in the British Museum. When Proiecta died— alas, as a young woman—she was declared by no less a personage than Pope Damasus to have "gone away, only to climb up into the eternal light of heaven."[44] It seemed as if such persons had left their fellow Christians far behind, even in the afterlife.

We learn of this development from elegant marble plaques, covered with long inscriptions in classical verse, replete with echoes of Virgil. It is not irrelevant that the cost of carving such inscriptions was roughly fifteen gold pieces for nine lines. And this was at a time when the average Christian grave plaque displayed barely a few phrases of distinctly homespun Latin.[45]

In the course of the fifth and sixth centuries, as we shall see, the distance between heaven and earth seemed to yawn more widely. From the time of Augustine onward, believers were encouraged to be more conscious of the burden of their sins. Their unexpiated sins were increasingly thought to expose them to danger in the other world. Altogether, average Christians felt further away from heaven than ever before. Their souls were imagined to travel more slowly and at ever-greater risk—past demons and through flames of fire—toward an increasingly distant heaven.

Manichaean Questions

But in 300 AD, all this lay in the future. Let us end this chapter by abandoning the little *tricliae* now buried beneath San Sebastiano and travel three thousand kilometers to the eastern frontiers of the Roman Empire—to Syria, Egypt, and Mesopotamia—to make the acquaintance of the followers of Mani, who are known to us as Manichaeans or Manichees.

It may seem like a digression to examine a Christian sect that originated in faraway Persian Mesopotamia, but to study Manichaeism is to be reminded of the Middle Eastern roots of Christianity itself. Mani was the product of a Christianity of the third world—of the world east of Antioch—that had spread far beyond the cultural and linguistic frontiers of the Greco-

Roman Mediterranean. He lived on the eastern edge of a linguistic zone that was characterized by the dominance of Syriac, the last and the most creative version of an ancient Aramaic that had once been the lingua franca of the Achaemenid Empire and that had been spoken by Jesus of Nazareth himself. From Mesopotamia to the Mediterranean, Mani and his followers addressed populations that spoke the same language as themselves. He wrote all but one of his works in Syriac.[46]

Because they shared in the religious lingua franca of Syriac Christianity, the Manichaean missionaries and leaders of local communities (known as "the Elect") mingled easily with bands of mendicant Christian ascetics who had already begun to walk the roads of the Middle East. Altogether, Mani and his followers were by no means exotic intruders. Mani regarded himself as the Saint Paul of his own times. The Manichees claimed to come as reformers of the Christian Church, not as its enemies. In many regions, Manichees settled down on the margins of the mainline Christian churches. They claimed to be the representatives of a superior, more spiritualized form of Christianity.[47]

An accident of survival has ensured that the bulk of Manichaean literature known to us from within the territories of the Roman Empire is in Coptic, the language of the ancient Egyptians in its last phase. For what we now possess of the literature of Manichaeism is what has been preserved for us, in the form of large papyrus volumes, in the bone-dry sands of Egypt. But these precious volumes are only the remnants (translated from Syriac into Coptic) of one of the great religious literatures of the Syriac world. For Manichaean literature was rapidly translated into Greek and Coptic in the wake of the astonishing advance of the missionaries of the "Holy Church" of Mani throughout the eastern provinces of the empire.[48]

Mani died in 277. Many of the Coptic Manichaean documents date from less than a century after his death. This seemingly exotic religious leader from Babylon and his disciples were almost exact contemporaries of the Roman Christians whose *refrigeria* and prayers to and for the dead at San Sebastiano we have just described. More astonishing yet, recently available Manichaean evidence from Egypt shows that the Manichees touched on the same issues, in the course of their sustained dialogue with local Christians, as did our Christian Romans. The memory of the dead was crucial to them also.

To be seen in conjunction with the Manichees might have startled the good Christians in the *tricliae* at San Sebastiano. Mani not only lived a long way away but the Manichees were a radical group. Like many extremist groups, they may not have drawn their recruits from among adherents of the mainline churches. Most of their converts may have come from dissatisfied splinter groups from within what were, already, radical communities. In their view of the ascent of the soul and its attendant perils, for instance, the Manichees were more Gnostic than the Gnostics.[49] The slow rhythms of a world of waiting souls were not for them. Rather, their image was of souls at risk, as they ascended, as quickly as possible, to the Kingdom of Light, past serried ranks of malevolent powers. Yet these souls also needed help from the living, and, when it came to this help, what the Manichees described and reinterpreted, so as to fit them into their own worldview, were the commonplace Christian practices that were believed to help the souls of the departed. Any pious diner at the *triclia* of San Sebastiano would have recognized these practices—the giving of alms, acts of memory, and intercessory prayer, and therefore they are directly relevant to our discussion.

So let us turn to the Manichaean text known as *The Kephalaia of the Teacher*. It was, originally, a mighty volume of more than one thousand pages. It was called the *Kephalaia* because it was a book of "chapters." Each had its own heading and was devoted to a specific topic. It amounted to an encyclopedia of Manichaean doctrine. The papyrus sheets that have survived date from around 400 AD.[50] The *Kephalaia* is claimed to be the record of an exchange of questions and answers between Mani and his disciples. In fact, they were written after his death in 277, but it is possible that they were not written too long after. This means that what we read in the *Kephalaia* are descriptions, from the inside, of a radical Christian sect as it engaged the religious practices of its Christian neighbors. The discussion concerns central aspects of normal Christian rituals connected with the dead as they were practiced in the decades immediately before and after the conversion of Constantine. It is a glimpse as unexpected and as revealing as are the humble graffiti discovered in the *tricliae* beneath San Sebastiano.

What we find is a heated debate on precisely the same rituals that are apparent in the graffiti and in other fragments of evidence for the care of the souls of the dead in the Christian community of Rome and elsewhere. We find the same rituals, if with slightly different names: the giving of alms (the *mñtnae*), the giving of a Eucharistic oblation (the *prosphora*), the celebra-

tion of a "love feast" (the *agapé:* the Greek and Coptic equivalent of the *refrigerium*), and the "making of memory" (r̄meue) on
behalf of "the one who comes out from the body."[51] But what is
most revealing is the tone of the questions. The questions that
the Manichaean rank and file—the catechumens—posed to
their teacher were very much the questions that any Christians
would have posed about the rituals of their own church: to put
it bluntly, do they work?

   This was the principal theme of *Kephalaion* 115. It is summed
up in the title:

> The Catechumen asks the Apostle: will Rest *(matnes)* come
> about for Someone who has come out of the Body, if the
> Saints [the Elect] pray over/for him and make an
> alms-offering (r̄oumn̄tnae) for him?[52]

The question touched on the very essence of the relation between the living and the souls of the departed:

> So now I beseech you, my Teacher, that you may instruct
> me about this matter, whether it is true.
>   For it [that is, almsgiving for the dead] is [a practice] very great
>   and honored among the people.[53]

   To which the teacher replied, in effect, "Make my day." He
reassured his questioner that, when performed in the Holy
Church of Mani, such practices worked. He told the catechumen
exactly why and how they worked—and that they worked on a
grandiose cosmic scale. Great powers would gather to protect
the soul: "And through your holy prayer, asking from God that,
to those in whose name the table [of the feast for the dead, or,

perhaps, the Eucharist] has been set up, a [heavenly] Power may come. And so, from the God of Truth, will a Power be sent; and it comes and helps the one for whom the offering—the *prosphora* [the Manichaean equivalent of the Eucharist]—has been performed."[54]

In this way, Mani linked the departure of the soul to a grandiose myth of the ascent of the soul through a cosmos filled with protective and hostile powers. Yet the rituals themselves, which Mani interpreted in this ambitious manner, were straightforward. Many were shared by Manichees and mainline Christians alike. We are looking into a world where alms offerings, oblations, and "the making of remembrance" for the dead were common practices. They were "very great and honored amongst [all] people."

Faced by the widespread and unproblematic presence of day-to-day Christian funerary and commemorative practices—alms, memory, the love feast, and the Eucharist—the issue for the average Manichee (as for every average Christian) was not really *how* these rituals worked, but *whether* they worked. It is on this point that Mani's cosmic explanation reassured the catechumen. Now the catechumen could be certain that:

> alms on his behalf and a remembrance on his behalf [of
> the one who has died], for his brother, for his father,
> or his mother or his son, or else his daughter or his
> relative who shall come out from the body . . . [If] he
> has made alms . . . He did not lack his hope.[55]

Indeed, Mani encouraged the catechumen to continue these practices.

What you are doing is a great good . . . you redeem it
[the passing soul] from thousands of afflictions.[56]

What set Mani apart was his conviction that only in his Holy
Church did rituals for the dead work. In *Kephalaion* 87, *On Alms*,
he made plain that the followers of "every sect" (by which he
meant all previous Christians—and, perhaps, also Jews and,
even, Zoroastrians) gave alms in the name of God. But only in
the Holy Church of Mani would these alms "find a place of rest"
in heaven: "It is the Holy Church [of Mani] that is the place of
rest for all those who shall rest therein; and it becomes a doorway
and a conveyance to the Land of Rest."[57]

Manichaean documents from Kellis, a town excavated beginning in the 1980s in the Dakhlah oasis of the Western Desert
in southern Egypt, show how important these rituals were in
the day-to-day life of Manichaeans. The letters and even the account books of Kellis are scattered with references to the *agapé*
offered for the souls of the dead.[58] It was a matter of sadness,
among the Manichees of Kellis, that one old lady should have
died without the consolation of such rites: "We are remembering
her very much and I am distressed that she died when we were
not with her and that she died without finding the Brotherhood
gathered around her."[59]

From Mani to Augustine

We would leave behind Mani and his ideas were it not for the
fact that, when we move forward in time for one century, to the
days of the aged Augustine, we find that the problems that Mani

had been called upon to answer had not gone away. In 422, Augustine came to write his *Enchiridion* (a *Ready-to-Hand Book of Christian Doctrine*). Like the author of the *Kephalaia*, he wrote the *Enchiridion* to address problems posed by a lay enquirer. It was written for Laurentius, possibly a well-educated resident of Rome. He was the brother of an imperial agent active in Africa.[60] Laurentius's uncertainties were exactly the same as those addressed by Mani: Did rituals for the souls of the dead work, and, if so, how did they work?

As we shall see in the next chapter, Augustine's answer—deeply pondered after thirty years of meditation and of pastoral work—was the opposite of Mani's. While Mani had expatiated in great detail on the cosmic processes that made rituals for the Manichaean dead efficacious, Augustine was remarkably reticent on how the Catholic rituals for the dead were supposed to work. His answer was, basically, "God only knows, and He is not telling." Augustine limited himself to saying that oblations for the souls of the dead were a custom handed down from the apostles. For this reason, Catholic Christians were to maintain them. Mani also had said the same.[61] But, when we ask how these oblations work in particular, and for what particular categories of persons, Augustine presents us with the immense silence of God.

The answers of Mani and Augustine may have been different, but we should note the convergence of concerns between the two men. Both were aware of a lacuna in their own systems. Clear on the otherworldly destinies of saints and of great sinners, neither could make sense of an ever-more pressing phenomenon—the average sinner. Both were challenged, in effect, to explain how the rituals of the living impinged on the vast majority of those who lived in the "grey zone" of Christian eschatology—in the tantalizing twilight between the glory of the saints and the black darkness of the reprobate.

For Mani, the lacuna in his system was particularly blatant. We learn from *Kephalaion* 92 that Mani had even drawn a complete picture of the universe. But his disciples pressed him to explain why, on this cosmic map, he had found no place for those of the Middle Way: "Why did he not depict the Middle Way of the catechumens. Why did he not show how the catechumen [rather than the saintly Elect] goes out of the body and how he is brought before the Judge?"[62]

Augustine found himself confronted by exactly the same questions. In order to reassure Laurentius, he took refuge in a trenchant formula. He offered what can best be called a Van Ness diagram of the other world. In this diagram, only in the area of overlap could ritual action by the living be thought to affect the fate of the dead. The prayers and oblations of the faithful were not relevant to the *valde boni*—the "altogether good," for they could be assumed to have reached heaven with no difficulty. Nor were they relevant to the *valde mali*—the "altogether bad," for they could be assumed to be either already in hell or surely destined for hell. The friction point of Christian eschatology, and of Christian pastoral care, was the fate of the *non valdes*—of the *non valde mali* and the *non valde boni:* the "not altogether bad" and the "not altogether good." Such persons could be helped by the prayers and offerings of the living, provided that they had "qualified" for such help in this life, by living reasonably good lives: "For there is a certain manner of living, neither good enough to dispense with the need for those offerings after death, nor bad enough to preclude their being of advantage to them after death."[63]

The lapidary phrases of the *Enchiridion*—which laid out this three-fold division of the faithful—achieved an almost gnomic authority in later centuries. Like well-worn stones, they slid smoothly into place, again and again, in all subsequent discussions of the fate of the soul and the offerings made on its behalf by the faithful. They have been acclaimed as "the first step in the hierarchization of sins" that would lead, eventually, to the three-fold division of the other world into heaven and hell, with purgatory in the middle, that characterized the Catholic Christianity of the West.[64]

But to say this is to jump ahead too fast. For Augustine himself, we can sense, behind the rocklike opacity of his answer to Laurentius, nothing less than the building of a dam. This dam was intended to hold back (and not to satisfy) the mute pressure of the *non valdes*—of the "not altogethers" of the Christian communities. Like the catechumens who questioned Mani in the *Kephalaia,* average Christians in Africa and elsewhere wanted considerably more circumstantial and, if possible, more reassuring answers than Augustine was prepared to give them. They wanted a clear place for their loved ones in the geography of the other world. They wanted to know that the rituals that they performed on earth on behalf of the dead had a direct and positive influence on their fate. Augustine denied them that certainty. Yet the issue could not be avoided. The church was on its way to swallowing Roman society whole. This meant that it was well on its way to becoming a church of the *non valdes.*

It is for this reason that we begin our next chapter with the reticences of Augustine. We will examine his hesitations on the issue of the relations between the dead and the living in dreams and visions, on the fate of the soul after death, and on the effect on the souls of the departed of the rituals performed on their behalf by the living. These hesitations were a response to continuous questioning by clerical colleagues and laypersons. The questions that he had to answer reflected more than mere theological dilemmas, they were the sign of the turning of an age.

Augustine himself would play no small role in bringing about this turning of the age. By winning his battle with Pelagius, he left a deep mark on the piety of Latin Christendom, in ways that intimately affected attitudes toward death and toward the need of the soul for expiation both in this world and in the next. But the constant questioning to which he responded showed how little even he had been able to solve the problems connected with the other world. For he had, if anything, made them more acute. Like many old men in the moment of their triumph, he ended his life with his face set against a future that he himself had done so much to bring about.

2

Visions, Burial, and Memory in the Africa of Saint Augustine

Augustine and His Questioners

In Chapter 1, we began with an examination of the implications of the basic early Christian notion of treasure in heaven. Then we found ourselves in a quiet world. We considered the manner in which Christian groups in late-third-century Rome remembered their dead. Finally, we moved to the eastern fringes of the Roman world to listen to discussions that took place at the same time between Manichees and Christians on the nature and effect of the funerary rituals (offerings, almsgiving, and prayers of intercession) that both groups shared. As the questions addressed to Mani showed, most believers agreed that these rites were somehow intended to shield the soul in its passage from this world to the next. But how difficult would this passage be? Would the rituals developed by the churches work? For whom would they work? And why?

The note of anxiety that accompanied the questions posed to Mani by his lay followers was widespread in Christianity as a whole. A century later, in the time of Augustine, this anxiety had not abated. For most Christian believers, the other world remained a place of mystery. The traditional rituals of burial, feasting, and intercession gave only the most tantalizing hints as to what exactly happened to the soul after death.

Questions abounded, but the questioners had changed. They were no longer small groups of disciples addressing their teacher, as within the radical sect of the Manichees. They included persons drawn from the upper reaches of Roman society, as Christianity edged its way to becoming the majority religion of the Roman world.

The questions came especially from the rich; or, at least, they concerned the rich. The rich, after all, had more treasure on earth than anyone else. They wanted to know what benefits might accrue to them in the other world by transferring all or part of this treasure to heaven. But the questions also came from critics of the rich. Many critics claimed that the rich did not give enough—that most of them notably failed to "sell all and give to the poor," as they had been urged to do by Jesus in the Gospels. Other critics claimed that the rich used their wealth to seek special privileges in burial and in commemoration. These privileges awoke suspicion, as they seemed designed to ensure special treatment after death for the souls of the wealthy.

In this chapter, let us see how one remarkable figure—Augustine, who was bishop of Hippo (Annaba, Algeria) from

395 to 430—approached the problems raised by this novel situation. We will look at his reticence when confronted with views of the other world that seemed to render it too comfortable—too transparent to the human imagination (through dreams and visions) or too easily thought of as controllable by human rituals (through forms of privileged burial). We will see what Augustine thought of the manner in which the traditional practices by which Christians remembered their dead—the giving of alms, prayers, and mention at the Eucharist—affected the fate of the soul.

In Chapter 3, we will see how Augustine's reaction to the views of Pelagius (as they began to spread in Africa after the sack of Rome in 410) led him to conjure up a distinctive attitude to religious giving. His insistence that the giving of alms was intimately related to the expiation of sins would become dominant in future centuries.

We will also see how Augustine's stark emphasis on the ubiquity of sin and on the permanent need for its expiation led him to attempt to answer, if in a studiously cautious manner, some of the questions that laypersons had continued to ask from the days of Mani to the very end of the Roman Empire in the West and beyond: What rituals performed by the living, what prayers and pious practices and, ultimately, what expectations of God's mercy might ease a soul burdened by many sins in the strange world beyond the grave?

By following Augustine on these issues we will be looking at a great figure from an unexpected angle. We will not see the author of great books—the *Confessions, On the Trinity,* the *City of God,* and innumerable volumes against various heresies. Rather we will see a man constantly responding to the questions of others. Those who raised these questions were usually fellow Catholics. They did not come to question basic dogmas, rather they wanted to be certain that what they imagined about the other world was correct. Above all, they wanted to know in what way their own notions of the effect of human rituals and human pious practices on the fate of souls in the other world corresponded to what really took place in that unknown territory. Augustine was expected to tell them.

It took a lot of his time to answer. Among the new letters of Augustine discovered by Johannes Divjak there is a particularly poignant note to his friend, Possidius, bishop of Calama (Guelma, Algeria), written in December 419, when Augustine was sixty-five. He told Possidius that he was preparing to get down again to writing the *City of God*. But he had been forced to put this project aside: "I am annoyed because of the demands that are thrust on me to write, arriving unannounced, from here, there, and everywhere. They interrupt and hold up all the other things that we have so neatly lined up in order. They never seem to stop."

In three months, Augustine wrote, he had dictated 6,000 lines of writing (roughly 60,000 words). Most of this had taken the form of immediate answers to challenges that came to him from all over Africa: the pamphlet of a recalcitrant Donatist bishop, Gaudentius, from Timgad, in the deep south, near the Saharan frontier of the empire; questions on the origin of the soul, involving a bishop from Spain and the treatise of a young man from the far west, from Mauretania (near Morocco); sermons edited on the nights of Saturday and Sunday, to be sent to Carthage.[1]

Not all the questions that Augustine answered concerned the fate of the soul. But a large number did. The *Enchiridion*—the *Ready-to-Hand Book of Christian Doctrine*—that Augustine wrote as an answer to the questions of Laurentius (to which we referred at the end of Chapter 1) was written in 422, only a few years after his letter to Possidius. It was one of Augustine's many answers to well-placed questioners. Laurentius's brother, Dulcitius, had been active in Africa. His measures against heretics had provoked the protest of Gaudentius of Timgad. Dulcitius also posed questions to Augustine. Many of these overlapped with those of his brother, in probing the problems of the afterlife and of the fate of differing categories of sinners at the Last Judgment. Augustine answered them all—and promptly. As we saw, it was from the *Enchiridion* written for Laurentius that all later ages of Latin Christians derived the three-fold division of souls into the *valde boni* ("the altogether good"), the *valde mali* ("the altogether bad"), and the *non valde boni* (the crucial "not altogether good") for whom rituals for the soul were deemed to be effective.

Writing such detailed replies was worth the trouble. For it was precisely by being the problem solver for a wide constituency of influential laypersons and clerical colleagues that Augustine bound the highest levels of society to the church of Africa. To an unusual degree (if we compare Africa with other provinces, where any number of bishops were active writers) Augustine was allowed to act as a one-man brain trust for the churches of Africa.

This means that we must approach his writings on this topic with a sense both of the limitations and of the opportunities connected with Augustine's situation. We must remember that we

are dealing with a highly educated man surrounded by a circle
of well-to-do questioners. Compared with the immense religious
population of Roman Africa as a whole, Augustine and his questioners were a small, self-chosen group. Not everyone had the
opportunity to talk at length with their bishop about death and
the soul.

We must constantly bear this fact in mind. In Africa, as in
all other regions of the late Roman world, the dead were everywhere, but only very few are now visible to us. Nothing reveals
more harshly the stratified nature of ancient societies than the
utter silence of the vast majority of the dead. Romans prized
memory and valued expressions of grief. Brent Shaw has calculated that, out of some 300,000 inscriptions that survive from
the Roman West, more than 75 percent were placed on tombstones.[2] But these tombstones ringed a vast black hole. Out of
875,000 graves in the Roman catacombs, only 27,688 had named
plaques.[3] In one catacomb (the catacomb of Priscilla) only 40
graves out of 40,000 were decorated with frescoes.[4]

If we turn to the recent excavations of burial areas in Carthage in the fifth century, we realize what this means. In the
well-to-do cemetery area of Bir el-Knissia, the dead were still
part of society: Their graves were well organized, and they spoke
to the living through inscriptions and through floor mosaics
placed in a great basilica. Outside the city wall, by contrast, the
dead huddled in rows beneath roughly stacked tiles: "there were
no recognizable paths between graves, few monuments and
markers, and no evidence for ritual activity . . . disturbance of
earlier graves by later ones was routine."[5] Only the ancient "obol
of Charon"—a small coin placed in the mouth to pay the cost

of the journey into the other world—was regularly found in these otherwise faceless graves. Apart from that, we have little idea of what rituals or representations of the other world were associated with these large cemeteries of the poor.

Those who went out to the graves of the poor may also have stood in the basilicas in which Augustine preached. But we cannot even be certain of that.[6] They certainly did not bring their questions to the great bishop in his study, to be answered by long treatises. Altogether, as every archaeologist knows, the dead speak to us only because of the money provided by the living. We meet them as members of the "chattering classes"—the rich and the relatively well-to-do who, for centuries, had filled the cities of the Mediterranean with vivid and poignant written stones.

But this should not lead us to underestimate what Augustine set out to do. His answers to the questions of colleagues and well-to-do laypersons consisted of a constant winnowing of current representations of the other world. He would reject some and urge caution about others. Above all, he would strive to identify a secure core of notions that, in his opinion, were consonant with the traditions of the church and with the correct reading of the words of scripture.

When it came to issues of the afterlife, Augustine's exegesis of scripture and examination of church customs was sternly minimalist. He gave his questioners little room to maneuver. He frequently warned them that there was no easy way by which hardened or negligent sinners might enter heaven. They were not to rely on some "magic bullet"—some ritual precaution, some form of protection given by the saints, some last minute act of mercy by God himself. In Augustine's opinion, only a narrow core of authorized representations (derived from the scriptures and from church custom) could bear the weight of the hopes and fears of humans as they faced the great unknown. Otherwise, the tender human imagination would weave any number of comforting illusions around the grave.

We can see Augustine at work in this way toward the very end of his life, in the second to last book of the *City of God*. This was written around 427. A remarkable book, it amounted to a handbook of popular illusions about the other world. To take one example, Augustine noted that many of the faithful with whom he had spoken were convinced that the souls of sinners (even, perhaps, of major sinners) might yet be saved at the very last moment, on the Day of Judgment, through the intercession of the saints. Augustine's interlocutors wished to believe that God would pardon even hardened sinners in response to the prayers of the saints, much as an emperor extended clemency to criminals in response to petitions. But Augustine did not wish them to be so sure. It was safer for the faithful that the other world should remain opaque: "it would be most perilous to define what those sins are which in themselves prevent attainment of the kingdom of God, while admitting of pardon through the merits of holy friends. I myself, at least, have given much thought to the question without being able to reach a conclusion. And it may well be that the answer is kept a secret for fear that knowledge might blunt one's zeal to make progress towards the avoidance of all kinds of sin."[7]

Much of Augustine's writing on the other world is marked by pointed caution. It often seems myopic to us, but this is because it was driven by questions that seem at first sight to be fussy or superstitious. But we lose a lot by seeing it in this way. What Augustine was doing, through his constant attention, one by one, to the small-print of the questions posed to him by a wide variety of questioners, was to undertake nothing less than the grooming of the religious imagination of vocal and influential members of the Christian communities all over Africa and, eventually, elsewhere.

Indeed, precisely because so many of Augustine's statements were prompted by the questions of others, we find that we are not dealing with a series of ex cathedra pronouncements issuing from Augustine alone. We are listening in to a vigorous conversation. We can hear the voices of Augustine's questioners almost as clearly as we hear his replies. To use a modern turn of speech, we can hear "where they are coming from." This gives us a wider field of vision than we might at first expect. For many of the concerns that Augustine addressed reached well beyond the privileged circle of his upper-class correspondents and readers of his treatises. They touched the "chattering classes" of Africa as a whole. They even reflected, at a distance, the hopes and fears of innumerable humble persons who (in the touching words of George Eliot's *Middlemarch*) "lived a hidden life and rest in unvisited graves."[8]

Death, Dreams, and the Presence of God at Uzalis

Let us begin with how Augustine faced the issue of human knowledge of the other world. He did not do this in the quiet of his study, but in an atmosphere buzzing with questions. At some time around 420 AD (just after Augustine's plaintive letter to Possidius), a series of small, poignant events took place in the little North African town of Uzalis (modern El Alia, Tunisia), forty miles north of Carthage.[9] A young man, the *notarius*—the stenographer—of Bishop Evodius of Uzalis, died suddenly. Evodius was deeply saddened. The boy would read to the old bishop, whose eyesight may have begun to fail him, "for some time at night when everything had fallen silent. And he did not want to pass over a passage if he had not understood it . . . I began to regard him not as a boy and a scribe, but as a close and dear friend." Now that he was dead, it was as if "he has entered my soul, and is there offering me a certain brightness by his presence."[10]

Evodius was not the only person touched by the death of the little notary. A devout widow dreamed of the preparation of a palace that shone like silver. It was the young man's "mansion in heaven": "And in the same palace there appeared an old man robed in white who ordered two men in white to take the body from the tomb and raise it up to heaven [and she saw] branches of 'virgin' roses—for closed buds are usually called that—spring up from the tomb."[11] The image of the roses in the tomb would soon occur in the famous legendary account of the death and passage to heaven of the Virgin Mary that had begun to circulate, at this time, in the Greek world. It is a reminder that, in Evodius's letter, we glimpse imaginative patterns that stretched from one end of the Mediterranean to the other.[12]

The boy also appeared to a monk. The monk asked the one crucial question: "*utrum fuisset a Deo receptus*" ("whether he had been received by God"). "And with great rejoicing [the boy] replied that he had been."[13] We should note this. Latin Christians of the third and fourth centuries spoke much of paradise—that is, of heaven. But, when those who were deemed worthy of heaven died, they wished to encounter first a person, and not a place. We can see this in the case of the martyr Perpetua. When Perpetua dreamed of her arrival in paradise with her companion, the priest Saturus, she dreamed of an encounter with a mysterious figure that was both intimate and awesome. Martyrs who had already arrived told Perpetua and Saturus what to do: "Come first, enter in and greet the Lord . . . And we came to a place whose walls seemed to be constructed of light . . . In this same place we saw an old man with white hair but with a young man's face . . . Entering with wonder, we stood before the throne: four angels supported us, and we kissed Him, and He touched our faces with His hand."[14]

Only then were they told: "*Ite et ludite*" ("Go and play"). They could now rejoice in paradise with the same raw vigor as the pagan Romans did when celebrating the games—the *ludi*—in honor of the emperor. The "play" of Perpetua and Saturus was no carefree frolic. It was a victory celebration. The association of victory with play was common in the Roman world. Even a gaming table, found in a Roman catacomb, bore the euphoric message:

> *Parthi occisi Britto victus. Ludite Romani!*
> Parthians killed off, the Briton conquered. Play Romans![15]

But the passage made plain that, before enjoying paradise, Perpetua and Saturus had first to meet Christ, *their* emperor, face to face.

The Christ of Perpetua was a deliberately ambiguous figure. His haunting combination of old age and youth spoke of a being who was above time and above human aging. The image was taken from the description of the Ancient of Days in Daniel 7:9 and from the Apocalypse—the Book of Revelation 1:14—of Saint John. By the time of Augustine, however, the image of Christ had settled down to a more unambiguous and up-to-date form of representation. Visually, Christ came to resemble a late Roman emperor. Despite some significant differences in iconography between representations of Christ and those of the emperor in the art of the fourth and fifth centuries (to which Thomas Mathews has drawn attention in his thought-provoking book *The Clash of Gods*), we should not underestimate the sheer gravitational puil of the image of the emperor in the religious imagination of the age. Christ was expected to look like an emperor and to act like an emperor.[16]

But emperors—even late Roman emperors—were not totally unambiguous figures. They also had many faces. The emergence of the image of Christ as emperor was not due entirely to a new, more rigid sense of Christ's majesty. It also drew on the studied ambiguity by which the late Roman image of the emperor combined great distance from the many with the thrill of personal intimacy for the few. Court ceremonial was not only about hierarchy, it was also about the gestures that bridged this hierarchy. For instance, those who were admitted to "adore" the emperor, through kissing the edge of his imperial robe, were not simply seen as abject subjects. Far from it: they were presented as having established, between themselves and their lord, a sense of face-to-face, personal bonding that echoed the combination of love and awe experienced by Perpetua as she approached Christ as the Ancient of Days.[17]

We can see this imaginative play at work in the long inscription on the tomb of Petronius Probus, one of the leading senators of Rome. Probus was a grandee of legendary wealth and equally legendary corruption. He had dominated the political scene in the western regions of the empire from the late 360s to his death in the late 380s. The inscription was found in the prominent mausoleum that Probus had built for himself outside the apse of the basilica of Saint Peter on the Vatican, and it lay as close as possible to the tomb of the apostle.

Given the fulsome tone of the inscription, modern scholars cannot be blamed for thinking that, for the prominent Probus—the great politico of his age—to go to heaven was simply to exchange an earthly for a heavenly court. He would be admitted to the presence of Christ, and he would sit down to dine with Him as he had once dined with the formidable Emperor Valentinian I. Heaven was Probus's ultimate promotion.

Yet there was more to it than that. Now baptized, Probus also came to Christ as a special friend. In the words of the inscription, "May he [Probus] perpetually see Christ's face turned in peace towards him, and, loved by Christ, hang always on His lips."[18] The last phrase—"hang on His lips"—was deliberately taken from Virgil's *Aeneid*. It described the manner in which Queen Dido of Carthage had hung upon the words of Aeneas, riveted by growing love for her hero.[19] This was what it meant for a Christian—whether a grandee or a little notary in distant Uzalis—to be *receptus:* to be "received" by Christ in a place where majesty and love were joined.

There was little doubt among the pious in Uzalis that this was what had happened to Evodius's notary. For at the time of the boy's death, an old man dreamed of a figure who carried a document and a laurel wreath. What the old man saw was one of the well-known *laureatae*. *Laureatae* were images of the emperor crowned with laurels. They made the emperor "present" in distant provinces. They often accompanied his edicts.[20] The little notary had been officially summoned into the presence of Christ.

Problems of the Soul

We know about the events at Uzalis from a rare document. Provoked by the bubbling up of visions occasioned by the death of a single, much-beloved person, Evodius reported them to his long-term friend Augustine. They raised problems for the bishop of Uzalis. How had it been possible for so many persons to have "seen" the young man or to have "seen" the preparations made in the other world for his arrival after death? The dreams reported by Evodius seemed to be more than mere dreams. They were "visits" from beyond the grave. If they were, indeed, direct visions of the other world, they immediately raised the issue of what could be known from them. For instance, did they prove beyond all doubt that good Christian souls were instantly "received" by God?[21]

But what if these visions could not be trusted? Must we conclude, then, that we can never know about the trajectory of the Christian soul after death? Evodius put it bluntly: *"Exeuntes de corpore qui sumus?"* ("Coming out of the body who are we?").[22]

Did the soul enter a world where everything was as clear as a rain-washed sky, from which the dark clouds of the body had been driven, as Evodius himself wished to believe? Or, in the absence of direct proof, was he forced to imagine a more depressing scenario? Did the soul merely fall asleep along with the body, deprived of all consciousness—"only hoping [for the resurrection], doing nothing, knowing nothing, especially not even active in a dream state?" To an aging bishop, who had just lost a dear young friend, the prospect of a mere "sleep of the soul" after death was "truly frightening." It was as if the soul itself had been snuffed out.

Coming from Evodius, this was a peculiarly poignant question. Over thirty years previously (in 388, just after Augustine's conversion) he had participated in a dialogue with Augustine recorded in *On the Greatness of the Soul*. In that dialogue, both men had agreed that heaven was the soul's rightful homeland. But how soon would the soul arrive at that homeland? Evodius found himself caught between two imaginative structures, almost between two ages of Christianity—between Tertullian's somber view of the waiting of the soul and the bright prospect of instant entry into heaven that had been more recently opened up for Christians by the spread of Platonic ideas. He wished to be doubly sure. He wished to believe that the dreams concerning the little notary proved that the boy's soul had, indeed, gone straight to God.[23]

Augustine's answer to his friend's letter was trenchant and quite remarkably discouraging. He simply brushed Evodius's questions aside. Dreams were dreams. There was no reason to assume that any dream was any more privileged than any other.

In his providence, God might form the imagery of a few exceptional dreams so as to communicate a message. This had been the case with the dreams and visions of the prophets.[24] But what happened in the Holy Scriptures was not likely to happen in small-town Uzalis. As far as Augustine was concerned, there was no way to know "what distinguishes the visions of those who are deluded by error or impiety [from true visions], as many events are described in them that are the same as those seen by pious and holy people."[25]

He warned Evodius to be careful. The problem of image formation alone—not to mention the problem of whether humans were able to discern the hand of God in some but not in other dreams—was a "wild wood."[26] Augustine had no intention of entering that wood. To read the exchange of letters between Augustine and his friend on the visions at Uzalis is like entering an unfinished and little-visited room in the far corner of a stupendous building. The letters document one of the many intellectual projects that Augustine—a man of many significant silences—decided not to pursue.

Because of the firmness of Augustine's reply, Evodius's questions have tended to be dismissed as superstitious or simply weird. But this is to accept too readily Augustine's side of the story. In fact, Evodius had touched on a very real metaphysical issue. How could a totally spiritual view of the soul (such as Augustine had embraced with such enthusiasm from his readings of the Neoplatonist Plotinus, who died in 270 AD) be reconciled with current images of the life of the soul after death? How could the soul in its pure state, once detached from the body, retain any recognizable features or pursue any recognizable trajectory? Even the most familiar and religiously acceptable representations (such as the "reception" of the soul into the presence of God) might turn out to be no more than representations—pictures formed in the human mind that bore little or no relation to reality. They would slide off the surface of another world that was so distant from human thought—so abstract, so placeless, and so faceless— as to offer the living no imaginative handhold upon it.

In his letter to Augustine, Evodius showed that he himself favored a more moderate form of Platonism. He suggested that, even when out of the body, the soul must be thought of as being accompanied by some material "vehicle" in the form of an envelope of infinitely fine matter.[27] Perhaps that was what the dreamers of Uzalis had seen. The ethereal but real body of their beloved friend had stepped into their dreams. Augustine dismissed this view out of hand. The soul must be totally immaterial. To speak of some sheathe made up of "spiritual matter" was to commit a "category mistake."

Modern commentators tend to follow Augustine in dismissing Evodius's notion of the vehicle of the soul as "bizarre."[28] In fact, Evodius's suggestion showed him to be a state-of-the-art Neoplatonist.[29] He was in many ways more up to date than was Augustine. The austere "immaterialism" of Plotinus had caused more problems than it had solved in Neoplatonic philosophical circles in the generations after Plotinus's death. For how could an entity defined in so absolute a manner as utterly devoid *of* matter have any relation *with* matter? Souls had to be thought of as being connected in some way with the fabric of the material world.[30]

Faced by this problem, the more advanced Neoplatonists tended to improve on Plotinus by positing some mediating body (spirit at its lowest and matter at its height of subtlety) that linked the soul, in an unbroken chain of being, to the material world. This ethereal link could survive death. Like the fine body of an angel, this "vehicle" preserved the lineaments of a distinct person even in the world of spirits. This was what Evodius proposed to his friend Augustine. His suggestion received a frosty reception. Augustine told him that the notion of a vehicle of the soul was "a most time-consuming problem" that some might have the leisure to pursue. He himself, he told Evodius somewhat abruptly, did not have the time to engage in such speculations.[31]

Augustine's impatience with Evodius was not shared by every Christian theologian. His radical immaterialism seems entirely natural to us, but it remained difficult for many serious thinkers to accept. For one of its most disturbing implications was that a totally spiritual afterlife lacked profile. If everything in the other world was pure spirit, there could be no clear heaven and no clear hell. An entirely spiritualized other world was like Oakland as described by Gertrude Stein: "There's no there there." For that reason, Augustine's extreme views were often treated with misgiving or quietly abandoned by a later generation of spiritual guides and preachers, as we will see in the case of fifth-century Gaul.

Visions and Religious Conflict in Augustine's Africa

There was more to Evodius's accounts of dreams and Augustine's brush-off than a metaphysical disagreement. Africa was a land awash with dreams. As Tertullian declared, two centuries before, "It is to dreams that the majority of mankind owe their knowledge of God."[32]

The notion that religious actions took place at the prompting of God or the gods through dreams and waking visions was shared by pagans and Christians alike.[33]

Above all, dreams had played an important role in the relations between the two, bitterly opposed, churches of Africa. Simply for the sake of convenience, I will call these "Donatists" and "Catholics." They were roughly equal to each other in number, and largely equal, also, in social and cultural profile. They were separated by no major theological or liturgical differences. But, because of a bitter schism that had happened in the early fourth century, the believers of each church considered their church alone to be the one, true Catholic Church, and treated the church of the other as a demonic travesty—an empty shell of a church, set up by the devil himself.[34]

More than that, each church was convinced that it alone was inhabited by the Holy Spirit, and with the Holy Spirit went the gift of dreams.[35] For many Donatists, their church was true because they had seen it to be true: "For this our brother and this our sister have had a vision to that effect, whether at a vigil or in a dream while asleep."[36]

This trust in visions was no mere "folkloristic" curiosity, restricted only to the Donatists. In 401, Catholic bishops legislated to control the spread of altars to hitherto unknown martyrs set up by Catholics in response to dreams: "And so may it please us that altars which have been set up all over the place, in the fields and along roads, in which there is no body of a martyr or relics . . . should be overturned . . . For altars that are set up through dreams or empty, pretended revelations are to be utterly rejected." And yet, in certain places, public opinion was so strong in favor of such shrines that the council ruled that the bishop might have to be content with simply preaching against dream-based shrines. Otherwise riots would occur.[37]

Altogether, the homely events at Uzalis stirred up larger issues that had implications far beyond the narrow circle of a bishop and his friends. Augustine's caution must be seen against the wider background of an eerie confrontation of visionary powers (accepted by some as otherworldly ratifications of their beliefs and rejected by others as demonic illusions) that may have gathered momentum in the desperate aftermath of the official suppression of Donatism in 411.[38]

In the course of his meditation on visions, Augustine had assessed a remarkable number of such experiences, news of which had circulated in the countryside and in the small towns of Africa. Many were full-blown visions of heaven and hell. Some of these even included views of the future punishment of living sinners (in the manner of Dante's *Inferno*).[39] These stories looked straight toward the Middle Ages. Many could have come from the works of Gregory of Tours. But Augustine refused to look that way. Such visions were epistemologically improbable. They might even be the work of demons. In any case, they were best left alone. The idea of a discomforting hiatus between representation and reality—between what humans imagined and what the world was really like—that Augustine had inherited from centuries of Greek and Roman philosophy held firm in the back of his mind. He still belonged to a mental world where "The innocence of direct representation was lost."[40] What even the pious saw in dreams and visions was not necessarily what they would get in the world beyond the grave.

Augustine, Paulinus of Nola, and Burial beside the Saints

Augustine could not escape the problem of the relation between the living and the dead. Only a few years after Augustine and Evodius's exchange yet another aspect of the problem came to be debated—this time in distinctly upper-class circles. Circa 420/424, Augustine wrote to his good friend Paulinus of Nola on a charged topic: What benefits did the souls of the departed derive from the actions of the living? Did any benefit whatsoever come from placing the dead beside the tombs of saints, so as to enjoy their protection at the time of the Last Judgment?

Paulinus had approached Augustine in response to a concrete situation. Cynegius was the son of Flora, a "most devout" noblewoman who, apparently, resided in Africa. He had died when abroad in Italy.[41] At Flora's urging, Paulinus had buried Cynegius beside the tomb of Saint Felix, the famous miracleworking saint of Nola. Paulinus even wrote the epitaph for the young man. Fragments of this epitaph have survived to this day. In elegant verses, it spoke of Cynegius in euphoric terms. Cynegius had been welcomed as "a guest at the house of Felix." Placed close to the tomb of Felix, the young man could feel safe when "the terrible sound of the trumpet [of the Last Judgment] shook the whole world."[42]

We must remember that, ever since his conversion to the ascetic life, in 394, Paulinus had poured vast wealth into rebuilding the shrine of Felix at Nola. This was the way in which he had chosen to place his treasure in heaven. But no one entering the splendid new building would have doubted for a moment that some of that imagined treasure had, as it were, dripped back to earth. With its shimmering, multicolored marbles, its blaze of candelabra, and a gilded roof that rippled like an ocean in the flickering light of innumerable scented lamps, it was a "mansion in heaven" set down in Campania, amidst the villas of the Roman aristocracy.[43]

Altogether, Paulinus's newly built shrine of Saint Felix was an advertisement to the power of religious giving, now practiced by a formidably wealthy Christian aristocracy. Cynegius's privileged burial at such a shrine revealed what the discreet weight of wealth could do to mold Christian views of the afterlife, for Paulinus's inscription seemed to have guaranteed in advance the safety of Cynegius's soul at the Last Judgment.[44]

But this was not Augustine's view of the matter. The treatise that he wrote to Paulinus, *de cura pro mortuis gerenda*—"What Care Should Be Taken for the Dead"—was discreet, firm, and (like his answer to Evodius) deeply discouraging. If Paulinus had wished for ratification from Augustine of his permission to bury Cynegius at the shrine of Felix, and if Flora had wished to be consoled by the thought that her son's proximity to Felix would help him in the Last Judgment, neither of them got any reassurance from the bishop of Hippo. The excellent study of Paula Rose, *Augustine and the Relations between the Living and the Dead,* makes plain the skill with which every word of Augustine's answer to Paulinus was weighted toward a negative decision.[45]

Though careful not to offend either Flora or his long-term friend, Paulinus, Augustine was blunt. Burial beside the saints did nothing whatsoever to aid the soul. All that such prominent burial did was to jog the memory of the bereaved by reminding them to resort with yet greater fervor to the traditional means of helping the departed—prayers to God and to the saints, almsgiving, and mention of the dead at the Eucharist. Despite the passing of one and a half centuries, we are still close to the little groups gathered at the *triclia* at San Sebastiano. *Memoria*—the hard, loyal work of memory—was what really counted in the relations between the living and the dead.[46]

Altogether, in disagreeing with Paulinus on this issue, Augustine challenged a baroque piety, focused on the newly developed cult of the saints, that had been fostered by a remarkable group of converted aristocrats in Italy, Gaul, and Spain, and that had already come to be adopted in many parts of the western Mediterranean. From around the middle of the fourth century (if not earlier) we can trace the creation of special groupings of tombs in close proximity to the graves of the saints.[47] The quiet presence of a saint did not only guarantee protection on the Day of Judgment, it was said to lighten the darkness of the tomb. The presence of the saint kept at bay the ancient dread of Tartarus—the personified figure of Death.[48] The physical closeness of tomb and relic shrine conjured up the possibility of a similar closeness in the other world. But the cost of such burial alone ensured that these were privileged burials, and that "holy space" was blatantly the space of the rich.[49]

The Power of Memory

Augustine would have none of this. He pointed out to Paulinus the serious error that might arise among those who drew incorrect conclusions from the decision to bury Cynegius beside Saint Felix. He did this in the name of traditional African commemorative practice. *Memoria,* "memory," was what the Christian dead of Africa were guaranteed.[50] They could have this without proximity to the saints. As Ann Marie Yasin has pointed out, the funerary basilicas of Africa were filled with tombs that bore the names of the deceased. They usually took the form of brightly colored panels of mosaic placed in the pavement of the basilica. But the lay elites did not necessarily enjoy any special proximity to the saints. Nor did all the marked graves in the great basilicas of Africa belong exclusively to the rich. Many were the graves of middling persons—minor town councilors and well-to-do artisans.[51] Having such graves demanded a certain outlay, but no outlay would have been as great as that required to place Cynegius beside the shrine of Felix along with a sarcophagus and carefully carved epitaph (not to mention the candelabra that probably burned beside his tomb). Prayer, almsgiving, and offering at the Eucharist were not expensive: They could be made by relatively humble persons on behalf of their loved ones. These actions alone—and not fancy tombs—had the power to alter the fate of the dead.

We often forget how deeply committed Augustine was to this traditional ritual structure. It comes as a surprise to realize that the vivid description of the passing of his mother, Monica, at Ostia, at the end of book nine of the *Confessions,* was not about her death at all: It was about the proper performance of the rituals associated with her memory.[52] Augustine described no dramatic passing of the soul accompanied by unearthly light and sweet perfume, as would be described in later centuries. Rather, having described the lives of Monica and her husband, Patricius, at the end of book nine of the *Confessions,* Augustine made a plea to his readers that they should be remembered in their prayers, just as they were remembered, also, at the Eucharist. Careful to preserve his mother's memory in such prayers, this was the only time that Augustine mentioned her by name— Monnica (the old African spelling, with a double n).[53] Had it not been for this tenacious memorial practice, which ensured that she would be named in prayer by all who read about her, Monica would have been as nameless a figure to us as was Augustine's former mistress. To be remembered in that way was all that her soul required. In a touching scene, at Ostia, she had surrendered her wish to join her husband in the family tomb in Africa. Memory alone—memory in prayer and at the altar—was enough for her.[54]

But this was also because memory at the altar was still needed. Augustine did not present Monica as a saint, far from it. She was presented as Everywoman, as a classic case of the *non valde boni*—of the "not altogether good": "I do not dare to say that, since the day that You [God] regenerated her by baptism, no word came from her mouth contrary to your precept . . . So now I pray for her sins . . . Forgive her, if there is any debt of sin that she carries after so many years since she passed the saving waters."[55] Ten years after her death, Monica still lived, somehow, in the other world, all too close to a dread shadow that needed to be kept at bay by the prayers of the living: "Let none wrest her from Your protection. Let not the *lion* or the *dragon* block her way, by force or by some craft."[56] It is one of the very few times that the devil makes an appearance in the *Confessions*.[57] The hint of that malevolent presence is all the more disturbing for being named through symbols alone.

Augustine wrote about Monica circa 397. At this time, the cloud of disquiet had been no more than the size of a fist. But by the time he wrote to Evodius and Paulinus, in the 420s, when he himself was in his sixties, the cloud had come to cover his whole sky. Why had this come about?

The short answer, of course, is because of Pelagius. For the Pelagian controversy (which erupted after 410) was far more than a conflict of ideas. It was a clash between two Christian landscapes—the landscape of Christian Rome (where Pelagius had taught and where he had found his principal supporters) and the landscape of Christian Africa. At stake were not only issues of grace and free will but of the nature and purpose of religious giving. For Augustine placed the distinctive mark of his own sharp preoccupation with sin upon traditional (and, until then, largely un-thought-through) notions of expiation in this world and the next through almsgiving.[58]

But how had this linking of almsgiving and sin come together in the first place? Why was the issue of almsgiving so charged, and why could it be swept, with such force, into the vortex of Augustine's notion of sin? And what would be the consequence of this novel, heightened sense of sin for notions of the fate of the soul after death? It is to these issues that we now turn.

3

Almsgiving, Expiation, and the Other World: Augustine and Pelagius, 410–430 AD

The Church, the Circus, and the Care of the Poor

In Chapter 2, we examined how Augustine dealt with concerns that he had in common with the third-century Christians of San Sebastiano and the Manichees of Egypt: a wish for access to the other world through dreams and visions; a concern with burial practices; and the assertion of the power of prayer and memory as the only certain bond between the living and the dead. We ended with Augustine's portrait of Monica in the ninth book of the *Confessions*. We would not have had so finely etched a portrait of a Christian woman if it had not been for Augustine's fierce loyalty to the traditional cultivation of memory—and especially of memory at the altar at the time of the Eucharist—that he shared with Christians as different from himself and from each other as the happy diners of San Sebastiano and the austere Manichees of the Dakhlah oasis.

With the Pelagian controversy, which escalated from 410 onward in Africa and elsewhere, we enter darker waters. Seen by Augustine, the Pelagian controversy was not only a controversy about grace and free will, it was about sin. But it was not only about the degree to which the human condition was tainted by sin, it was about what could be done about this situation. That is, it was about those modes of expiation for daily sin that Augustine considered to be fundamental to the Christian search for salvation. Among the most prominent of these modes of expiation was the giving of alms to the poor.

For Jews and Christians alike, almsgiving for the remission of sins had involved the perpetual circulation of wealth within the religious community for the benefit of the poor. Augustine claimed that Pelagius's view of the perfectibility of human nature led to a denial of the need for such expiation. Why give alms so as to expiate sin if Christians were capable of living without sin in the first place? Whether Augustine accurately reported the ideas of Pelagius is far from certain. Rather, he presented Pelagius's ideas in such a way so as to ensure that the Pelagian controversy was not only about sin, it was also about the use of wealth to expiate sin.

As we will see later in this chapter, Augustine's decision to fight the Pelagius on those terms had two immediate consequences. The first was the frank acceptance on his part of the fact that the church was a church of the *non valde boni*—of the "not altogether good": of twilight persons, rendered incomplete by sin. In the great Van Ness diagram of Christian souls that

Augustine propounded in his answer to Laurentius in the *Enchiridion*, ordinary Christians, as sinners, occupied the ever-widening zone between the saints and the reprobate. The victory of Augustine over Pelagius was their victory.

But, second, we will see at the very end of this chapter that this was a victory that created as many problems as it solved for Augustine and for those who consulted him in his old age. How could a soul so burdened with recurrent, almost subliminal sins ever be purged before death? Or would the soul have to pass through some form of purgation after death before it could enter heaven?

These problems (and especially those that involved purgation in the afterlife) were largely unexpected ramifications of a controversy that began, after 410, with the issues of sin, expiation, and wealth. But why, in the first place, should the emphasis on almsgiving to the poor be so charged in Augustine's Africa? In order to understand this, we must step back a decade, and look, for a moment, at the nature of giving in the secular world. Roman North Africa was one of the last provinces of the western empire to have maintained a high standard of civic life. This was especially true of the region best known to Augustine: Carthage and the cities of the Medjerda Valley through which he traveled regularly on his way from Hippo to near-annual councils of the African church at Carthage. Throughout the fourth century, buildings were renewed, theaters were repaired, and great circus games were performed in Carthage and elsewhere.[1]

Behind this last Indian summer of the African cities there lay an ancient ideology that determined the horizons of those who had continued to fund civic activities. This ideology has come to be called, by modern scholars, "civic euergetism." Civic euergetism involved a potent constellation of ideas and practices that had dominated the minds and actions of the upper-class inhabitants of the classical Mediterranean for over a millennium. It only began to lose its grip in late antiquity. The ideology of civic euergetism effectively governed the patterns of public giving among the rich, who were technically free to spend their money as they wished and rich enough to spend it on any number of different causes. When it came to the public use of wealth, the rich were "hard wired" for civic euergetism and for very little else.

In the late 1970s, two brilliant monographs—that of Paul Veyne and that of Evelyne Patlagean—drew attention to the tenacity of this ideology in late antiquity and made clear its sharp and distinctive profile.[2] What Veyne and Patlagean showed was that the notion of civic euergetism had always assumed a strictly civic (one might almost say political) model of society. The wealthy were expected to spend their money on their city and on the comfort and entertainment of their fellow citizens—and on those only. It was a model that tended to look through the economic structuring of society. Poverty, in itself, gave no entitlement. Those who received benefits from the wealthy received them not because they were poor but because they were citizens.

Thus, for Christian bishops such as Augustine to preach in favor of almsgiving to the poor was to do far more than stir the wealthy to occasional acts of charity and compassion. It was to undermine the entire traditional model of society that had directed their giving habits up to this time. Civic notables were challenged to abandon the notion of citizen entitlement. They were urged to look beyond their fellow citizens and to switch their giving toward the gray immensity of poverty in their city and in the countryside around them.

Altogether, to accept Christian preaching was to make a major shift in one's image of society. In terms of the social imagination, it involved nothing less than moving from a closed to an open universe. We begin, in the classical world, with a honeycomb of little cities, in each of which the rich thought only of nurturing their fellow citizens, with little regard to whether any of them were poor. We end, in Christian times, with an open universe, where society as a whole—in town and countryside alike—was seen to be ruled, as if by a universal law of gravity, by a single, bleak division between the rich and the poor. The duty of the Christian preacher was to urge the rich no longer to spend their money on their beloved, well-known city, but to lose it, almost heedlessly, in the faceless mass of the poor. Only that utterly counterfactual gesture—a gesture that owed nothing to the claims of one's hometown or of one's fellow citizens—would earn the rich "treasure in heaven."

To put it mildly, this was a notion that thousands of well-to-do persons in the little cities that covered the Roman Empire still needed to be persuaded to accept. We cannot understand the prodigious output of Christian sermons from all over the empire, advocating almsgiving to the poor, unless we bear in mind that we are dealing with a church and with a society for whom the horizons of the possible had, relatively suddenly, been blown open.[3]

This widening of horizons affected the church quite as much as it affected the elites of the empire. The conversion of

Constantine made the Christian Church a privileged institution. But the quid pro quo of this privilege had been an opening of the churches to the care of the masses. Christians no longer limited their activities to the somewhat cozy care only of impoverished fellow believers. The new obligation of outreach to the poor as a whole placed a totally novel burden on the bishops and clergy, for which many churches were ill prepared.[4]

As for the lay elites, they had to be persuaded to abandon, or at least to moderate, their most intimate and deeply rooted code of public behavior—the civic code of euergetism, which had been as much a matter of noblesse oblige to them as chivalry would be for knights in the Middle Ages. They found that they were being urged to direct some, at least, of their wealth in a markedly different direction from that to which they were accustomed—toward the faceless and unglamorous poor.

Despite many assertions in conventional accounts of the fall of Rome, there is little evidence that the later empire passed through a marked crisis of poverty in the course of the fourth century.[5] Nor, alas, is there any evidence that Christians were suddenly engulfed in a wave of spontaneous compassion for the poor. What we are dealing with is a far more charged and interesting situation. An entire society found itself wrestling with its self-image. As a result, the division between rich and poor, and the insistence on the duties of the rich to the poor, took on an imaginative charge that had been lacking in any earlier period of the ancient world.

This was the situation that Augustine found in Africa when he became bishop of Hippo in 395 AD. He took the task of preaching on the relations between the rich and the poor very seriously. His audience may not always have included large numbers of the poor, but his preaching left those who heard him in no doubt as to their duties toward the poor.

We have received recent confirmation of Augustine's commitment to charity and the care of the poor. A series of sermons written by Augustine on almsgiving have only recently been discovered in the cathedral library of Erfurt, and they have been admirably edited and commented upon by Isabella Schiller, Dorothea Weber, and Clemens Weidmann in *Wiener Studien.*[6] These sermons show that Augustine had planned an entire campaign of preaching on the topic of almsgiving. The sermons preserved in the Erfurt manuscript have a particular value for us in that they are not rhetorical showpieces, as were many of the sermons that Augustine preached in Carthage in the 400s. Rather, they were model sermons that were written for his own clergy to preach on a regular basis. In these sermons, Augustine did not urge the clergy to appeal only to the compassion of their Christian hearers, far from it. The clergy were to go straight for the jugular and attack the rival system of giving—the ideology of civic euergetism. It was this euergetism, and the model of society that euergetism underpinned, that needed to be demystified and eventually replaced. Augustine implied that only by setting the church on an imaginative collision course with the circus could the rich ever be persuaded to notice the poor.

For this reason, the clergy were to preach directly against the circus games. These games were the most spectacular—and understandably the most popular—demonstrations of the civic notable's love for the citizens of his hometown. They were not simply occasions for riot and debauch; they had a serious purpose: reassuring the citizen body—the *populus*—of every city that the rich still loved them, and them alone. At the games, at least, the people were king.[7]

Augustine expected his clergy to confront rich members of the congregation who supported such games, who presided over them, or who contributed to chariot races and wild beast shows. They were to be "condemned, rebuked and changed for the better." The only use of their crazed displays of generosity was to challenge Christians to engage with equal enthusiasm in giving to the poor: "lazy members of our churches are to be challenged to action, seeing that they barely break a single loaf of bread to feed the starving Christ [in the poor], while those who lavish wealth on the theater [spend so heavily that they] leave hardly a loaf of bread for their own sons."[8]

Augustine had long preached in this way against the games and in favor of almsgiving. In late 403, for instance, he had combined a visit to Carthage with a series of sermons that coincided with a splendid civic occasion—the gathering of the priests of the imperial cult in Carthage, in a magnificent display of public loyalty to the emperor. The occasion would be celebrated in the traditional manner by public banquets, chariot races, and pitting human huntsmen (*venatores*—the equivalent of modern matadors) against lethal beasts (lithe leopards or ferocious, shuffling bears).[9]

Augustine's sermons at that time amounted to a direct challenge to the ideology that had rendered the poor invisible to the non-Christian and even to the Christian rich: "Driven crazy by this and puffed up with pride . . . they even wish to lose their fortunes by giving—giving to actresses, giving to cabaret artists, giving to wild beast hunters, giving to charioteers. They pour forth not only their inherited fortunes, but their very souls. Yet they draw back with disgust from the poor, because the People [the *populus*—the citizens gathered in the hippodromes and amphitheaters] do not shout for the poor to receive largesse. But the People roar for the *venator* [the matador] to have his prize."[10]

Augustine as a Preacher of Almsgiving

We must, however, remember that many of Augustine's sermons against the games were showpieces, preached at Carthage on special occasions. But it was not enough to define Christian almsgiving against its weighty rival in this way, almsgiving itself had to become an everyday habit. It is fascinating to see how Augustine set about making this happen. His business was similar to that of any other bishop in the Christian world. To use the words of Jaclyn Maxwell, describing the preaching of John Chrysostom at Antioch, the time had come for his congregation "to pick up habits . . . the Christian ethic had to become a [form of] commonsense."[11]

We can see Augustine's method in his choice of metaphors. In order to inject the notion of a transfer of treasure from earth to heaven through almsgiving with a thrill that it may not have possessed in the minds of many, he appealed to the sense of risk that was part of the adrenalin of wealth for the landowners, artisans, and merchants of coastal cities such as Carthage and Hippo. "God wishes you to invest what you have [by sending it to heaven], not to throw it away," was his refrain.[12] He preached to persons who were used to the tense hiatus that the treacherous seas placed, every year, between their own landed wealth—their grain, olive oil, and fine pottery—and the hope of profit through successful sales on the far side of the Mediterranean, in Italy and elsewhere.[13] His audiences were accustomed to the complex loans that helped them to handle this situation. To give to the poor, Augustine explained, was no different: They were sending their wealth to a distant land. They should think of almsgiving as a form of *traiecticium*, a cash purchase in advance that could lead to a "killing" elsewhere: "Our Lord God wishes us to be merchants of a kind. He proposes a long-distance deal. For example, a merchant says to his friend: 'Take gold from me here and give me oil in Africa.' He travels without travelling, and has already gained what he wanted."[14]

Such images were more than mere jeux d'esprit. They were part of a molding of the consciousness not unlike that which ancient philosophers had always recommended. Philosophers had encouraged their disciples to make reality look different. They were to do so by telling stories to themselves about the nature of things—life, death, honor, wealth, and poverty—that were different from the usual stories. These countercultural stories were supposed to subvert everyday common sense by turning conventional values on their head.[15] Augustine did the same, but his novel stories were about the paradoxical joining of wealth, heaven, and the poor. They caught a mood—the mood of Africa in the last days of its glory as the center of gravity of the economy of the western Mediterranean. He encouraged his hearers to think in blatantly commercial terms. They were to treat placing "treasure in heaven" as if it was an advanced purchase. They were to think of the poor as dockhands, loading wealth aboard for a distant port.[16] They should regard a gift to the church as if it were that part of the family inheritance that would have gone to a dead son. Seeing almsgiving in this way involved a series of "small and easily accomplished" thought experiments that roused Augustine's audience to cheers.[17]

But above all, Augustine had to present almsgiving as regular and dependable. His hearers were to think of almsgiving as a *machinamentum*, a well-known device in Africa. It was a wheel whose constant turning caused a chain of buckets to move up and down, like the *noria* of Spain or the *shaddûf* of Egypt. The perpetual horizontal movement of a wheel (pushed by an animal or a human) was transformed, by a complex set of gears, into a vertical motion that drew the chain of buckets so that they poured water taken from a low river or canal on to the higher fields.[18] Working ceaselessly to place water where no water was to be found, alms were the *machinamenta occulta*—the "hidden devices"—that raised treasure to heaven.[19]

Pelagian Attitudes to Wealth

This is how we find Augustine, in 410, at the moment when Pelagius and many of his upper-class patrons began to arrive in Carthage as refugees from the Gothic sack of Rome. Their arrival not only brought ideas on sin and free will that Augustine considered to be dangerous theological novelties, but it threatened to upset the patterns of religious giving in Africa.

We have just seen why this might be so. For over a decade, Augustine had struggled to create among the elites of Africa—but also among the less well to do—a habit of steady giving that

marked a novel departure for many of them. As he made clear
to his clergy in the Erfurt sermons and in his preaching as a
whole, the notion of "alms" came to embrace three pious causes—
care of the poor, support for the clergy, and the building and
maintenance of churches.[20] None of these, except, perhaps,
church building, involved spectacular outlays. The cost of a
church could be around 2,500 *solidi*—solid gold pieces. By contrast, the cost of public games at Rome (though probably not in
Africa) could be as high as 144,000 *solidi*.[21] Rather, what mattered was to maintain a steady flow of funds to the poor and to
the church through the insistent schooling of all members of
the congregation—both the rich and those of modest means—
in the proper, Christian use of wealth. They had to develop both
habits of the heart and habits of the hands.

By contrast, what the refugees from Rome brought with
them to Carthage was from another world—a world of upper-
class Romans where wealth itself had been problematized. Pelagius had addressed circles of men and women who suffered
from a plethora of riches. He was close to Paulinus of Nola, and
also to the senatorial heiress Melania the Younger and her husband Pinianus.[22] Only five years previously, in 405, this young
couple had shocked Roman society by selling their possessions.
This fortune amounted to some 120,000 *solidi* a year. On one
occasion, they had been comforted by a dramatic dream: "One
night we went to sleep, greatly upset, and saw ourselves, both
of us, passing through a very narrow crack in the wall. We were
gripped with panic by the cramped space, so that it seemed as
if we were about to die. When we came through the pain of that
place, we found huge relief and joy unspeakable."[23]

Here were two young persons who had felt, as if in a nightmare, the pain of passing through "the eye of a needle" in order
to enter "the kingdom of heaven."[24] Yet, when they arrived as
refugees in Africa, they did not come as paupers. They emerged—
much as Paulinus had emerged at Nola a decade earlier—as patrons on a grand scale, endowing churches and founding large
monasteries.[25] Far from being delighted, the bishops were made
uneasy. Augustine and his colleagues approached Melania to tell
her, in effect, to cool it: "The money that you now furnish to
monasteries [they told her] will be used up in a short time. If
you wish to have a memorial for ever in heaven and earth, give
one estate and its income to each monastery."[26] One can understand the anxiety of the bishops. In their urge to disperse their
wealth, the pious couple was burdening the church with foundations for which there was no proper endowment. This has remained up to this day the nightmare of many a charitable or
learned institution.

At the same time, radical Pelagian tracts, such as the *de
divitiis*—the relentlessly argued "Treatise on Riches"—had advocated the total renunciation of property by the rich.[27] The
author of this tract extended his plea for total renunciation to
include a consequential denunciation of the existence of wealth
in the first place: *Tolle divitem et pauperem non invenies* (Get rid
of the rich and you will find no poor) was one of his many pro-
vocative slogans.[28] The *de divitiis* made plain that the only way
for rich Christians to reach heaven was through the total renunciation of their wealth, as Pinianus and Melania had done.

In 414, a summary of the ideas canvassed in the *de divitiis*
was passed on to Augustine from Sicily: "A rich man who

remains in his riches will not enter the Kingdom of God unless
he sells all that he has: nor will those be of any use to him [in
securing salvation] even if he uses them to fulfill the command-
ments [that is, by giving alms]."[29] Augustine instantly understood
the implied threat that such radicalism posed to traditional habits
of religious giving. It was not so much that the rich should not
exist, it was that they could not be saved. Unless they gave away
everything, their regular almsgiving would be of no avail.

Expiatory Almsgiving in Judaism and Christianity

Because of their radical nature, Augustine was determined to
take a stand against Pelagian ideas on wealth. Almsgiving was
more than a way to support the poor and to show the financial
muscle of the church in competition with the urban elites and
their ideal of civic euergetism. As we have seen, almsgiving had
a supernatural dimension. Augustine now emphasized this supernatural dimension ever more strongly. He insisted that almsgiving was an obligatory pious practice because it had an expiatory function. Alms atoned for sins. The command of the prophet
Daniel to King Nebuchadnezzar was a command to every Christian, as it had been to every Jew: "Redeem your sins with alms
and your injustices by compassion on the poor."[30] Like Jesus's
great image of the transfer of treasure from earth to heaven, the
notion of the redemption of sins through the giving of alms was
calculated to startle the average person. In the words of the later
rabbis: "Come and see how merciful God is to flesh and blood.
For a man can redeem himself from the heavenly judgment by
paying money, as it is said: *O king . . . redeem your sins with alms.*"[31]

This citation from the book of Daniel was widespread among Christian writers and preachers of the time. In order to understand its implications, we must go back, for a moment, an entire millennium—to the world of the Achaemenid Persian Empire and the succeeding, Hellenistic kingdoms of the Middle East. It was against this background that the story of Daniel was set (as a dramatic historical novel written many centuries later). In the centuries after the end of the Achaemenid Empire (roughly the third and second centuries BC) many Jewish writings came to speak about almsgiving and expiation.

When we turn to these writings we realize that we have passed one of the most significant imaginative frontiers in the history of ancient Judaism. Sin came to be spoken of in financial terms. Sin was no longer seen as a load that could be lifted only by the heavy rituals of sacrifice associated with an archaic, agrarian society. Sin was a debt.[32]

As a result of this imaginative change, sin itself took on a quicksilver quality. Like money, sin could be calibrated: Small acts of sin and negligence could be identified and handled expeditiously, without requiring the massive communal action involved in the flow of blood and the heavy smoke of sacrifice. Above all, sin was reversible. As Jesus ben Sirach, the author of *Eccelesiasticus,* insisted: like water putting out fire, alms extinguished sin with the certainty and speed of a natural process.[33]

The image of God Himself changed. God became, as it were, the "debt manager" of the believer. He could set the terms for the repayment of the debts of sin. Better yet, He could remit those debts—canceling the arrears of a lifetime in a splendid moment of forgiveness. He could also repay good deeds like any other creditor who had received a loan. But He did so at rates of interest far above those current in the real world. To say that "he who is kind to the poor lends to the Lord" was to be certain of a repayment whose generosity broke all the rules of a zero-sum economy.[34]

We often speak with disapproval of the "ledger-like" attitude to the expiation of sin that these metaphors seemed to imply.[35] But this is not how contemporaries saw the matter. Rather, the imaginative patterns that presented sin as debt (in a frankly monetary manner) gave pious Jews and Christians a way of speaking of the unbounded mercy of God. It was Satan who was the Scrooge-like accountant. The devil was often presented, in late antique visions of the other world, carrying a large and ominous account book.[36] By contrast, commercial metaphors brought a touch of fluidity to the notion of God's relation to human sin. They conveyed a sense of infinite possibilities. As a result, what seems at first sight to modern persons to be a crass commercialization of the religious imagination became one of the great "metaphors to live by" of the Jewish and Christian worlds. It infused relations with God with a sense of the infinite—of infinite reward, of infinite capacity for change, of the infinite possibility of settling accounts—that echoed, in all later centuries, the breathtaking expansion of the horizons of the possible that had accompanied the first expansion of a monetarized economy from the sixth century BC onward.

This was the view of the relation between sin and almsgiving that Augustine advocated after centuries that had already witnessed "The slow but sure penetration of the metaphor of sin as a debt into every aspect of Greek- and Latin-speaking Christianity."[37]

Augustine and Daily Sin

Let us see how Augustine deployed this conglomerate ideology when confronted with the challenge of the spread of Pelagian ideas. Briefly, he performed a remarkable feat of intellectual "splicing." Well-established pious practices were harnessed to a brand-new thought. He grafted his own, distinctive notion of sin on to the widely accepted notion of the expiatory nature of almsgiving and of similar good works.

There is little need to linger on Augustine's notion of sin. He had long been convinced that the life of a Christian was a life of continual penance."[38] The pious Christian was a human hedgehog. He or she was covered from head to foot with the tiny, sharp spines of daily, barely conscious *peccata minutissima*— with "tiny little sins."[39] It was to expunge these tiny sins that the Christian should pray every day *Dimitte nobis debita nostra:* "Forgive us our sins."[40] One should note how, in the Latin of the Lord's Prayer, "sins" were usually termed *debita*—"debts." They were debts that could be cancelled.

To Augustine, from 412 onward, these words of the Lord's Prayer—"Forgive us our sins"—provided the answer to Pelagius's doctrine of the freedom of the will. Pelagius had offered a freedom to be perfect. Augustine countered this perfectionist message with the argument that the Lord's Prayer itself denied the possibility of perfection in this life. No one could claim to be perfect—to live without sin. Still less could they claim to have gained this perfection through the exercise of their will alone. The Lord's Prayer was a daily reminder of a state of sinfulness that cried out for daily forgiveness. To deny this was to strike at the very heart of Augustine's religion.[41] By the 420s, Augustine's view of the future of Christianity was simple in the extreme: It consisted of the prospect of ever more churches filled with the thunderous sound of chest beating, as congregations recited the Lord's Prayer.[42]

But there was a concrete, financial corollary to this insistence on daily penance for daily sin. Like all other Christian preachers of his generation, Augustine never doubted that prayer for forgiveness should be accompanied by almsgiving. Almsgiving provided the "wings" that brought the *Dimitte nobis* of the Lord's Prayer up to heaven. Without such wings no prayer could fly.[43]

This meant, in effect, that perpetual giving was the counterpart of perpetual sin. Challenged by the perfectionism of Pelagius, Augustine expanded the traditional notion of almsgiving as a payment for sin to include the more daring notion of the need for the daily expiation of sins. It seemed to Augustine that the human condition demanded this. The soul was a leaking vessel on the high seas. Little trickles of daily sins constantly seeped through the timbers, silently filling the bilge with water that might yet sink the ship if it were not pumped out. And to man the bilge pump was both to pray *and* to give alms: "And we should not only pray, but also give alms . . . Those who work the bilge-pump lest the boat go down . . . do so [chanting sea-shanties] with their voices and working with their hands . . . Let the hands go round and round . . . Let them give, let them do good works."[44]

Religious giving was part of daily life, because daily life itself was defined by sin. It took place against the noise of the steady creak of the bilge pump of prayer, fasting, and almsgiving.

Furthermore, daily sin, wealth, and almsgiving were drawn together by a half-hidden homology. Augustine always stressed the way in which daily sin piled up, in, and around the human person in a largely unconscious manner—like sand, like drops of water, like fleas.[45] But, for the good Christian, wealth did much the same. Surplus wealth also seemed to pile up almost insensibly in the form of small sums that could be disposed of with little difficulty or regret in the form of alms or contributions to the church. The good Christian could learn to dispose of these small sums in a manner that was as painless and as much to be taken for granted as was the regular trimming of one's hair.[46] Furthermore, the daily sins to which Augustine referred were also sins due, largely, to the subliminal buildup of a surplus of negative drives that accrued in the course of normal social living. The "daily sins" that could be expiated by alms alone were not the big, cold crimes of violence, fraud, avarice, and adultery. They were the humdrum sins of everyday life. They also grew like hair—or like the prickles of the humble hedgehog.

Though small, these sins were peculiarly significant for Augustine. They reminded the faithful that, though relieved from the burden of original sin through baptism, all members of the church were still spiritual convalescents. The effects of the terrible, first sin of Adam and Eve still lingered in them. Human beings had been irreparably weakened. It took time for healthy skin to form over the deep scar of Adam's fall.[47] Nothing showed this more clearly than did the surplus, almost unconscious energy that still led to little bursts of anger and pride, to inappropriate sadness at the loss of material things, and (for the married) to moments of excessive energy in bed.[48]

Augustine did not linger on these small sins of excess because he was unnaturally scrupulous. Rather, he did so because he was optimistic. He regarded them as precisely the sort of sins that could be dealt with by almsgiving. Everyday sins and their remedy—everyday almsgiving—slid together in his mind. Wealth—the almost insensible buildup of a surplus—could be used on a day-to-day basis to counter sins that were, themselves, the result of a daily bubbling up of surplus energy—of largely insensible tendencies to sin—that still lingered in the veins of all human beings since the fall of Adam.

As we follow this constellation of metaphors in Augustine's preaching, both before and after his clash with Pelagius, we find that he stressed, above all, the value of daily, almost subliminal actions as remedies for equally subliminal sins. Such metaphors would only have carried weight with his audience if the sums of money involved in almsgiving had been modest. He did not expect heroic renunciations of wealth. Rather, "small change" sins were met by "small change" outlays to the poor.

Sin and Religious Giving in Augustine's Africa

The congregations of Africa—rich and poor alike—heard Augustine's message with a certain relief. Augustine's preaching fitted in very well with the realities of their social condition. Even if they were good Christians and wealthy, none of them suffered from the overabundance of wealth that characterized super-rich Roman Christian families. They had no wish to be told to renounce their wealth in its entirety, as the Pelagius in the *de divitiis* urged that they should do. Rather, rich and poor alike were encouraged to save their souls, on a regular basis, by forms of giving that were as regular as the daily repetition of the *Dimitte nobis* of the Lord's Prayer.

This attitude had social repercussions. Augustine never discouraged heavy giving by the rich, but his insistence on the expiatory nature of giving ensured that the rich did not see themselves as special. Their giving was associated with penitential habits that they were assumed to share, as fellow sinners, with all other members of the congregation. Hence there was a significant contrast between the two forms of giving. A citizen gave to the city, quite frankly, so as to show his own glory and that of his family. Citizens were not supposed to give in that way to the church. Rather, one gave "for the remission of sins." Augustine received some quite substantial legacies for the church of Hippo. But he always insisted that they had been given because the donor was "mindful of the eternal safety of his soul." This language brought to the gifts of even the wealthy a note of human fragility, a sense of risk and of a need for safety for the soul, such as could be shared by all Christians, rich and poor alike.[49]

There was room in such a view for relatively humble donors. Everyone was a sinner, and, so, everyone could give. Such a donor was Umbrius Felix, a schoolteacher in the little town of Mina (modern-day Ighil Izane, Algeria), far to the west of Hippo, on the inland road that crossed Caesarean Mauretania. In an inscription carved between two rosettes, he wrote in 408 AD: "from the Gifts of God and Christ, Umbrius Felix, the *magister*, made this. He has repaid his vow to God. Let prayer be made for him and may he have salvation from his sins."[50]

In this way, Augustine gave his Christian contemporaries a doctrine for the long haul. Driven as it was by the perpetual motion of the need to expiate sin, religious giving endured. Sin was permanent, and for that reason, religious giving also had to be permanent, regular, and devoted, above all, to the expiation of sin.

Sin and Purgation in the Afterlife

But how was the zest with which Augustine propounded this ideal of religious giving consonant with his notable reluctance to commit himself to a clear view of the destiny of the soul after death? On this issue, we come closest to Augustine if we look at his reactions to the challenge posed by the rigorism of Pelagius and his followers.

In their exhortations, Pelagius and his radical followers had shown zero-tolerance for sin. They argued that to be entirely free was to be free to abandon all sin as abruptly as one was supposed to abandon all wealth. Those who failed to do so were not simply weak, they were rebels and *impii*—impious persons. They were as far from the mercy of God as were out-and-out pagans. Confronting Pelagius in the Holy Land (to which Pelagius had come in 416, having passed rapidly through Africa), Jerome professed to be horrified by this doctrine. In his opinion, only unbaptized non-Christians could be called *impii*. By contrast, the baptized Christian had the rare privilege of being a *peccator*—a "sinner."[51] As a mere "sinner," he or she could hope for the mercy of God right up to and perhaps even beyond the Last Judgment.[52] Unlike the "impious" (so Jerome insisted),

Christian sinners would always receive "judgment tempered by mercy." In the warm words of Brian Daley: "It is Jerome at his most generous."[53]

Along with Jerome, Augustine insisted that average Christians were not *impii*. They were merely *peccatores*, for whom he had sketched out an entire lifetime of penance, prayer, and almsgiving. Indeed, they were the *non valde boni* for whom the prayers and almsgiving of the faithful might be expected to be effective in the other world.

Augustine and Jerome almost certainly caricatured Pelagius's real position on sin. But they both did so in order to make a point. They wanted to find ample room in the church for those of "the Middle Way." As in the time of Mani and his disciples, in the early fifth century the fate of the average believer—caught in the twilight zone between the certainty of heaven and the certainty of hell—was of far more concern and lucubration than the fate of out-and-out saints and sinners. By the 420s, the twilight zone had widened to embrace the majority of the population of an officially Christian Roman Empire. The Christian Church had become a church of the *non valdes*—of the "not altogether good" and the "not altogether bad" believers.

Writing in 421, against the last and most tenacious of his Pelagian opponents, Julian of Eclanum, Augustine offered a portrait of the sort of Christian who might yet get to heaven. It is a glimpse of the average Christian of his own days and of centuries to come:

> Who indulge in their sexual appetites, although within
> the decorous bonds of matrimony, though not only for the

sake of children, but even because they enjoy it. Who put up with insults with less than complete patience . . . Who may even burn at times to take revenge. Who hold on to what they possess. Who give alms, but not very generously. Who do not grab other people's property, but who defend their own—although they do it in the bishop's court and not before a secular judge. But who, through all this, see themselves as small and God as glorious.[54]

But how far would God's mercy for sinners extend? Could Christian souls as heavily laden with small, almost subliminal sins (as Augustine had presented them in his sermons against Pelagius) ever hope to expiate all those sins in this life alone? Would the process of expiation have to extend beyond death, so as to admit some form of purgation in the afterlife? Augustine was increasingly driven by Pelagius to face this problem. He had to peer, once again, into the world beyond the grave.

Among the letters of Augustine discovered by Johannes Divjak, there is a letter written to none other than Cyril, patriarch of Alexandria, in 417. In this letter, we see Augustine from an unusual angle. The bishop of Hippo is hardly known to us as one who was easy on sin. And yet, in this letter, Augustine presented himself as having been accused by the followers of Pelagius of being soft. He claimed that the Pelagians had accused him of believing that "not all sinners are punished by the eternal fire."[55]

Augustine accepted the accusation with gusto. He insisted that those who had sinned lightly would not go straight to hell, suggesting that they even had a chance to change in the other world, at some time in the uncharted period between their death and the Last Judgment. To prove this, he cited from Paul's First Letter to the Corinthians (1 Cor. 3:14–15):"A fire will test the quality of each person's work. If the work of one who is built on the foundation [of Christ] survives, they will receive their reward. And if the work of one is burned up, they will suffer loss. But the person will be saved, as if by passing through fire."

But he was careful to add: "These words of the Apostle are to be understood as not referring to the fires of the Last Judgment [which would be eternal] but of some fire that precedes the judgment, whether in this life or after death. But, however that may be [that is, purgation in this life or in the next] at any price we must avoid the error of thinking that all sinners are destined to go to eternal fire if they have not lived on earth a life totally exempt from sin."[56] This letter, addressed to a distant and formidable prelate, shows that Augustine was prepared to envision some form of purgation beyond death, if only to rescue the average Christian from the inflexible rigor of the Pelagians.

Augustine was always careful to explain his notion of an *ignis purgatorius*—of "a purging fire"—to the patriarch Cyril and to others by means of a scrupulous reading of the words of Saint Paul. He did not admit (or he did not realize) that he had raised a problem for all later ages: How long would it take for souls to pass through that purging fire? In the words of Claude Carozzi, the notion of an *ignis purgatorius* changed the idea of time in the other world. It created a sort of enclave of "suspended time" in the middle of eternity.[57] For Augustine did not see purgation in terms of the pain that its fire might inflict, he saw it in terms of time. He stressed the element of "delay" that such purgation imposed on souls who, otherwise, might have passed on directly to the presence of God—as the little notary of Uzalis was believed to have done. It was in this twilight zone, between human time and eternity, that Augustine suggested that the prayers and offerings of the faithful might be most effective.

This sense of an intermediate existence of the soul brought Augustine into largely unexplored territory. When Paul implied that the fire would burn away the "wood, hay and straw" (1 Cor. 3:12) that some had built on the foundation stone of Christ— that is, their lives—he gave no hint as to whether such buildings of straw would follow their creators into the stillness of the other world. But this is what Augustine came to expect. He could imagine that the *non valde boni* might, indeed, enter eternity carrying with them an entire life, straw and all. That straw would have to be burned off before the soul was considered worthy to enjoy the presence of Christ.

Writing in the *City of God* on the notion of a purging fire in the afterlife, Augustine was prepared to be studiously open minded: "I do not argue against this view, for perhaps it is true."[58] But his willingness to entertain such a notion had wide implications. Every soul had a specific destiny—one might say a biography of its own—in the other world that was directly related to the aspirations and failures of their former selves. Every soul among the *non valdes* could be prayed for in terms of precise features—of bits of straw still to be purged by fire. Augustine himself had already sketched such a figure with great delicacy, but with a surgical firmness, when he portrayed his mother Monica at the end of book nine of the *Confessions*.

Only among Neoplatonic philosophers, to whose debates on the soul Augustine constantly paid attention if only to rebut them, was the issue debated as to what happened to souls who brought part of their life with them into heaven. The Neoplatonic solution was that souls still weighed down with past sins must descend again, through metempsychosis, to have these sins purged by a new existence in the body. Augustine went out of his way to reject this view.[59]

But the problem remained. For a late pagan Platonist, the souls of the truly great—of great philosophers such as Plotinus—came once and for all to heaven. Their past slipped from them in blessed amnesia. It was believed that such great souls would not even remember the heaving sea of matter from which their souls had escaped, much less that they would feel any downward pull of their past life. But for the average soul, one had to ask what unpurged residues of a former life had caused them to slip back into the cycle of rebirth.[60]

This was no sheltered speculation. Ever since boyhood, Augustine had read, in book six of Virgil's *Aeneid,* about the *dira cupido*—the "fateful urge"—that caused once-ascended souls to leave the Elysian Fields and to plunge yet again into the body. If the "dire longing" to return to a lower life did not happen out of sheer cosmic necessity, then the return to bodies of imperfect souls implied that they had brought some part of their own past, unpurged, into eternity. It was this tenacious remnant of their past life that condemned them to return to purgation in the body.[61]

Augustine, in the long hours spent in his study, must have grappled with this solution. No matter how much he rejected it and drew on other sources for his speculation on the purging of the soul, the philosophical debate on metempsychosis remained present to him. It hovered always at the back of his mind.[62] This would at least account for the paradoxical presence in eternity of the traces of an earthly identity among weaker souls who had not wrenched themselves entirely free from the world at death. These needed purgation of some kind. Platonic philosophers thought that these blemishes caused them to descend again to earth.

Augustine rejected this view with scorn. Nonetheless, he was inclined to think that souls with too much "straw" around them might have to face some kind of purgation. The pagan Platonists chose a redescent of souls into other bodies as a means of purgation. Augustine, by contrast, chose the passing of souls through some searching, purifying fire. But both were providing answers to a shared conundrum: What could be done with the presence of imperfection, "tracked in," as it were, by human lives, in a space associated with absolute perfection?

We should not, however, lean too heavily on Augustine's views on the *ignis purgatorius*. We tend to do so because of the later development of the idea of purgatory in the Latin Church. Much excellent scholarship has been done on this topic.[63] At the time, however, it was not a notion on which Augustine himself wished to linger. He spoke of it always with the reticence of a scientist who realizes that he made a discovery that might be used to create a devastating secret weapon.

We see this in a long sermon that Augustine preached at Carthage as early as 403. In this sermon he took his audience carefully through the crucial passage of Saint Paul. A sharp note of anxiety hangs over the sermon. It is one of the set of sermons in which Augustine had challenged, head-on, the ancient codes of civic euergetism and had advocated the giving of alms to the poor. But what he now told his congregation was that they themselves must not slack off. They had to maintain their own battle with their own sins. He wanted them to know that a mistaken reading of Paul's words might lead them to reduce their efforts in the hope of some easy purging in the never-never land of the other world. He insisted that, beyond the possible, somewhat minor, scenario of some form of otherworldly purging, there still lay the immovable, undoubted fire of the Last Judgment. That fire would not go away: "Brothers, I wish to be more than usually fearful . . . It is better not to give you false security. I will not pass on to you what I do not receive. Struck with fear, I have to terrify you. I would willingly make you feel safe if I myself felt safe. The eternal fire is still there. That is what I must still fear."[64]

God's Amnesty

There was one easy solution for the expiation of the sins of the *non valdes* that Augustine would not consider. This involved an appeal to the image of Christ as an emperor. As we have seen, this image had become firmly established in the Christian imagination in the course of the fourth century. It was widely accepted, especially among members of the upper class, for the figure of Christ as emperor seemed to solve at one stroke the problem of the tenacious sins of the average Christian. An emperor showed his power at its most stunning by exercising the prerogative of mercy. *Clementia* had always been presented as a central imperial virtue. At any time, an emperor could respond to petitions for mercy by a gesture of amnesty—by granting remissions of tax arrears or by cancelling sentences or reducing them either permanently or intermittently.[65]

In many circles, the root metaphor of imperial amnesty determined representations of Christ's mercy to sinners. Circa 400 AD, Prudentius, a poet who had been a provincial governor, wrote the *Cathemerinon*—his "Daily Round" of prayers for the pious Christian. In one of these poems, Prudentius claimed that every Easter (and maybe, even, every Sunday) the souls of those in hell would enjoy respite from suffering: "Hell's force abates, its punishments are mild, and the people of the dead, set free from the fires, rejoice in the relaxation of its imprisonment, nor do the sulphurous rivers boil as hot as they are wont."[66]

Prudentius may well have been echoing a contemporary *Apocalypse* that was already believed to have made its way from Asia Minor to the court of Constantinople—the famous *Visio Pauli* (the *Vision of Paul*). In this vision, Paul was said to have seen Christ come down to hell in the full panoply of an emperor—diadem and all. There He solemnly granted respite from punishment on every Sunday to all the souls caught in that dread prison.[67]

Augustine knew of these imaginative options, including the *Vision of Paul*. He set his face against them. This was not, as we might suppose, because such representations replicated in too crass a manner the social structures of this world. Rather, he was a conscientious bishop. He knew that images based on the almost whimsical exercise of the imperial prerogative of mercy would encourage Christians to put too much trust in that mercy. Images of amnesty especially affected upper-class Christians (such as Prudentius), who had seen firsthand how imperial mercy could be implored by petitioners, often through the intercession of powerful patrons. As we have seen, the saints were thought of as the otherworldly equivalents of such patrons.[68] The image of Christ as the ever-generous, good emperor and of the saints as supportive patrons would encourage sinners to lie low and wait until Christ declared a general amnesty at the Last Judgment.[69]

But there was more to it than that. Augustine had remained a Platonist. He yearned for the eternal presence of God.[70] Time— even the suspended time that his notion of a purging fire implied—was the last enemy of eternity. He wished all time to cease, so that he could live forever in the presence of his God. As he wrote to Laurentius in 422 AD:

> There is no harm in their thinking, if this gives them plea- sure, that the penalties of the damned are at certain in- tervals of time somewhat eased.
>
> But even if these physical punishments [from which Christ was believed to have granted a respite, as in Pru- dentius and the *Visio Pauli*] were the slightest that can be imagined, to perish from the kingdom of God, to be alien- ated from the presence of God, to be deprived of the abun- dance of God's sweetness . . . So great is *that* punishment, that no torments we have ever experienced can be com- pared to it.[71]

Eight years later, in 430, Augustine faced death. He would have wished to go to the sweet presence of God, much as the little notary at Uzalis had done. But he was not a man to cut his corners. Possidius of Calama, the friend and biographer of Augustine, described his last days:

> He often told us in intimate conversation that the reception of baptism did not absolve Christians, and especially priests, from the duty of doing fitting and adequate penance before departing from this life. And he acted on this himself in his last and fatal illness. For he ordered those Psalms of David which are specially penitential to be copied out and, when he was very weak, used to lie in bed, facing the wall where the written sheets were put up, gazing at them and reading them, and copiously and continuously weeping as he read.[72]

In Chapter 4 we move to Gaul and follow, among very different persons, in very different circumstances, and in a landscape very far from Africa, the further unfolding of the issues to which Augustine was forced, by his innumerable Christian questioners, to bend his mind.

4

Penance and the Other World in Gaul

Salvian of Marseilles

As we saw in Chapter 3, Augustine's intervention in the Pelagian controversy mobilized an entire conglomeration of ideas—some ancient, and some very new—that suffused the practice of religious giving with a dark dye. Giving was about sin. Like the insistent creak of a pump, regular almsgiving, along with regular prayer, was a constant reminder of a fallen human condition that demanded constant expiation. There would never be a moment when the good Christian did not need to say *Dimitte nobis*—"Forgive us our sins." Nor would there ever be a time when the flow of alms to the poor and to the church, which made such prayers effective, would cease.

We also saw that Augustine's emphasis on the need for the constant expiation of sin in this life posed questions about the afterlife. Yet, on the issue of how the soul passed into the other world, the extent to which the souls of the dead required further purgation, and, above all, how the prayers and rituals of the church affected the fate of the soul beyond death, Augustine retained a heavily charged silence.

It is only in the next centuries (and especially in the Gaul of the fifth and early sixth centuries) that we meet figures such as Salvian of Marseilles, Faustus of Riez, and Caesarius of Arles, for whom the other world had taken on more clear and palpable features. Each of them, in a different way, was driven by an overriding concern with penance, expiation, and reform. This concern led them to bring the other world into this world, so as to rebuke the sins and to redress the injustices of their own times, and to secure the souls of believers in the world to come. How and why they did this is the theme of this chapter.

But, first of all, we must remember that the Western Roman Empire in its last century was a very big place. History seemed to happen at a different pace in each of its many regions. Seen from Gaul, Africa was an *alter orbis*—"a world of its own."[1] Indeed, up to the end of Augustine's life, Africa still appeared to be caught in a time warp. Roman rule and a large measure of old-world prosperity had continued unchallenged.

At exactly the same time, by contrast, the provinces of Gaul and Spain had already passed, at headlong speed, through a convulsion brought about by a deadly combination of civil war and barbarian invasion. This began in Gaul with the collapse of the Rhine frontier after 406. The civil wars that accompanied these raids, and the hurried attempts of rival emperors and barbarian kings to carve out regional centers of power, left the Roman order irreparably damaged in Gaul (as also in Spain and, even more irrevocably, in Britain).

By the 450s, Roman rule in Gaul was reduced, effectively, to what it had been before the wars of Julius Caesar. A deeply Romanized Mediterranean coastline looked up into a wide and uncertain world to its north and west, where the emperor's writ no longer ran. Though Marseilles and Hippo faced each other across the Mediterranean, they were in different historical time zones.[2]

There is one vivid figure whose career and writings sum up the extent of the convulsion that had passed through Gaul, making the Christianity of the region very different from that of Augustine's Africa—Salvianus, known to us as Salvian of Marseilles. Salvian was born in the Roman Rhineland. As a young man, he had seen his world collapse around him, when the Roman defenses of the Rhineland crumbled in 406. He had witnessed with his own eyes the rows of corpses strewn outside the burned out city of Trier.[3] While his aunt remained in Cologne, a virtual captive of new barbarian overlords, he had headed for the south.[4] Arriving in Provence, he was captivated by the newly established monastic settlement of Lérins, off the Côte d'Azur. He settled in Provence and became a priest in Marseilles. He died in the 470s, having witnessed the end of the Western Roman Empire. His works are suffused by a new sense of urgency, driven by the fear of God's judgment in this world and in the next.

Salvian wrote his most famous work in the early 440s. It was entitled *de gubernatione Dei (On the Providential Rule of God)*. It is revealing that this scathing tract was called, by contemporary admirers of Salvian, *de praesenti iudicio:* "judgment in the here and now."[5] For Salvian, the ruin of the empire was a judgment of God, clear for all to see, upon the Christians of his own time. The aristocracies of Gaul had refused to repent and to expiate their sins. They had not learned "to redeem sins by means of scattered coins."[6] They got what they deserved: Barbarian armies had marched across the Roman provinces, bringing judgment to every region as if they were the footsteps of an angry God.[7]

It was to urge the rich to avoid God's judgment in this life and in the next that Salvian wrote his first tract in 435—the *ad Ecclesiam* (an *Open Letter to the Church*). It is hard to believe that this work appeared only five years after the death of Augustine. It seems to belong to a different world. Salvian's *Open Letter* shows that not only in politics and military affairs had fifth-century Gaul lurched suddenly toward the Middle Ages: Gallic Christianity, also, had taken on a new tone.

The churches of Gaul faced a situation that was very different from that of Augustine's Africa. In particular, the wealth of the church in Gaul came from a different source. As we saw, Augustine had preached and written in Africa so as to maintain regular, low-profile giving among large and relatively prosperous congregations. He appealed both to the rich and to ordinary men and women—to members of the self-respecting *plebes* of still vigorous cities and villages. He looked back to a very ancient church, where religious giving by all classes had been kept buoyant by the overall prosperity of the Roman Mediterranean. He could still cite, as if it were Holy Scripture, an early Christian text that expected Christians to allow their few coins "to gather sweat in their hands," as they made up their mind to part with them to deserving causes.[8]

In southern Gaul, by contrast, a different Christian landscape had emerged. The leadership of the churches had begun to pass into the hands of the local nobility. These well-to-do figures were supposed to bring much of their wealth with them. Thus, what was at stake for Salvian when he wrote on religious giving was not the creation of humdrum habits of giving among the rank and file but the movement of entire fortunes. He wrote to persuade the truly rich—and especially the rich who had joined the clergy or who had adopted the monastic life—to bequeath a considerable part of their wealth to the church in order to atone for their sins.[9]

In order to do this, Salvian conjured up a gripping vision of the other world. He urged potential donors to think of the serried ranks of angels and demons who awaited them in the world beyond: "Behold, the staff of the Sacred Tribunal awaits you as you leave this life. The torturing angels and the ministers of undying punishments stand at the ready."[10] Only by generous donations to the church could the rich entertain "one tiny flicker of hope" that they might be saved from this grim tribunal.[11] It is as if we were suddenly transported, across half a millennium, to the scenes of bliss and terror that decorate the portals of the Romanesque churches of France. Never before had wealth and the afterlife been brought together in so menacing a manner.

How had this imaginative change come about? The reasons for this change were both local and more general. On the local level, the presence of the island monastery of Lérins was the bearer of exotic and frightening views of the afterlife. Salvian and those to whom he habitually wrote had passed through the island monastery of Lérins in the 420s and 430s. Founded around 400/410, Lérins had brought a touch of the desert of Egypt to within sight of the coast of Gaul. Its monks had been "reared

on Eastern values, Eastern preoccupations and Eastern metaphors,"[12] and, with this touch of the East, came the dramatic
notions of heaven and hell that had circulated among the monks
of Egypt.

In Egyptian monastic literature, merciless demons were
thought to lie in wait for the soul as it left the body. They would
close in around it, like relentless creditors or tax officials, armed
with large, meticulously kept account books. They demanded
payment for every sin recorded in these books. If this debt of
sin had mounted too high, the ranks of angels sent from heaven
to protect the soul would step aside. They would leave the soul
to its fate. The demons would take the sinner to a very Roman
prison—a stifling waiting pen in which criminals were confined
before the governor issued his final sentence. At the Last Judgment, Christ would condemn them to hell.[13]

The monastic life as a whole was supposed to be lived out
under the shadow of the approach of the Last Judgment:

> A brother asked Apa Ammonas: "Give me a word." The
> Old Man said: "Go, have such a thought as evil-doers
> have in prison. They always ask those around them where
> the governor is and when he will arrive [to deliver final
> sentence]. And they weep in expectation. So should a
> monk always pay attention and search his soul, saying:
> 'Woe to me: how shall I stand before the Judgment Seat of
> Christ' . . . If you meditate all the time on this, you can be
> saved."[14]

It was to tableaux such as these that Salvian appealed, in 435, in
his *ad Ecclesiam*.

Death and the Protection of the Soul

Scholars usually ascribe this new, gripping sense of peril in the other world to the monastic environment of Lérins. We take for granted that such grim images could only emerge "from within the narrow, tomblike confines of the monastic cell."[15] I suspect, however, that such a view misunderstands the origins and extent of these fears. It overrates the role of monks in the Christian imagination of the time. Monks functioned less as innovators than as catalysts. Rather than purveying an entirely new piety, they were revered because they had taken seriously, and brought into dramatic focus, notions that they shared with other, more average Christians.

The recent work of Mariachiara Giorda has shown that even in Egypt itself, the monasteries were never worlds of their own. They lived in constant symbiosis with the beliefs and expectations of the lay Christians who supported them and who turned to them constantly for spiritual advice.[16] Far from radiating a distinctive, "monastic" Christian piety that injected a toxic current of dread into the laity, monks and nuns (in Gaul quite as much as in Egypt) shared with the laity an inherited conglomerate of Christian representations of the other world.

For this reason, we should set the changes in Christian representations of the other world against a wider background than that of the monasteries. Throughout the Mediterranean—in Italy and the East quite as much as in southern Gaul—Christians entertained expectations on the fate of the soul in the other world. Not all these expectations were reassuring. We should not be misled by the studied serenity of early Christian liturgies for the dead. In these liturgies *un climat festif et pacifié*—"a festive and peacefully resigned mood"—seems to predominate, but such prayers left much unsaid.[17] The sunny face presented by early Christian prayers and epitaphs only told half the story. "Tartarus," the ancient personification of the underworld—a source of faceless dread—had lost little of its imaginative force.

To understand this undercurrent of fear, we should look beyond the monasteries. We should also look at the growing practice of burial beside the saints that had developed all over the Christian West. Such burials betrayed the fear of dangers lurking in the other world. They even rendered these imagined dangers more explicit by claiming to offer protection from them. The saints beside whom believers were buried were thought to protect those buried close to them on the Day of Judgment, as was the case with Cynegius, the son of Flora, who was buried beside Saint Felix at Nola (as we saw in Chapter 2). Burial beside the saints also offered immediate protection. The saints would help the soul to confront the malevolent forces that hovered around it at the moment of death. In a sermon circa 400 AD, Maximus of Turin claimed that the saints sheltered those who were buried beside them from *Tartarus furens*—from "raging Tartarus."[18] This phrase was echoed, two centuries later, on a tombstone in Trier. The echo of the sermon of an Italian bishop of the fourth century on a tombstone of the sixth century, far to the north in Trier, shows how anxieties that were already present around the year 400 gathered momentum in the ensuing centuries.[19]

Altogether, we are dealing with a widespread phenomenon. It was not linked exclusively to monastic piety, nor was it recent. As we saw at the end of Chapter 1, the anxieties addressed by Mani in his *Kephalaia* circa 300 AD as to the efficacy of the death rituals of his Holy Church played on a lasting sense that the soul needed all the protection that it could get as it made its way "out of the body."

Death (and the demonic forces that lurked in the underworld) was not to be treated lightly. Even the story of the death of the little notary of Uzalis (with which we began Chapter 2), for all its gentle, homespun quality, was tinged by a sense of danger. The boy's soul had required safe conduct, guaranteed by an imperial summons, laurel wreath and all, in order to reach heaven. The tombstone of a nun in fifth-century Vicenza speaks with evident relief of the journey through which she was believed to have passed: "Now you rest in the bosom of Abraham, Jacob and Isaac. No places of punishment hold you back, no Hells filled with horror."[20]

These fears came together in a legend that may have originated in Palestine at some time in the mid-fourth century and that later became well known in the West. It was the story of the *Transitus Mariae* (of the passing of Mary). In this legend, even Mary, the mother of Christ, was said to have expressed fear, at the moment of her passing, of what would await her in the other world.[21] She prayed, "That no power of Satan or of Hell should come to meet me, nor should I see the dark spirits standing in my way." Her prayer was not granted: "You will see him [the Devil] due to the common law of humankind by which you are fated to die. But he will not be able to harm you."[22]

Thus, the fears relating to the other world that Salvian invoked were not an entirely new departure for the Gaul of the first half of the fifth century. Nor were they of purely monastic origin. Like the breaking crest of an ocean tide, Salvian's dramatic tableau of the sinister powers that await the soul at the moment of death had been prepared by a mighty swell of dread that had gathered momentum for more than a century before the 430s—that is, generations before Lérins was established and the Roman order collapsed in Gaul.

Altogether, the fears to which Salvian appealed and the need for expiation that these fears engendered were not the hothouse products of a single monastery. The notion of expiation through giving (such as Salvian proposed for the rich in his *Open Letter*) simply placed a Christian face on the fears of innumerable men and women, all over the Christian world, at the prospect of death.

Conversion and Public Penance in Gaul

What we have to understand is not so much how these grim notions about death came to be, but rather how they came to play so public a role in the Christianity of Gaul from the time of Salvian onward.

In order to do this, we must go back in time for almost a generation before Salvian wrote his *Open Letter*—to the 410s and 420s. We must shift our attention to a widespread and ancient Christian practice—to the practice of public penance. We will see how a discourse of conversion and reform developed around this practice in southern Gaul in the course of the fifth century.

Until recently, the institution of public penance in the Christian churches of the fifth century—in Gaul and elsewhere—was treated by scholars as a spiritual dinosaur. They presented it as a relic from the heroic days of the early church. It was believed that these were days of zero-tolerance for sin. Major sins committed after baptism could only be atoned for—and that only once—by a fully public humiliation of the sinner, followed (after a long period of exclusion) by his or her formal reception back into the church by the local bishop. On this heroic model, penance amounted to virtual exclusion from social life. It involved the abandonment of sex for married persons and, in the case of upper-class men, the snuffing out of the public persona through retirement from office and through the adoption of a low-key style of dress. Penitents became nonpersons, condemned to live, for a period, on the margins of the Christian community.[23]

Presented in these terms, so drastic a system seemed like taking a sledgehammer to crack a nut. Major sins that affected the community as a whole might be made subject to public penance. But there were so many other sins committed by so many other, small-time sinners. Did they all have to be dealt with in the same drastic manner? It has usually been assumed that once Christianity became a majority religion and the church was filled with very average and pertinacious sinners (the "not altogether goods" who claimed Augustine's constant attention), the early Christian system of public penance became unworkable. It survived only as a grandiose and increasingly awkward legacy from the heroic days of the early church, which had lost touch with present-day realities.

Or so the story goes. We are left with a sharp contrast between two ages—a heroic, but increasingly unrealistic, early Christian system of public penance that finally came to be replaced, in the early Middle Ages, by the more flexible system of "private" penance, linked to private confession, that characterized the Catholicism of the Middle Ages and of modern times. This contrast is deeply ingrained in the historiography of the Christian Church in the West.

The roots of this contrast between the two ages of the church reach back to scholars and polemists of the early modern period—to the debates between the Jansenists and the Humanist *dévots* in seventeenth-century France. Already in 1655, the Franciscan François Bonal defended the moderate confessional practices favored by the *dévots* of his own day against what he perceived to be the Jansenist idealization of the drastic penitential regime of the early church. He accused the Jansenists of exaggerating and idealizing the penitential practice of the early Christian Church. He claimed that the Jansenists presented a "melancholy, tearful and wretched" image of early Christian penance, so as to contrast its salutary rigor with the all-too "dainty," undemanding practices of modern times, of which they disapproved.[24]

The recent works of Éric Rebillard, Mayke De Jong, and Kevin Uhalde have made plain that this presentation of the early Christian institution of penance has little basis in reality.[25] The system did not fail. It never existed in the first place in the dramatic form that we had imagined. However, we still have to explain the emergence, in fifth-century Gaul, of a powerful "discourse" of penance. In this discourse, a drastic notion of public penance was used as a template for an equally drastic notion of conversion. Penance was about change—about the shedding of past sins through conversion to a different life. It became clear that it was possible, indeed eminently desirable, for certain men and women both to change their lives drastically and to show this change in public as a guarantee, as it were, of their future good behavior.

This notion of penance gave contemporaries a language with which to speak of the emergence of a new class of leaders dedicated to the preaching of moral reform in the churches of Gaul. For, like penitents, these were persons who had broken dramatically with their past. Thus, it could be believed of a contemporary of Salvian, Bishop Eutropius of Orange, that he had performed drastic penance when a young deacon. As a ratification of the effects of this penance, he had a terrifying vision. He dreamed that he was lying on his back and that a column of black birds flew out of his penis. Fire from heaven burned them all up. A little later, he dreamed that a cloud of flies came out of his chest. These also were burned up. With such a penance behind him, Eutropius could become a bishop. He came to his bishopric thoroughly purged of his past sins of sexual desire and of evil thoughts.[26]

The discourse of penance, with its emphasis on clearly marked transitions from one state of life to another, was very different from the ideal of a life of daily penance advocated by Augustine. That had been a gray world, marked by no clear breaks, but by the slow, creaking alternation of prayer and almsgiving. But the drama of penance suited the churches of southern Gaul. Let us see why that was so.

Honoratus and the Monks of Lérins

In Provence in the 420s and 430s, major changes took place in the structure and the personnel of the churches. Many episcopal

sees were taken over by monks from Lérins, and these monks
were often recruited from the local nobility. But their nobility
was not the identity to which they were now committed. They
wished to be known as persons who had put their old selves behind them. In turn, the lay nobility patronized these monks precisely because they had passed through the drastic penitential
discipline of a monastic life and had made themselves radically
different from their worldly peers. They had erased their former
identity as members of the upper class. They appeared, instead,
as members of a new "out class," and they did this by appearing
in public as figures who were as discontinuous with their former
selves as any penitents were imagined to have been.[27] Arriving in
Provence, the young Salvian came to know and greatly ad-
mire such persons. He addressed his treatises to them. To Salvian and to many others, this new "out class" represented the
wave of the future.

The first steps in the conversion to the religious life of these
young Provençal aristocrats usually took the form of a fully public
adoption of the lifestyle traditionally associated with penitents.
As a young man, around the year 400, Honoratus, the future
founder of Lérins, had done this. He had cut his flowing, well-
curled hair of a nobleman and replaced his bright silks with a
dull, coarse robe: "*ita repente totus ex alio alius ostenditur*": "and
so he was suddenly shown to be completely changed from one
person into another."[28]

Honoratus then went on to found the island monastery of
Lérins (the modern Île Saint-Honorat, opposite Cannes) circa
400–410 AD. Lérins was spoken of as a "Circe's Isle."[29] It was a
place where sons of the gentry were changed, as if by magic, into

members of a new monastic "elite." Well and truly shorn of their past, they emerged from the island ready to take over the bishoprics of southern Gaul. In 426, Honoratus himself became bishop of the turbulent governmental capital of Arles—not long after a predecessor had been murdered by a faction of the military!

Such self-professed outsiders were welcome in the cities. In his funerary address for Honoratus, in 429, Hilarius (usually known as Hilary—Honoratus's eventual successor to the see of Arles) stressed the manner in which Honoratus, as a monk-bishop, had gained the support of the laity. It is significant that Hilary did not only stress Honoratus's preaching and his impact on public affairs. He praised in particular the role of Honoratus in furthering the care of the souls of the departed.

Honoratus did this through careful administration of the gifts to the church that laypersons had made for the safety of their souls. He imposed a monastic austerity on the finances of the church so as to ensure that the wealth of the church was spent mainly on the poor and on offerings for the souls of the departed. In doing this, (so Hilary insisted) Honoratus "bestowed the treasures [of the church] on those who had recently died. Those who made offerings once again sensed the *refrigeria*—the "respites" to the souls of the dead—which their gifts had sought."[30] From then onward, the finances of the church of Arles flourished, for the bishop enjoyed the *gratia*—the "goodwill"—of a rich laity. In this very direct manner, the bishop of Arles established himself as the guardian, par excellence, of the bond between wealth and the other world on behalf of the well-to-do members of his congregation.

We should linger on this aspect of the life of Honoratus. The church of Arles did, indeed, become a wealthy church. It did so because the bishops of Arles upheld the notion that the wealth of the church was unlike any other form of worldly wealth. It existed to serve the two highly charged and paradoxical poles of the Christian imagination: the socially dead and the physically dead—the poor and the souls of the departed.

Above all, the wealth of the church not only supported the poor but had the power to obtain the forgiveness of sins. We know this from a later writer connected with the church of Arles—Julianus Pomerius, a refugee from the former Roman province of Mauretania. Looking back to around 500, Pomerius pointed out that the wealth of the church (in Arles and elsewhere) was made up in a unique manner. It consisted of the "patrimonies of the poor"—that is, of estates given for the support of the poor. But these estates were given as a result of "the vows of the faithful, as the price for sins." For this reason, they were sacrosanct. Paradoxically, the near-invisibility of the poor and the total invisibility of the afterlife provided the increasingly visible wealth of the church with a protective shield that no other property enjoyed.[31]

Julianus was an admirer of Augustine. One could not have had a more clear statement of the manner in which the linking of gifts to the poor to the expiation of sin (on which Augustine had built his case against Pelagius) had hardened, over the years, into a full-blown ideology of church property. And this ideology worked. Looking back as he wrote his treatise *On the Contemplative Life,* in 502, Pomerius noted that Honoratus's friend and successor, Hilary, had greatly expanded the wealth of the church of Arles through gifts from the faithful.[32] Shorn of their own past and former wealth, monk-bishops proved to be charismatic fund-raisers among the members of their own class.

We can see why this was so in the case of Hilary of Arles. Hilary had been a monk at Lérins. He was bishop of Arles from 430 to 449. He had a dramatic career, marked by almost constant conflict as he built an ecclesiastical empire based on Arles. But what his later biographer made clear was the manner in which Hilary had brought the other world into the present, much as Salvian, his younger contemporary, had done. And he did so as a preacher of repentance. He was renowned for his hellfire sermons on the subject: "Who could have shown more vividly the terrible ordeal of the Last Judgment? Who could inspire such terror by conjuring up the dark fire of Hell? Who could express the agonies of the searing river of fire, as it swept the sinners away?" And when his congregation tended to drift away before such sermons began, he would cry after them: "Go out, go out. For over there [in the other world] you will not be able to make an exit from Gehenna [from Hell]." A fire that soon devastated the city gave weight to Hilary's words. It was God's revenge on an insouciant populace who had refused to listen to a preacher of repentance.[33]

This was penance as it was understood in southern Gaul in the first half of the fifth century. It was not so much a system as a part of a general call to repentance, associated with the preaching of a remarkable group of charismatic bishops.

Faustus of Riez

The momentum of the penitential drive continued in widening circles in Gaul up to the beginning of the sixth century. It is

well summed up in the person of one of the very last products
of Lérins. Faustus was a person quite as strange as his older contemporary, Salvian. He had probably come to Lérins as a refugee, as Salvian had done. He did not come from the Rhine
frontier, but rather from a ruined enclave of "Roman" values in
the far west—either from what remained of Roman Britain or
from the Romano-British settlements of Brittany. From around
434 onward, he was a monk and abbot of Lérins for thirty years.
Then, circa 460, he became bishop of Riez, a little town, now
surrounded by fields of lavender, separated from the Riviera by
the sharp crests of the Alpes de Haute-Provence, but still close
enough to Lérins along a Roman road. He was bishop until the
late 490s. Like Salvian, he outlived the Roman Empire in the
West.[34]

While bishop, Faustus wrote on issues calculated to cause a
stir among contemporary theologians. In 474 he wrote the *de
gratia (On Grace)* as a firm rebuff to the teachings of extreme
supporters of Augustine.[35] He also wrote on the nature of the
soul as a critique of the excessive "immaterialism" of Augustine's
Neoplatonic notion of the soul.[36] He also wrote letters to leading
laymen on the nature of penance.[37] Let us linger for a moment
on these works, for they enable us to gauge the mental furni-
ture of a bishop from the school of Lérins.

First and foremost, Faustus insisted that a bishop had a duty
to rebuke and change the world around him. This meant taking
on the nobility of Gaul. He pitted his status as a member of the
"out class" against the pride and ruthlessness of unrepentant
members of his own, upper class. One of his most warm admirers
was Sidonius Apollinaris. A member of the upper echelon of

Gallic aristocratic society (and acutely aware of the fact), Sidonius knew a proud nobleman when he saw one. His principal
praise for Faustus was that, as a monk-bishop, Faustus had
learned "to flout the high handed habits of the great" (*tumidos
maiorum temnere mores*).[38]

Faustus's writings were of a piece with his sense of duty as
an active bishop. In his view, a bishop was there to make an impact on the leaders of his age. He was a militant, both in his
day-to-day activities and in his theology. His *de gratia* was an
uncompromising statement of what has been called the "Gallic
consensus" on grace and free will.[39] This was a consensus that
favored direct action in the world.

The details of Faustus's theology need not concern us. What
matters is that his view of the relation between God and human
beings was based on a metaphor of social relations that carried
great weight among the petty nobility of Provence. Faustus insisted that Christians should not see themselves as mere slaves
of God who had surrendered their will entirely to a higher
power—as some of the extreme supporters of Augustine were
suspected of believing. They were God's free clients, and He was
their patron. It was not that they were not dependent on God.
They were profoundly dependent on Him. But they had approached God in the first place as free persons.

That thin sliver of freedom meant everything to Faustus and
his supporters. The difference between being a client and slavery
was particularly charged in a world where real slavery was still
widespread. If clients were dependent on the great, it was because they had freely chosen to be dependent. What they could
offer in return was the willing, uncoerced service of free men.

It was the same with relations with God. Human beings did not simply "serve" God like slaves, or like possessed persons whose identity had been totally taken over by the divine. They were not God's robots; they were God's collaborators.[40]

This robust opinion lay at the root of Faustus's surprisingly activist view of the church. He made it very plain that God did not intend to act "by Himself alone, as a one-man show [*solitaria procuratione*] . . . Not at all! But with the whole body [of the church], with its members arranged around its bishops and pastors, with those who can say [with Paul]: *For we are God's fellow-workers* [1 Cor. 3:9] . . . Surely the church is built up in no other way than by the labors and good offices [*officia*] of bishops and by the activities and good examples offered by the saints."[41]

But how was this militancy to be sustained? Faustus's answer was unambiguous: through penance and through forms of meditation that encouraged penance. This austere notion of penance gave him a lever on the hearts of the great. Thus he approached Magnus Felix, former prefect of Gaul and a friend of Sidonius Apollinaris, with "a letter of exhortation to the fear of God, suitable to a person disposed to do penance with full commitment [*pleno animo*]."[42] For Faustus, this "full commitment" was to be achieved by drastic thought experiments. The pride of the converted nobleman could only be overcome "if the whole tableau [the *historia*] of a former life worthy of shame is brought before the eyes and the guilty conscience is made present to the quivering senses."[43] The Last Judgment, also, was to be made present in the mind: "in the hidden depths of the self, pictured in advance, [so that] you lift your eyes always to the throne of the Judge."[44]

"Acknowledgement of sin, fear of judgment and terror at the eternal fire" were Faustus's prescriptions for the spiritual education of the great who held the fortunes of Gaul in their hands.[45] For Faustus, there was no other way. He told Paulinus of Bordeaux (a nobleman from the same family as the great Paulinus of Nola) in no uncertain terms that a mere moment of regret on one's deathbed was not enough.[46]

It was because the work of the imagination was of such importance to him that Faustus also rejected the Augustinian notion of the immaterial soul. He was not the only thinker of his time to do so. John Cassian, whose works on the monastic life in Egypt (written in Provence in the 420s) had inspired the monks of Lérins, was of the same opinion. Only God was totally immaterial, totally "spiritual," and, so, totally boundless.[47] All His other creatures were delimited by a body of some kind, even if this body was as fine as the ethereal fire of angels.[48]

For Faustus, Cassian's notion of the "body" of the soul served to give gripping concreteness to the work of the imagination. Hell was no ethereal abstraction or a mere *façon de parler*. It was there. The vertiginous abyss that separated heaven from hell was also there. Those who doubted this would learn: "amid the searing steam, the soul will feel and see, all too late, that it *is* a material thing."[49]

Faustus's views on the soul brought upon him a reply from yet another friend of Sidonius, the Neoplatonic philosopher and clergyman Claudianus Mamertus of Vienne, in the form of an unusually aggressive pamphlet—the *de statu animae (On the [High] State of the Soul)*.[50] For Claudianus, to deny the total immateriality of the soul was an intellectual regression. It was to turn one's back on the highest thoughts of the ancient world.

As Claudianus saw it, the history of ancient thought had cul-
minated first in Plato—the "Prince of Philosophers"—and, then,
in Christian times, in Augustine's daring reelaboration of
Plato's view of the total immateriality of the soul. For him,
Augustine was a *spiritalis sophista* (a genius in defending the
spiritual nature of the soul).[51]

We have tended to agree with Claudianus Mamertus. Faustus's view of the soul has been made to seem primitive compared
with the more "spiritual" vision of Augustine. Yet, at the time,
the issue was far from clear. Faustus had Cassian on his side,
along with a long tradition of Stoic thought.[52] To him, the "immaterial" soul of Augustine was dangerously faceless: Identity,
linked to a precise body, slipped off it. And with identity went
responsibility for sin. As Tertullian had already pointed out, in
200 AD: "Immateriality is freed from every kind of limiting re-
straint, and is immune from punishment."[53]

Augustine's notion of the soul seemed to Faustus to be dis-
turbingly unlocalizable, and, for that reason, incapable of gripping the imagination. How was it possible, with so abstract, so
ethereal a thing to bring the tingling reality of heaven and hell
into the present?[54]

Faustus's position demands closer attention than it has received from historians of early medieval religion. It is now almost taken for granted that the piety of fifth- and sixth-century
Gaul became more primitive and more crassly "materialistic" as
the centuries wore on. The views of the afterlife that emerged
in Merovingian Gaul strike us as improbably concrete. We in-
stinctively assume that the upholders of a more "spiritual" view
of the soul must, somehow, be superior, for they seem more like
modern persons.

Yet those who read Faustus at the time would have seen matters rather differently. His appeal to Cassian against Augustine was a call to responsibility. It was a product of his urgent need to ensure that the reality of heaven, of hell, and of eternal punishment sank deep into the souls of the great. As we will see in Chapter 5, this tradition endured. The writings of Gregory of Tours are filled with grippingly concrete stories—with *historiae*. These vivid tableaux brought the realities of heaven, hell, and the Last Judgment into the here and now in a manner of which Salvian of Marseilles and Faustus of Riez would have thoroughly approved.

Caesarius of Arles

The positively last major figure from Lérins to preach in Provence was Caesarius, bishop of Arles from 502–542.[55] Caesarius is known to us for his loyalty to the memory of Augustine. He regularly used the sermons of his master in preaching. At the council of Orange, in 529, he secured the condemnation of views that Faustus had maintained with verve.[56]

Yet Caesarius and Faustus were a lot closer to each other than we usually think, for they were drawn together by a shared sense of urgency. Both saw themselves as preachers of repentance. Both wished to awaken their flocks to the reality of the other world and to the approach of the Last Judgment. Caesarius was known for his "unceasing voice" as a preacher. He hectored his flock on a regular basis.[57] Unlike Hilary when he preached at Arles a century earlier, Caesarius did not merely remind members of his congregation who slipped off before the sermon that they would not be able to do this when in hell. He actually locked the doors of his cathedral so that they could not escape![58] He wished his message to them to become *impectoratum*—to "sink deep into the breast" of those who listened to him.[59]

It is far from certain that Caesarius did all this from a position of strength. His authority in Arles was frequently challenged and ignored. If his was an "unceasing voice," it was often the voice of a prophet in the wilderness.[60] A recent careful and humane study by Lisa Bailey of a collection of sermons preached at Lérins and in Provence (known as the *Eusebius Gallicanus*) has shown that not every preacher in circles close to Caesarius adopted the same confrontational and invasive stance toward his congregation.[61]

Although Caesarius's sermons may not have been far reaching, there is no doubt that Caesarius was committed to what he preached. The *Life of Caesarius*, written by priests close to him, revealed that the bishop had wrestled even in his dreams with the stark alternatives of heaven and hell: "Then in his sleep he would shout with a slow voice. *Duo sunt, nihil est medium:* There are two places. There is nothing in between. Either one goes up to heaven or down to hell."[62]

Penance and the Last Days in a Postimperial World

There is a danger, when we study the religious history of Gaul, that we allow our attention to be riveted on the brilliant circle connected with Provence and with the monastery of Lérins. And yet, the urgency that characterized these writers and preachers was considerably more widespread than in southern Gaul alone. A sense of hurry settled over Western Christianity as a whole

at this time. Evidence for it turns up in unlikely places. We even
meet it in distant Ireland. When, at some time in the mid-fifth
century, Patricius (none other than our Saint Patrick) wrote his
Confessio to justify his mission to the pagan Irish, he showed his
credentials by writing out the traditional statement of the Creed.
But when he reached the phrase that Christ "will come again"
to judge the living and the dead, he went out of his way to add
one crucial word: *mox*. For Patrick, Christ was coming "soon."
It was a voice from the edge of the known world. Without necessarily having any contact with Lérins (despite later legends that
connected him with that monastery), Patrick shared a sense of
the approach of Judgment that had already developed across the
continent of Europe. It overshadowed not only individuals but
entire communities.[63]

Again, as with our examination of the development of a
menacing view of the other world in Provençal circles, we should
not limit our field of vision to Gaul alone when examining this
conviction in the approach of the "Last Days." We are dealing
with the Gallic reception and adaptation of ideas current elsewhere. Products of Lérins, such as Faustus of Riez and Caesarius, had tended to concentrate on individual conversions.
But as Patrick and others were well aware, the preaching of
penance had always involved wider issues. The Christian people
as a whole were seen as one great sinner who had to be called to
repentance.

We can see this most clearly in a visionary text, the *Apocalypse*, or *Vision, of Saint Paul* (known briefly as the *Visio Pauli*).
The *Visio Pauli* began to circulate in Italy and Africa in the time
of Augustine (as we saw at the end of Chapter 3).[64] By the 500s,

parts of it had become known in Gaul and were cited by Caesarius.[65]

The *Visio Pauli* originated in the East, possibly in southern Asia Minor. It is an elusive text. One should not exaggerate the extent of its circulation, but it does reveal a distinctive and widespread mood. Let us look at it for a moment.

The *Vision* took the form of a gripping travelogue in which the Apostle Paul was shown the torments that awaited sinful souls in the other world. The horror of these scenes of torture has tended to eclipse the overall intention of Paul's vision. The basic message of the *Visio Pauli* was not that God was cruel, rather that He was remarkably patient. He had rejected accusations against the human race made by the elements themselves. The Sun and Moon had complained to Him that human sin was polluting the entire lower air. The Earth and the Sea had asked God to allow them to wipe out humanity. Yet God had refused to do this: *patientia mea sustinet eos* (my patience puts up with them).

God insisted that the human race should be granted yet another respite.[66] Paul was to return from his vision to preach repentance for one last time. The bishops of Gaul were to be the Pauls of their age. It was not only the individual but society as a whole that was challenged to return to God before it was too late.

It would be tempting to see the circulation of the *Vision of Paul* as an apocalyptic reaction to the fall of the Roman Empire. But this is, perhaps, to exaggerate the impression made upon the Christians of Gaul by the final disappearance of the empire in 476. Rather, the circulation of the *Vision of Paul* in Gaul was a postimperial phenomenon. It was one sign among many of the rallying of society after the severe dislocation of the first half of the fifth century. As far as bishops and preachers were concerned, the Roman Empire might vanish from the scene, but the human race remained. It was as much in need of penance as ever before. Far from wiping them from the face of the earth, God had granted the inhabitants of Gaul and elsewhere yet another period of respite in which to repent their sins. What this meant in practice was that the leaders of a post-Roman society, sensitized by generations of the preaching of penance and by gripping scenarios of the afterlife and of the Last Judgment, could settle down to business as usual—to penance, almsgiving, and the elimination of sin. Altogether, the mood of the late fifth and the early sixth centuries was not one of apocalyptic dread, it was a strenuous mood of reform. Gallic society had survived, and now it had to be licked into shape so as to face the judgment of God with better hope than before.

A vivid incident shows this change of attitude. In 467, Lupicinus, a hermit, descended from the caves of the Jura to denounce a powerful Roman for oppressing the poor. This Roman had become a successful politician at the court of the king of the Burgundians, who had taken over the region. He mocked the hermit: "Are you not that impostor whom we have known for some time, who, ten years ago [that is: around 457—just after the great raid of Attila], was talking down the majesty of the Roman order in your arrogant pride, proclaiming that the land of our ancestors was threatened with imminent ruin? Why . . . have such terrible predictions not come true?"[67] In the 450s, Lupicinus had plainly been the Salvian of his region. He had threatened the end of the Roman Empire as part of the judgment of God "in the here and now" on the sins of the local Romans, as Salvian had done, from Marseilles, at roughly the same time. Now, ten years later, it appeared that this threat had not materialized.

Lupicinus, of course, reminded the courtier that his prophecy of doom had not been proved entirely wrong. The empire had, indeed, disappeared, leaving the proud Roman as the subject of a barbarian king. But, on a deeper level, the Roman grandee was right. The sense of imminent catastrophe that had characterized the generation of Salvian had dissipated. The establishment of barbarian kingdoms had not brought about the end of Roman society.

On the contrary, these kingdoms brought law and order to regions that had suffered for decades from a perilous vacuum of authority. Indeed, the term "barbarian kingdoms" is a misnomer. Supported and largely staffed by the local Roman elites, these kingdoms were downsized versions of the empire.[68] It was time for their rulers and their largely Roman officials to show that they meant business in a world without an empire.

With the fall of Rome came a significant change in geographical perspective. When it came to the flexing of the muscles of royal power, other kingdoms beyond the hyper-Roman enclave of Provence come to our attention. The center of gravity of the Frankish kingdom—soon to be known as Francia—lay to the north. After the reign of Clovis (486–511), the Frankish kings who strove to make good the losses of the previous generation by a *mise en ordre* from above ruled all of Gaul. This renewal of control also involved the Gallic church as a whole, creating a wider world, with non-Mediterranean as well as Mediterranean horizons.

For the bishops, the recovery of order went hand in hand with the continued preaching of the need for penance driven by the fear of hell and of the Last Judgment. Like the long span of a great bridge, penitential piety, which had already gathered force in the age of Augustine and characterized the monks and bishops of Provence, joined the last days of the empire to the first centuries of the postimperial kingdoms of the West.

Furthermore, the Frankish kings took over from the Roman Empire the notion of a Christian ruler that had developed since the days of Constantine. They joined the bishops as partners in preaching repentance and in punishing sin.

Conventional accounts of the end of the Roman Empire in the West have tended to overlook this rallying of the powers that be. Popular stereotypes present the fall of the Roman Empire as a single, irreversible catastrophe. These stereotypes assume that, once the fall had happened, it was downhill all the way. It is still widely believed that the barbarian kingdoms of Western Europe (and especially the kingdoms of Frankish Gaul, ruled by members of the Merovingian dynasty) were failed states. They were doomed polities, caught in a downward spiral of aimless violence that continued without remission throughout the sixth and seventh centuries.[69]

Yet, this was by no means what happened. Recent major studies by Christopher Wickham and Jairus Banaji on the economy of Merovingian Gaul have shown that a restoration of control took place after the convulsions of the fifth century.[70] The peasantry of northern Gaul was brought to heel. The result was increased agrarian production based on forced labor. The study by Stefan Esders on the nature of the Frankish state also shows that the authority of the state was reaffirmed in the hands of Frankish kings and their Roman servants.[71] By the year 600, crown, nobles, and the church had come together to form a single ruling class in which Franks, Romans, Burgundians, and other groups mingled easily. They collaborated to create what was for them (if not for their serfs) one of the most prosperous polities in the Christian world of its time. The elites of northern Gaul emerged (in the words of Jairus Banaji) as "the first truly medieval nobilities of Europe."[72]

A Governmental Mood

Against this background of the recovery of order and the emergence of new elites—especially in northern Gaul—in the course of the sixth century what we might call a religious "governmental mood" developed. This governmental mood can be clearly seen in the public proclamations of the Merovingian kings. Urged by their bishops, the Frankish kings fastened rapidly on the notion of group penance. They declared that it was their duty to suppress public sins that brought down the anger of God on the community as a whole. If the preaching of the bishops did not work in provoking repentance and the abandonment of sinful ways, royal governors would finish the job, fining well-to-do sinners and flogging slaves and peasants for breaches of Christian behavior.[73]

The *Praeceptum* of King Childbebert (511–558) made this clear. It was the king's business to "give thought as to how the vengeance of God might be brought to bear on sacrilegious persons"—even on those who did no more than "dance from farm to farm on Sundays."[74] In 585, King Guntram of Burgundy asserted his power by an edict that was even more explicit: "Therefore, while we deliberate on the stability of our kingdom and the salvation of our region and its people, we know that every crime [against Christian morality] is perpetrated within our kingdoms . . . and, without doubt, because of this, by the wrath of heaven, men and beasts are known to perish by different calamities and die of disease and by the sword . . . and [the people] not only lose their present life sooner [than they might have done] but also sustain the tortures of hell."[75]

We should not exaggerate the impact of these laws. They did not turn Gaul into a moral police state. In modern parlance, these laws were "aspirational" laws.[76] There was an element of window dressing about them in that they spelled out a blueprint for an orderly Christian community without necessarily enforcing it with great rigor. The list of crimes was straightforward—magic, profanation of Christian feasts by folkloristic junketing, work on Sundays, pagan practices, and incest.[77] Nonetheless, the laws were symptoms of a significant turn of the tide as Gaul passed from a classical Roman to a post-Roman society in a development that affected bishops and rulers alike.

To put it briefly, by taking notice of sins, the Frankish kings showed that they could act like the Christian Roman emperors of the West in the fifth century and like the formidable Roman emperors of the East in the sixth century. They continued the

imperial mandate to suppress paganism, to ensure that the Jews
kept a low profile, and to impose Christian notions of public
morality.

But there was more to it than simply maintaining the image
of a Christian Roman Empire. This legislation gave a message
to the local populations that, by suppressing sin, the kings proclaimed themselves at the head of a single Christian community. All Christians could sin. Every Christian could go to hell.
The entire community could be affected by sins that brought
down the anger of God upon the entire people. As a result, the
kings could claim that they had as many subjects as there were
potential sinners in their kingdom—which meant, in effect, that
everyone was their subject.

So stark a view imposed a great simplicity on what, otherwise, were complex polities, where Franks jostled Romans,
churchmen jostled the laity, and where many of the ancient land-
marks of status inherited from the Roman past (such as citizen
entitlement) had been washed away. In an untidy society, made
up of different, conflicting groups, at least all members of a
Christian kingdom could be treated as potential sinners whose
behavior needed to be patrolled. As a result, all could be treated
as members of a single "Christian people," subject to the admo-
nition of a single Christian king.

It is in this paradoxical manner that the dramatic sense of
the perils of the other world, of the fires of hell and of the approach of judgment, to which Salvian and others had appealed
in southern Gaul in the early fifth century, took root, in the sixth
century, in the extensive kingdom of the Franks and elsewhere,

to form the basis of a call to order in this world. Otherworld and this world had come to be intertwined.

With the emergence of the notion of a Christian kingdom, subject to the impending judgment of God, we enter a new age in the church of Gaul. In order to understand what this meant for views of the afterlife, let us turn to the abundant and vivid works of a figure from the latter half of the sixth century, to Gregory, bishop of Tours from 573 to 594 AD.

5

The Other World in This World:
Gregory of Tours

WHAT WE HAVE SEEN so far, in the Gaul of the fifth and early
sixth centuries, has been the development of a sense of the
looming prospect of the Last Judgment. It was in the name of
preparation for the Last Judgment that the preaching of repentance gathered momentum in the monasteries and cities of
southern Gaul. Among the bishops and monastic leaders of
Provence, a discourse of moral reform, based on the language
of the penitential system, was elaborated. By means of this discourse, an articulate "out class" of converted aristocrats sought
to distinguish themselves from the impenitently profane and
high-handed members of their own class who still ruled in what
remained of Roman Gaul.

From the time of Salvian of Marseilles onward, this "out
class" produced an abundant literature of exhortation and rebuke addressed, largely, to members of their own class. In the

case of Salvian's *Open Letter to the Church* and his *de guberna-tione Dei*—*On the Providential Rule of God*—this tradition of rebuke produced masterpieces of social criticism. The one had warned the rich of the "judgment [of God] in the here and now" that had been made plain for all to see in the ruin of Gaul. The other warned them of the ranks of punitive angels that would gather at the deathbeds of the rich, if they neglected to expiate their sins by gifts to the church.

But Salvian's acute sense of "judgment in the here and now" was the product of a moment of crisis in his own times. Most of the writing and preaching of the monk-bishops of Provence concentrated, rather, on the Last Judgment. They wished to make the Last Judgment present to their readers and hearers through gripping representations of heaven and, especially, of hell.

The Last Judgment still lay in the future. Held back by the mercy of God (as we saw in the *Visio Pauli*), the threat of the Last Judgment stretched over Gaul as all embracing, but as dis-tant, as the sky. It was the duty of bishops and kings to look up to that threatening sky and to warn their subjects not to try the patience of God any further. As we saw at the end of Chapter 4, the strenuous collaboration of kings and bishops to bring order to Gaul after the Roman Empire had disappeared encouraged a "governmental mood." This governmental mood involved the moral policing of the Christian subjects of each kingdom in the name of avoiding the further descent of the wrath of God on the entire community.

This was the world into which Gregory of Tours was born, in 538. He grew up in a transitional zone, between the Midi and the north of France—in Burgundy and in the Auvergne. He spent his youth and early manhood in an old-world region, still heavy with memories of great senators such as Sidonius Apollinaris, among churches whose crypts, porticoes, and adjoining mausolea were filled with great marble sarcophagi that dated from Roman times. He moved further north, to become bishop of Tours, in 573. He died in 594.[1]

Gregory is our principal source for the imaginative world of late-sixth-century Gaul. He wrote his *Libri historiarum*—his *Books of Histories*—in installments between 575 and 594. At much the same time, he continued to write his *Libri septem miraculorum—Seven Books of Miracles*.[2] Having written these two works, he insisted that they should be read together. For both great collections were written for a single purpose—to warn the powerful (Romans and Franks alike) that, through the saints, Christ was still present in their world and that He would return in the last days to judge them.[3]

For Gregory, the Last Judgment would not occur only in the future: He came to believe as passionately as had Salvian in "judgment in the here and now." The other world did not lie only at the edge of time, waiting to be revealed in its full majesty and terror at the Last Judgment, it had already infiltrated Gaul, through miracles of healing and judgment at the shrines of the saints. This is what made the works of Gregory so distinctive: He wished his readers to witness, in their own times, the frequent irruptions of the other world into this world, through miracles associated with the saints of Gaul and through dramatic turns of fortune among the rulers of Gaul. It is for this reason that he insisted that his audience should read his *Books of Miracles* alongside his *Books of Histories,* for in both the other world

was woven into the texture of this world with a circumstantiality that had not occurred before in Latin Christian literature.
Of all the preachers of penitence and the Last Judgment in Gaul,
Gregory was the most insistent, and his chosen media the most
idiosyncratic. He preached through history and through tales
of the saints.

Gregory turned to history early in his career, with good
reason. He faced a world where signs of the justice of God in
the here and now were sorely needed. On becoming bishop of
Tours in 573, he found himself in the right job at very much the
wrong time. Though an outsider to Tours himself, he claimed a
long family connection with the city. What he had not antici-
pated was that Tours and its region would become the storm
center of what Ian Wood has called "the worst period of civil
war in sixth century Francia."[4]

These civil wars were not as destabilizing for the Frankish
kingdoms as a whole, nor were they as widespread in their effects as has been thought (largely on the strength of a naïve
reading of the *Histories*). But the fact that Tours lay in the Loire
Valley, at a crucial joining point between northern and south-
western Gaul, placed these wars on Gregory's doorstep. Furthermore, though limited, they were particularly vicious. Basically,
each of the rival brothers from the Merovingian family attempted
to extend his kingdom by persuading or frightening individual
cities or whole regions to submit to his lordship and to abandon
that of his competitors.

Such warfare was not catastrophic. Few major battles were
fought. No cities were sacked. But it was warfare of a peculiarly
nasty kind, reminiscent more of the feudal warfare of the Middle

Ages than of the murderous civil wars of Roman times. Relatively small armies would descend on a region, as in the *chevauchées* of the Hundred Years' War. They aimed to cause sufficient damage to persuade the locals to switch their allegiance from one brother to the other. These brutal gangs were largely paid through the right to pillage. They would return home laden with prisoners to ransom, sacks of grain, and precious silverware taken from exposed churches and monasteries in the countryside. In this way, fortunes could be made from the spoils of war, quite apart from the rewards that a successful king would hand out to his upper-class intimates and to those local leaders whose loyalty he had bought. It was a situation in which the *potentes* (the "men of power"), Romans quite as much as Franks, throve.

But there was money in it also for the little men. To take one example, in 576, one such band of pillagers took over a church farm across the Loire from Tours. They were the "men of Le Mans"—that is, they were the urban militia of the city of Le Mans who had pitched in to get even with their neighbors in Tours. They dismantled the wooden house—and, most likely, its great barn—so thoroughly that they returned home with their purses stuffed with the nails taken from its planks![5] The boisterous participation of the "men of Le Mans" in this time of mayhem is a reminder that we must never think of the civil wars of Gaul as being fought only among "Franks." The "Roman" population, both aristocrats and commoners, were equally implicated.

With the countryside around Gregory's city systematically terrorized in this way, these were hard times for the bishop. If we can rely on Guy Halsall's ingenious reconstruction, we gain a new understanding of the Easter sermon that Gregory preached on the subject of civil war in 576.[6] Halsall suggests that this sermon formed the basis for the preface of Book 5 of Gregory's *Histories*. Whether this is the case or not, the message of the preface of Book 5 was plain: The wars between brothers of the Merovingian dynasty were not simply "barbarian" family feuds, they had been fuelled by the avarice of the upper classes of every kingdom, Roman and Frankish alike.

Gregory gives us an unexpected view of the Gaul of his times. He does not lament an irreparably ruined country. Rather, he reveals a society where the rich had become indecently affluent:

> What are you doing? What do you seek? What do you not have in abundance? Your houses are overflowing with luxuries: wine, wheat and oil abound in your storehouses; gold and silver are heaped up in your treasuries. You lack one thing, that in not having peace, you are deprived of the good favor of God . . .

> What is worse, we now see the beginning of that time of sorrows, which the Lord foretold: *Father rises up against son, son against father, and brother against brother* (Matt. 10.20).[7]

Driven by avarice to war, the kings, and with them the aristocracies of Gaul (Franks and Romans alike) had lurched into the chill shadow of the "time of sorrows" that heralded the end of the world.

Gregory was not the only bishop to preach in this manner. At just this time, his colleague Germanus, bishop of Paris, had written in the same apocalyptic tone in order to persuade Queen Brunhilde to ask her husband Sigibert to call off a *chevauchée* against the Île de France: "Lo the days of our tribulation and loss are coming. Woe to us, for we have sinned."[8]

But Gregory did not only preach. He took to the pen. He revived an ancient skill and became the first major Latin historian of his own times in over a century.[9] In embarking on this unaccustomed venture, Gregory turned to the great Christian chroniclers of late Roman times—to the Latin version of the *Chronicle* of Eusebius of Caesarea and to the continuation added to it by Jerome. He did this so as to place Gaul against the background of world history. For Gregory, Gaul was only one part of a wider Christian world. He was determined that the history of his times should be seen as part of the history of the world, from the Creation to the Last Judgment. And he did this because it seemed to him that time was running out for humanity as a whole.[10]

For this reason, Gregory opened his *Histories* with a chronological survey that reminded his readers, abruptly, that the end was near. He pointedly left to others speculations as to the exact date of the coming of the Antichrist and of the Last Days. Rather, Gregory did his sums. The human race had lasted 5574 years, patiently calculated from the making of Adam to the death of King Sigibert in 575.[11] This was already a long enough respite to make one feel anxious. Gregory may well have known the *Visio Pauli*.[12] How much longer would God's patience last?

In the preface to the first book of his *Histories*, Gregory made clear why he had made such calculations: it was "*propter eos, qui adpropinquantem finem mundi disperent.*"[13] But what exactly did this phrase mean? Current translations imply that Gregory wrote to reassure those who were driven to despair by the prospect of the end of the world. The standard German translation of Rudolf Buchner renders the phrase as "*um derentwillen, die da banget vor dem herannahenden Weltende.*" The English translation gives the same rendering: "For the sake of those who are losing hope as they see the end of the world coming nearer and nearer."[14]

Our historical stereotypes about the nature of Merovingian Gaul cause us to expect Gregory to have said this. We think of him as witnessing a dysfunctional society as it stumbled ingloriously into the Dark Ages, men and women alike driven to despair by fear of the last days. But Gregory meant no such thing. In late Latin, the verb *disperare* frequently lacked the subjective overtones of fear and desperation that accompany the modern notion of "despair." Instead, *disperare* meant, literally, *de-sperare*—to "un-hope" oneself. It meant to give up hope, to cease to expect, even, quite bluntly, to give no thought to. Salvian of Marseilles had used the word in this sense of the Romans of his own times: "Everything in human life is conducted through the expectation of some return. Only from God do we expect nothing—*solus Deus est de quo desperatur.*"[15] Bluntly, the Romans castigated by Salvian in his *de gubernatione Dei* acted as if God did not exist. They did not expect Him to intervene in their affairs.

It was the same with the powerful whom Gregory addressed in his *Histories.* They were not panic-stricken persons, living in a world of gathering gloom, far from it. They had put the Last Judgment out of their minds. From Gregory's point of view, they were the sort of persons who were notoriously difficult for any preacher of repentance to deal with. Franks and Romans, laity, clergy, and, even (alas!) monks and nuns—all too many of the characters who appear in Gregory's *Histories* and in his *Books of Miracles*—were confident persons, only too happy with the things of this world. They gave no thought to the coming judgment of Christ. Gregory wrote to remind them that the patience of God was not endless. Sooner or later, this judgment would come.

We should stress this aspect of Gregory. Those who come to his works often come with the conviction that he offered something new—some vision of a world on the threshold of the Middle Ages. As a result, Gregory's world seems separated by a chasm in our imagination from the ancient world. But for Gregory the bishop no such chasm existed. It was a matter of "business as usual." In his own, distinctive manner, he was the spokesman of a Christian piety of repentance that reached back, without a break, to the last days of Augustine and to the preachers of fifth-century Provence. Christians should be ready for the Last Judgment.

Gregory was not the only one in Gaul to give voice to this ancient message. A later book of legal *Formulae* from northern Gaul—the *Formulae of Marculf*—provides a model specimen that showed how pious persons should make up their wills: "Clear signs show and evident proofs are known that the end of the world is near, as disasters become more frequent, and the predictions of the Lord in the Gospels [made] some time ago . . . are known to be at hand." Duly warned, the donor knew what to do—give to the church: "Give alms, and all things are clean" (Luke 11:41).[16] This legal formula bluntly compresses a tide of Christian piety that had already run for almost two hundred

years. Let us see, in greater detail, what Gregory wished the daily
expectation of the Last Judgment to mean to his readers.

A Debate on Resurrection and the Afterlife

Gregory primarily wanted his readers to believe in the Resurrection and the coming of the Last Judgment because of events
in the present. The miracles performed at the tombs of the saints
proved, in the here and now, that their souls lived on undimin-
ished. Not only did the charged tombs of the saints prove that
there was life after death, but the sheer vigor of their souls, as
revealed by their miracles, proved that some great transformation lay in store for them, and—so Gregory hoped—for all good
Christians, at the time of the Resurrection. Indeed, to witness
miracles of healing at the shrines of the saints was to catch a
glimpse of the Big Future—of the mighty transformation that
would take place at the end of time. In a world overshadowed
by the grim prospect of God's judgment, the Resurrection maintained the fierce hope of a better world beyond that judgment.
It was the light at the end of the tunnel.

When it came to the topic of the Resurrection, Gregory
claimed to be no more than an upholder of ancient certainties:
God would make all things right. But even this ancient certainty
still needed to be defended. We are often tempted to think of
Gregory's Gaul as becalmed in an intellectual Saragossa Sea, a
brutish civilization, bound by unthinking traditionalism. But
this was by no means the case. Questioners still abounded, as
in the days of Augustine. There was a good reason for this: The
more sixth-century society became "clericalized"—in that ser-

vice to the church became one of the principal career paths for
young civilians—the more the clergy itself became a diverse and
potentially contentious body. Persons who might have been
rhetors, teachers of grammar, doctors, and small-town lawyers
in earlier times now found a place for themselves in the church.
They were as mixed and as restless a bunch of persons as they
had always been. But now it was the bishop who employed them.
It was the bishop who had to put up with them as part of his
own clerical entourage. And it was the bishop who had to deal
with their doubts and criticisms. In the words of Bruno Dumézil:
"Christianity had become sufficiently universal to retain in its
own bosom those who challenged it."[17]

It is, therefore, not at all surprising that a member of Gregory's own clergy declared, in 590—that is, in the last years of
Gregory's own life, when he had already been bishop for almost
two decades—that he did not believe in the resurrection of the
dead. Gregory reports his debate with this priest in the last book
of his *Histories*.[18] It was a surprisingly up-to-date debate, sparked
by a specifically late antique theological dilemma: How much
could average Christians expect to share in the glory of the heroes and heroines of their faith? Or were they debarred by their
dull, fallen nature from a glory that only Christ and the saints
enjoyed?

Let us look at this debate for a moment. The priest was quite
prepared to accept that Christ, as God incarnate, had risen from
the dead. He may even have thought, in the back of his mind
(though Gregory's account does not say this), that the great saints
of the church would also be raised up at the end of time. But,
in his opinion, the anger of God lay too heavily on the remainder

of mankind. God had said to Adam: "dust thou art, and to dust thou shalt return" (Gen. 3:19). This dust could not expect to rise again. The blinding glory with which sixth-century piety had invested Christ and the saints had cast a dark shadow over the graves of ordinary persons. They might rest in peace in their tombs, but there they would remain: "For the wind passes over him and he is gone" (Ps. 103:16).[19]

Similar issues had been raised a century earlier, at the height of the Christological controversies that had rocked the eastern empire. Again, the issue was to what extent normal human beings could share in the Resurrection of Christ. This, in turn, depended on how extraordinary a being Christ was thought to have been. Upholders of a more moderate view of the relation between the human and divine in the person of Christ criticized their enemies (usually known to us—but not to themselves—as Monophysites) for positing too total an absorption of Christ's person into that of God. They claimed that this view implied that Christ was a being so far removed from humanity—so fully charged with divinity—that He could not extend to a fallen human race the benefit of his divine nature.[20] Humanity and divinity were incommensurable. Divinity could not touch fallen flesh, and so Christ could not extend his own victory over the grave to the millions of Christians who lay in the earth, subject to the curse of Adam.

We now know that the debate at Tours between Gregory and his priest was not an isolated, small-town controversy. The recent book of Matthew Dal Santo, *Debating the Saints' Cult in the Age of Gregory the Great*, has shown that similar debates were happening in contemporary Constantinople. They were addressed with vigor by Gregory's namesake and younger contem-

porary, Pope Gregory the Great, whose book of *Dialogues* on
the saints of Italy appeared in 594, a little after Gregory's debate took place in Tours.[21] Both men were concerned to show
that the vibrant souls of the saints were still very much alive,
and that the souls of average Christian believers would also enjoy
a vivid afterlife, even if, in their case, their continued life beyond the grave was less evident than in the case of the saints.
Not only did saints and average Christians remain alive after
death, ripples of energy flashed from the tombs of the saints in
the form of miracles of healing. These miracles were hopes made
concrete. The dramatic changes associated with miracles were
visible manifestations, in the here and now, of the hoped-for
transformation of all things at the Resurrection.

In defending what he presented as the inherited conglomerate on the resurrection of the dead, Gregory brought the distant past into his own age. The souls of those who would be res-
urrected at the end of time were, even now, fully active both in
the other world and in this world. This meant, in effect, that
the past was never past. Long-dead saints were still present and
active at their shrines, they constantly intervened to show their
existing power. As a result, time itself became, as it were, "con-
certinaed": Past, present, and future came together. The power
of Christ, first displayed by the miracles in the Gospels, reached
directly into the present through the saints in whom He "dwelt."[22]
This was particularly the case of Gregory's hero, Saint Martin.
Martin had been the charismatic bishop of Tours, who had died
in 397. But, for Gregory, Martin was far from dead. Up to the
present, Christ's mighty hand lay behind the hand of Saint
Martin as it reached out from his tomb at Tours to heal the sick.[23]
In turn, the hand of Martin could be physically felt resting on

the hand of Aredius (a pious friend of Gregory's in Limoges), as Aredius made the sign of the cross to heal a sufferer.[24]

In the same manner, the future glory of the Resurrection could reach back in time for a moment. It entered the present. Crippled bodies bloomed again, as they would bloom at the end of time.[25] The face of Gregory's own great uncle, Gregory of Langres, glowed like a rose as he lay on his bier—this was flesh already bathed in the dawn light of the Resurrection.[26]

The Passage of the Soul

Despite Gregory's insistence that he did no more than pass on an unchanging tradition, many of his representations of the other world betrayed significant shifts since the age of Augustine. It is notable that, for Gregory and his contemporaries, the fate of the soul after death had come to seem ever more fraught with danger. As we saw in Chapter 4, this was by no means a new development in the Christianity of the West. This urgency had already emerged in the still confident days of the fourth-century empire and was by no means a sign of the approach of the Dark Ages. But Gregory added an autumnal sharpness to the theme. He picked up stories that spoke of the passing of the soul as a long and perilous journey. It was a journey increasingly inter-rupted by demonic "checkpoints" where souls were challenged to give accounts of their sins. These stories reveal the extent to which anxieties concerning the passing of the soul after death had intensified over the years.

When, for instance, in 397, Sulpicius Severus (who wrote the classic *Life of Saint Martin* around 397) dreamed of the death of

Martin, he had seen his hero rising rapidly to heaven (as in an ancient scene of apotheosis), to vanish beyond the stars. Sulpicius had also described how, when on his deathbed, Martin had turned only for a moment to the devil who shadowed him: "Hold off, you bloodthirsty beast! You will find nothing of yours in me!"[27]

Gregory knew the work of Sulpicius Severus well. But he had also heard a somewhat different story. On the day that Martin died, Bishop Severinus of Cologne was celebrating Mass. He heard a choir of angels singing, then suddenly the singing stopped. It was like the unnerving jolt of a train making an unexpected stop. Only later did the singing resume. During that time of silence, Gregory was told, Martin had been forced to halt so as to render account of himself to the devil and his angels. To this Gregory added: "What will happen to us sinners, if the evil powers could wish to harm even him?"[28]

Gregory was told a similar tale by "old men" at Artonne, in the Auvergne. They told Gregory that, when Martin was on his way to Clermont, he had passed the tomb of a consecrated virgin, Vitalina: "Holy virgin [Martin asked], have you already deserved to be in the presence of the Lord?" As we have seen, this was an old-fashioned, early Christian question, such as had occurred in the dream that followed the death of the little notary of Uzalis in the time of Augustine. But Vitalina's answer was not reassuring:

> "One thing [*una causa:* already the vulgar Latin was close to the modern French, *une chose*] that seems a light matter (*facilis*) in the world is an obstacle to me. On Good Friday,

ᵉ

when the Redeemer of the world suffered, I washed my face in water." As Martin left the tomb of the virgin, he said to his companions: "Woe to us who live in this world! If this virgin, who was dedicated to God, incurred this obstacle . . . what are we to do, whom a deceitful world everyday persuades to commit sins?"

On his return from Clermont, having prayed on her behalf, Martin went back to the tomb and said: "Vitalina . . . rejoice now, because after three days you will be presented to the majesty of the Lord." After that, the old men said, Vitalina became an active presence in Artonne. She appeared in dreams. Miracles began to happen at her tomb. She even revealed the day on which her festival should be celebrated. "This must be understood [Gregory added] in no other way than that she had deserved [to be in] the presence of the Lord's majesty, because of the plea of blessed Martin."[29]

Intercession and Amnesty at the Last Judgment

The moral of this story was plain. Except for a few saints, no passage to heaven was easy. The soul required all the prayers that it could get, and especially the prayers of holy persons, whether living or dead, to reach the presence of Christ after death. The prayers of the saints were even more necessary when the soul faced Christ at the Last Judgment.

Hence there was a decisive change in the image of the Last Judgment itself. We do not know if Gregory knew Augustine's *City of God* well. If he did, he certainly paid no attention to

Book 21. In this book, as we saw, Augustine had disassociated himself from views that, in his opinion, exaggerated the power of the saints to obtain amnesty from Christ. Augustine had also dismissed the possibility that the souls of sinners might be allowed to pass only for a short time through the flames of hell— to take a brisk dip, as it were, in purging fire—as a result of the intercessions of the saints.[30] As we saw, the views combated by Augustine were far from eccentric. They circulated among well-educated and highly placed persons, such as Prudentius. They rested on the current image of Christ as an emperor, exercising the supreme imperial prerogative of mercy in response to the intercessions of the saints.

It was precisely this possibility—one that Augustine had rejected in his *City of God*—that Gregory envisioned when he thought of the Last Judgment. For Gregory, the Last Judgment was the occasion for the final grand scenario of amnesty in an imperial mode. This in itself marks a change of emphasis. In the account of the Last Judgment in the Gospel of Matthew (Matt. 25:31–46), Christ had separated the sheep from the goats. He had told the goats to "go away into eternal punishment." His judgment had been final. But for Gregory and his contemporaries, the Last Judgment was not the day of the sheep. It was the day of the goats. It was then that sinners had one last chance to reverse the seemingly irrevocable judgment of Christ by pleading for mercy, as if to a Roman emperor or a contemporary Frankish king. They hoped that they would be aided in their plea for mercy by the intercession of the saints: "And when, at the Last Judgment, I am to be placed on the left hand [among the goats], Martin will deign to pick me out from the middle of the goats with his sacred right hand. He will shelter me behind his back, as the angels tell the King: 'This is the man for whom Saint Martin pleads.'"[31]

Those for whom the saints had to plead did not expect instant promotion to glory, either when their souls left their bodies or at the Last Judgment. Gregory made plain that he himself expected little more than forgiveness: "At the moment of the Judgment, when eternal glory surrounds the martyrs, forgiveness—*venia*—will come by their mediation or a light punishment only will pass over us."[32]

It is this high-pitched view of the Last Judgment that accounted for the mounting fortunes of the church. Contemporary records of donations to the church showed this with increasing clarity. Those who gave alms to the poor and endowments to the churches and monasteries did so, quite bluntly, *pro remedio animae*—"to heal and protect their souls" in the afterlife and, above all, at the Last Judgment. A *remedium* meant more than simply a therapy for the soul. In Gregory's world, *remedia* protected quite as much as they healed. The word was used both for healing substances and for amulets that kept at bay the onslaughts of malevolent powers.[33]

The great of the land—with Gregory among them—sought protection for their souls through gifts to the church. They did so with a dramatic scenario of mercy and intercession at the Last Judgment at the back of their minds. Thus, when the great politician-bishop Bertram of Le Mans drew up his will in 616 AD, he hoped only for what Gregory had hoped. He did not dare to hope to join the saints in glory. All that he wanted was *vel venia*—"forgiveness at the very least"—gained by the prayers of the saints.

In order to gain the favor of the saints who would plead for amnesty on his behalf at the Last Judgment, Bertram drew up a list of bequests and pious foundations that included seventy-four villas, drawn from a fortune that amounted to 300,000 hectares of land. Bertram owned half of one percent of the entire landmass of the Frankish kingdom. These holdings and the bequests derived from them were originally recorded on a papyrus scroll that was seven meters long![34]

Venia—"mere forgiveness"—was costly for the great. But, then, we must remember that, for a grandee like Bertram of Le Mans, to declare oneself a sinner and to make elaborate preparations for one's death was as good a way as any to display one's present wealth and power—and to do so in an eminently acceptable manner: as a repentant fellow Christian.

Episcopal Authority in Late Sixth-Century Gaul

What made Gregory distinctive was not his view of the Last Judgment and of the elaborate precautions that were needed to ensure the intercession of the saints on that great day, it was the intensity with which he insisted that the other world breaks in upon the human race also in our time. He was also convinced that, through the saints, the judgment of God occurs frequently and palpably in the here and now. His belief in the power of the saints as the bearers of God's justice was harnessed to the pursuit of a serious program of reform and consolidation in Gaul. How had this attitude developed in Gregory and in the world around him?

In a recent, most illuminating article, Steffen Diefenbach has pointed to a significant change in the texture of the Gallic church that had happened since the days of Faustus of Riez and Caesarius of Arles.[35] Up to the middle of the sixth century, most of the articulate preachers of penance and leaders in the church in Gaul had come from the local nobility—and especially from the nobility of the highly Romanized regions of southern Gaul. They had based their authority on ancient models of aristocratic role reversal. As with philosophers in pagan times and holy men in Christian late antiquity, a large part of the fascination that such persons held for their contemporaries was that they had broken pointedly with the values and lifestyle of the aristocracy while maintaining the prestige, the poise, and the authoritative tone of voice of the class that they had abandoned. In this way they had marked themselves out as an "out class," as discussed in Chapter 4.

But, as in all forms of charisma based on dramatic role reversals, there had to be a role to reverse. The aristocrat-turned-monk carried with him (almost as a second halo) the memory of the wealth and status of his profane past. The monk-bishop was seen to have rejected a constellation of social expectations that everyone recognized as pertaining to the old Roman nobility of Gaul—a confident tread, flowing hair, fine dress, frequent baths, and a mastery of classical Latin.[36]

By the age of Gregory, however, this semiotic system had evaporated. Altogether, there was nothing to be gained by pointedly inverting the lifestyle of an old-world Roman grandee if there were no such grandees around to render this inversion significant. A new *Gesamtadel*—a "melded aristocracy"—had emerged around the courts of the Frankish kings. An increasingly homogeneous ruling class, drawn as much from Frankish as from Roman and Burgundian families, had begun to emerge. These men had begun to take over the church of Gaul. At the very top of society, around the court, "Barbarian" and "Roman" families had become inextricably mingled. Even Gregory of Tours himself, though he bore the very Roman name of Georgius Florentius Gregorius, had a great uncle on his mother's side (a *dux*—"a military man") called Gundulf.[37]

As a result, the bishops of Gaul increasingly looked to the saints as the sources of their authority. Memories of Roman birth were no longer enough. It was in the shadow of Saint Martin that Gregory ruled at Tours. He did so by claiming to be the representative of a saint who was more alive in his tomb than he had ever been when on earth. Gregory did not rely to any great extent on his somewhat frayed senatorial pedigree. He was a churchman and a devotee of Saint Martin first, and a descendent of senators second.

This was something new. As Diefenbach has pointed out, much has been written about the *Bischofsherrschaft*—the "Bishop's Lordship"—in sixth-century Gaul. Those who write about this "lordship" stress the unbroken continuity between the former Roman senatorial class and the powerful bishops of the time of Gregory of Tours.[38] But family continuity (which might still have counted for much in the fifth century) was less widespread and potent an element in the make-up of the Gallic church by the late sixth century. The church of the Merovingian kingdoms was characterized by an awkward mixture of representatives of faded Roman families and energetic courtiers (Roman and Frankish) who had made their careers in the entourage of the Frankish kings.[39]

Altogether, the Gallic bishops of the age of Gregory of Tours were a diverse and somewhat drab body of men. But what they claimed to have behind them, as guarantors of their authority, made up for their lack of social status. They presented themselves as the living representatives of a *Herrschaft der Heiligen*—of a "lordship of the saints." This was a lordship based on the other world. It reached out to all classes and joined all ethnic groups. From being an "out class," distinguished by what they did not share with their peers in a specific (highly Romanized) segment of the aristocracy, Gregory and his episcopal colleagues (Franks as well as Romans) settled down, in the various Merovingian kingdoms, as members of a progressively homogenized ruling class.

In this situation, Gregory knew very well where his authority was supposed to come from. It did not come from his senatorial background, and still less did it come from flamboyant gestures of ascetic renunciation. Rather, it was the quiet presence beside him of "his" lord, Saint Martin, that gave Gregory his authority. One incident shows this clearly. In 585, Gregory arrived at the court of King Guntram to plead for rebels who had sought sanctuary at the shrine of Saint Martin at Tours. Guntram was in no mood to pardon men whom he regarded as "tricky foxes." But Gregory persisted. "'Listen, mighty king,' I said. 'I have been sent by my lord to give you a message. What answer shall I carry back to him . . . ?' Guntram, amazed [and possibly suspicious that Gregory had been set up to make this request by some noble faction] said: 'And who is that lord of yours who sent you?' I answered with a smile: 'It was Saint Martin who sent me.'"[40]

So let us now look at what were the principal aims of the program that Gregory hoped to carry through under the shadow of the "lordship of the saints," and at how the need to assert the presence of these "lords" in this world affected his view of the other world.

The Poor, the Anger of God, and the Wealth of the Church

First and foremost, Gregory presented the justice of God as deeply immanent. Those who insulted the saints and their shrines suffered instantly, in the here and now. The nature of their deaths left no doubt as to their ultimate destination. A tax collector who had denied the exempt status of the herds of Saint Julian at Brioude died of a fever, blackened by heat and panting for water: "About him there is no doubt as to what place he found himself in over there [*huc:* "in the other world"] who left this world [*hic*] with such a judgment upon him."[41]

Secondly, Gregory saw the justice of God at its most forceful when it acted in defense of the poor. In order to understand the particular intensity of the notion of the poor in Gregory's Gaul we have to step back, once again, to the fourth century. In the Chapter 3 we saw how the evaporation of the traditional classical model of society—where the most significant binary had been that between citizen and noncitizen—had left rich and poor to face each other as the charged, incommensurable poles of a Christian society.

By the sixth century, this brutal polarization had invested the poor with an aura of hidden power. The poor represented the nadir of the human condition. They were the ultimate

victims. But Christ had identified Himself with these victims. Bishops were supposed to take this identification seriously. Gregory wrote with particular warmth about Bishop
Quintianus of Rodez: "This holy bishop was magnificent in
his giving of alms. Indeed, when he heard poor men cry out he
used to say: 'Run, I beg you, run to that poor man . . . Why are
you so indifferent? How do you know that this poor man is not
the very one who [Christ] ordained in his Gospel that one
should feed Him in the person of the poor?'"[42] To oppress the
poor was to do no less than trample upon Christ.

This poignant piety was supported by weightier considerations than mere compassion. As we saw in Chapter 4, the wealth
of the church was regarded as wealth held in trust for the poor.
As a result, by the sixth century, the notion of the poor as perpetual victims, identified with Christ, served to sacralize ecclesiastical property. The growing estates of the church were ringed
with the equivalent of an alarm system, calculated to go off at
the slightest touch. Any attack on the lands of the church was
an attack on the poor. And an attack on the poor was an attack
on Christ Himself. For it was from the estates of the church that
the poor were supposed to be fed. Those who attempted to appropriate church lands, or who had held back legacies made to
the church, were regularly denounced as *necatores pauperum*—
as "murderers of the poor."[43]

It is worthwhile lingering on this distinctive phrase. It occurred frequently in the councils of the church and in the writings of Gregory, for it implied that the growing wealth of the
church did not come from donations made exclusively for
the safety of the souls of the dead. The vast kinetic energy of

the early Christian notion of the poor as the privileged benefi-
ciaries of Christian giving ensured that, in sixth-century Gaul,
gifts for the soul continued to be seen to operate through the
poor. This meant that gifts to the church were expected to work
in society at large, through the provision of food, clothing, and
shelter to the destitute. They were not simply gifts to specialized
ritual experts, such as priests, monks, or nuns, whose effects
would be felt in the afterlife alone.

Though they were administered by the church (and, in fact,
contributed greatly to its endowment) gifts for the soul invariably took the form of gifts to the poor. Those who robbed the
church or withheld donations to it were never said to have put
the souls of the deceased at risk. Rather, they were denounced
as murderers or despoilers of the poor, who were fed from the
products of estates given by laypersons to the church as a remedy
for their souls.[44]

We are tempted to be cynical about such claims. After all,
when Bertram of Le Mans distributed his fortune, barely one
tenth of it found its way directly to the poor—and that largely
in the setting up of somewhat *boutique* almshouses, usually built
for no more than twelve members each, and never for more than
forty.[45]

It is difficult to measure the amount of wealth that went directly, through the church, to the care of the poor in Merovingian Gaul. What we can know, however, is the symbolic role
that the poor played in Gregory's imaginative world. The fate
of the poor stirred Gregory's acute sense of the immanence of
God. For him, the oppressed poor remained an ominous, supernatural presence at the very bottom of society. The poor were

like the earth. The mute anger of the earth at the sins of humankind (as expressed in the *Visio Pauli*) was frequently shown by the failure of harvests, by the appearance of strange signs, and by the spread of disease.

Gregory noted these disturbing events with care.[46] The poor played a similar role in his imagination. The failures of nature and the laments of the poor came together in his mind. Both were the growl of a God whose patience was running out. When plague struck the royal court in 580 AD, robbing Queen Fredegund of her children, Gregory reports the Queen as exclaiming: "God in his pity has endured our evil goings on long enough. Time and time again, he has sent us warnings . . . Now we are going to lose our children. It is the tears of the poor which are the cause of their death, the sighs of orphans and the widows' lament."[47]

In this manner, the resolutely this-worldly nature of Gregory's descriptions of the vengeance of the saints against oppressors of the poor brought the Last Judgment down to earth—much as (four centuries later) the figures of evil knights tumbling into hell on the great Romanesque portal of Sainte Foye at Conques reflected the charged atmosphere of the Peace of God movement of around the year 1000.[48]

Gregory's Conception of Miracles

Gregory expected Gallic society to be called back to order by miracles that showed the active presence of the saints on earth. For Gregory, miracles were not only private benefits bestowed by the saints on individuals but public portents that proclaimed the restoration of peace and concord in society at large.

To understand this aspect of Gregory's worldview, we must enter into the great density of his conception of miracle. For him, miracles had many layers. There was the immediate, stunning act of power—as sudden and vivid as the sparking of a high-tension wire. But to see miracles in that light only would have been, for Gregory, to take a superficial view of the miracles of the saints. Miracles were always more than that. Giselle de Nie has frequently pointed out, with the aid of modern studies of medical anthropology, that, for Gregory, miracles were metaphors of order and deliverance come true. They worked by triggering—almost by subliminal association—scenarios of resurrection and, above all, of release from bondage. Release from bondage had a social as well as an individual dimension.[49]

Furthermore, the scenarios of healing described by Gregory derived much of their cogency from being firmly rooted in body fantasies that were widespread also in secular medicine. For sixth-century doctors, healing was associated with the removal of dire blockages and with release from forms of acute constriction. Paralytics were said to be "bound" by cramping humors. Sufferers from fever were seen as being in the grip of a pattern of heats and chills that was as inexorable as a chain.[50]

As a result, descriptions of miracles of healing followed the same imaginative paths as did healing in secular medicine. We are dealing with an imaginative world patterned to a marked degree (in contemporary medical knowledge quite as much as in hagiographic literature) by the antithesis of rigidity and release. The miracle brought release. Sometimes this was inner release. Penance, for instance, could be seen in terms of inner release from the terrible, "blocked" rigidity of the unrepentant. Looking at the shrine of Martin, Gregory found no difficulty in viewing the physical healings that occurred around it as mirrors of the inner changes that he most hoped for within himself and in the Christian people as a whole. What he looked for both in physical healings and in the conversion of sinners were moments of blessed release from constriction, marked by outbursts of tears. For tears showed that the hardened will itself had melted. This was the greatest miracle of all—the inner miracle of repentance: "tears at last flow loose and genuine remorse follows . . . sighs rise from the bottom of the heart, and guilty breasts are beaten."[51] In this way, inside and outside were joined in miracles around the shrine. What one saw happen here and now was a direct reflection of the healing that might come to the soul over there—in the other world: "For we believe that just as the saints here lance all kinds of illnesses here [*hic*], so they deflect the ruthless penalties of torment there [*illic*]; that just as they alleviate bodily fevers here, so they quench the eternal flames there; that just as they clean out the horrible ulcers of leprosy here, so through their intervention they obtain release from the blemishes of sins there."[52]

It is revealing that, in this forceful passage, Gregory never talked about a dichotomy between "immaterial"—spiritual—and "material"—physical. He spoke, rather, of "here" and "there." In his imagination, the material world flowed easily into the other world.[53] One wonders how much he owed to the robust materialism of Faustus of Riez (which we discussed in Chapter 4). Certainly, his view of the relation between physical miracle and its invisible homologies, between this world and the next, is marked by the same gripping concreteness, by the same need to conjure up the other world in vivid physical images—in tableaux—that Faustus shared.

The Miracle of Peace

Gregory's sense of the many levels of miracles meant that, for him, the basic scenario of deliverance from bondage was not limited to individual miracles of healing. Miracles had a public dimension. They could be regarded as living metaphors for the restoration of social order. We see this most clearly in Gregory's frequent descriptions of miracles of breaking chains. Here the antithesis between rigidity and freedom was at its most intense. He tells us that the shrine of Saint Medardus (Saint Médard) in Soissons was surrounded with broken chains, offered in gratitude by freed prisoners and former slaves. At such a shrine, surrounded by such concrete testimonies of deliverance, it was easy for a woman to believe that her paralyzed hand, "fettered" by swelling, might at last be set free, "By the power of Medardus, who had released the chains of wretched men."[54] Miracles of release from prison and from chains were part of what Steffen Diefenbach has appropriately termed a *Befreiungssymbolik*. They provided a symbolic backdrop to Gregory's day-to-day activities as a bishop. Release was his business. He was constantly attempting to secure release for persons who had fled to sanctuary at the shrine of Saint Martin. He also had to intervene frequently to protect victims of arrest, imprisonment, or oppression.[55]

But, once again, we must remember the differing layers of Gregory's notion of the miraculous. Public miracles gained an added dimension from the belief that freedom from chains in this world echoed the vast release of freedom from the chains of sin in the next. When the chains that held the priest Wiliachar, falsely accused of treason, miraculously dropped from him, Gregory's reaction was characteristic. He hoped for a similar release from bondage for himself: "If only the blessed Martin might deign to show such power to me, so that he might release the bonds of my sins just as he crumbled those massive heavy chains on top of Wiliachar."[56]

But Gregory did not only think about himself. He continued to hope for yet bigger, more public miracles. Such miracles could be read as mighty portents of better things to come. The most daring miracle of all occurred in the midst of the civil war that had overshadowed the early years of Gregory's life as a bishop. It was a miracle of peace announced through a miracle of release from bondage. In 574, the armies of two rival Merovingian kings met each other peaceably near Paris. They parted without fighting. On that same day, three paralytics were healed at the shine of Saint Martin in Tours. Gregory recorded the fact in both in his *Books of Histories* and in his *Book on the Miracles of Saint Martin:* "Another lame man named Leuboveus . . . arrived [at Tours] after dragging himself along the ground . . . One day, while he was weeping outside . . . his knees and his feet were straightened, and as the people watched, he received his health. It is well known that these three miracles [that of Leuboveus and two others] occurred when the most glorious king Sigibert crossed the Seine river and made peace with his brothers . . . Even that was a victory for the blessed Martin."[57]

And why? For Gregory, as we have seen, to be cured from paralysis was for heavy chains to drop from the body, "like a shower of broken tiles."[58] In 574, for a miraculous moment, it appeared that even the chain of sin that had dragged the Frankish upper classes into war had shattered. What Gregory saw in a human body freed from illness was very much what he hoped

to see around him—an entire society whose fabric had been restored, because the rival kings and their followers were no longer
"fettered" to avarice and violence.[59]

Yet it is precisely in nourishing such robustly this-worldly
hopes that Gregory showed himself to be already a little out of
date. By the end of the sixth century, the civil wars that he had
decried so vehemently had achieved what civil wars often do
achieve (as they had done at the end of the Roman Republic
and in the Roman Empire of the third and fourth centuries):
They had thrown up a new governing class. These persons were
rich, confident, and (as Gregory knew only too well from his
daily observation of their behavior) very few of them were
troubled by thoughts of the Last Judgment. Faced by the new
Gesamtadel—the Romano-Frankish aristocracy that had formed
around the court of the Merovingian kings—Gregory, for all his
intense engagement with the contemporary scene, seemed like a
voice from the past. In the Epilogue we will see why this was so.

Epilogue:
Columbanus, Monasticism,
and the Other World

Columbanus in Gaul, 590–615 AD

As bishop of Tours, Gregory looked out on a very public world. The intrusions of the other world in the here and now that most held his attention took place at the tombs of saints in crowded shrines, open to all comers, or in the course of fully public confrontations between bishops, kings, and sinful men of violence. Miracles of conflict-resolution, the loosing of chains, and the opening of jails were acclaimed by urban crowds who were still touched by the raw desire for justice of an ancient Roman *populus*. These events took place against the background of a largely urban environment. The tombs of the saints often lay in ancient cemeteries just outside the walls of their city. Their distribution reflected the map of the old Roman cities of Gaul.

Gregory had traveled frequently to northern Gaul and knew many of its leading bishops and politicians, but these were journeys to a land with an as-yet-uncertain future. It was there—in Francia proper—that the Merovingian kings most frequently held court, at the center of a new, increasingly northern governing class of their own creation. By contrast, Gregory's own roots still lay in the south. His memories of the saints stretched down toward the Mediterranean, to a very ancient landscape. The stories he listened to were told largely in southern towns.

In this Epilogue we turn toward the north to follow the monastic movement initiated by an ascetic star from the very furthest Christian region of the West—by the Irishman Columbanus. In doing so, we find ourselves in the afforested ridges and upland valleys of the Vosges; in the lush, well-watered countryside of northern France; and at estuaries that looked out over the English Channel and the North Sea.

Above all, this is a world where the crowds have melted away. We no longer follow Gregory's intent gaze as he recorded the stunning intrusions of the other world at shrines filled with swarms of worshippers. Rather, we follow the repercussions of a fierce quest for sanctity among the very few in the deep, notional quiet of great new monasteries and convents. The literature produced in seventh-century Gaul by the monastic followers of Columbanus and others reveals the other world in the quietest of all places—in the passing of the lonely soul at the moment of death. The other world was thought to step, for an instant, into this world at the deathbeds of the saints, not at their blazing, fully public tombs. Even for saints, death was thought to mark only the beginning of a prolonged journey into the other world. In this Epilogue we encounter the first complete visionary accounts of this journey.

These developments can easily be summarized in a brisk narrative that stresses what was new about them. But, in reality, the changes of this time were slow and complex. The Christianity of Gaul was already an old religion. It was a richly sedimented conglomerate that varied greatly from region to region and from person to person. The world of Gregory of Tours was not the only world in Gaul. He would not have devoted so much energy to spinning around his readers a near impenetrable web of gripping stories if he had not sensed that there were other stories—told by other persons, in other regions, in other situations or in other social niches—that were different from his own.

Nor did Columbanus and his followers initiate a totally new departure—some irrevocable switch from a late antique to an early medieval Christianity. Rather, the spread of Columbanian monasticism ensured that, in the rich earth of Christian Gaul, yet another layer of soil came to the surface, adding a new and vivid streak of color to ancient fields.

With the emergence of that streak, we have come full circle. In the Introduction I showed how a distinctive representation of the afterlife that would come to be shared by medieval Latin Christians was summed up by Bishop Julian of Toledo in his *Prognosticon*—his *Report on the Future of the Soul*—of 688 AD. By the end of this Epilogue I will trace the last stages of the process by which the imaginative building blocks of Julian's "futurology" of the soul after death came together between 250 and 650 AD. All that is left is to say a brief good-bye to the ancient worldview that this new representation of the afterlife had slowly but surely ousted from the minds of Latin Christians. But now let us return to Columbanus.

Gregory of Tours died in 594. Only sixteen years later, in 610, a strange group of monks from a region that Gregory had never mentioned spent a night at the tomb of Saint Martin at Tours. They were mainly from Ireland and were led by a remarkable Irishman—Columbanus. Exiled by a Frankish king, they were expecting a ship to take them from Brittany across the Irish Sea, back to their homeland. They left behind one monastery—at Luxeuil, in the Vosges, on the eastern edge of Frankish rule—now safely in the hands of their non-Irish disciples.

The meteoric career of a holy man from an exotic land appeared to have come to an end. Columbanus and his companions had come from the monastery of Bangor on the shores of the Lough of Belfast. They arrived in Gaul in 590, just as Gregory was finishing his *Books of Histories*. At first, their extreme asceticism and proud indifference to the customs of the country in which they found themselves riveted the attention of Frankish kings and of the local elites who came into contact with them. But, as was often the case with the arrival of wandering holy men, this enthusiasm soon cooled. Local bishops came to suspect their clannish adherence to Irish monastic customs (as Gregory of Tours, who had suffered enough in his time from charismatic wanderers, would certainly have done, had he been alive). The Frankish king, Theuderic II, who ruled in Burgundy, was alienated. He saw Columbanus and his monks as guests on his lands. Now these guests had outstayed their welcome. They could go home to where they belonged.

But this is not how the story ended. A rival Frankish king summoned Columbanus and his company back from Britanny.

Theuderic II soon suffered a stunning defeat. The old Irish abbot returned to Luxeuil as a token of peace restored to Burgundy and the eastern regions. But both Columbanus and those who patronized him were careful to channel their energies away from Francia proper and toward its frontiers. Columbanus passed through Bregenz, at the eastern end of Lake Constance, and eventually settled in Bobbio, on the edge of the Lombard kingdom of northern Italy. He died in 615. A man born in Leinster in southern Ireland ended his life in the monastery that he had founded at the foot of the Alpine passes over which Hannibal had led his elephants against Rome.[1]

As can easily be imagined, this vivid story has held the attention of historians. But what is truly remarkable about the career and later influence of Columbanus is less easy to discover and more decisive for the history of Christianity in Europe. Like a new form of vaccination, the radical monastic option represented by Columbanus "took." Within a century, northern Gaul was covered with one hundred monasteries and convents of nuns derived from the monastic experiments first initiated by the Frankish disciples of the great Irishman.[2] These monasteries and convents were prominent institutions. They did not hide along the peripheries of settled life—in cemeteries outside city walls, in woods and caves, or on offshore islands—as the monastic settlements of an earlier time had done. Rather, they stood out in the midst of rich farmlands and on busy estuaries. Many were surrounded by deep ditches, thick hedges, and palisades that marked them off as holy places. They echoed the great monastic "cities" of Ireland, which were the triumphant successors of the tribal sanctuaries of pagan times. Many of these monasteries lasted into the modern age. For the first time in the history of

Western Europe, we can speak of a "monastic landscape" directly continuous with that of all future centuries.[3]

It was not Columbanus himself but the rallying of the laity of northern and eastern Gaul to the piety represented by his followers that truly marked the watershed between late antiquity and the Middle Ages. And so our brief history of ideas about the other world in late antiquity ends with Columbanus, with his Frankish and Burgundian disciples, and with the lay patrons who supported the "Columbanian" monasteries and convents with their wealth and physical protection.

What did Columbanus bring to Gaul? Strangely enough, he brought back an older Gaul. Like many charismatic leaders, he was not totally exotic to the society to which he came. Rather, he awakened old dreams. At first sight, this seems unlikely. Columbanus was an outsider. He arrived in Gaul surrounded by Irishmen and Bretons. He was tenaciously loyal to the monastic customs of his country and played with great skill on the fact that he came from the furthest edge of the known world.

But that was only half the story. As befitted a learned man in an Irish monastic environment, Columbanus was a man of his books. These were Latin books. They had come from Gaul (either directly to Ireland or through the surviving "Roman" regions of western Britain). These books brought to little enclaves in Ireland, perched on the edge of the Christian world and still hemmed in by an overwhelmingly pagan culture, a vision of what Christian monasticism should be. Like a mammoth preserved in permafrost, the worldview of the great writers and preachers of southern Gaul of the fifth century, with which we began Chapter 4, lingered in the libraries of distant Ireland. In his many years on the Continent, Columbanus added to this radical Gallic core, but it remained central to his message.

Columbanus had absorbed the monastic ideals of Cassian. He appealed to the works of Faustus of Riez (of all people) as "the most perspicuous and polished teaching" known to him.[4] When it came to what really mattered—the hard art of weeding vice from the soul—the passing of the centuries and the distance between Ireland and southern Gaul meant little to Columbanus. A line of sight led, directly, through the books that he read, to Faustus of Riez and to the upholders of the "Gallic consensus" of the fifth century. He derived both his Latin style and his stance toward the world from the great tradition of Gallic preachers of repentance. As we saw, this tradition ran straight from Lérins through Faustus of Riez and Caesarius of Arles. It also filled the very different works of Gregory of Tours with a sense of urgency and a desire to see the judgment of God in the here and now.[5] In this at least, Gregory of Tours would have recognized Columbanus as one of his own. As Columbanus wrote to the bishops of Gaul in 603: "And since the Day of Judgment is now nearer than it was then, it is up to you to embark upon a more exacting interpretation of the precepts of the religion of the Gospel."[6]

Such a challenge did not necessarily endear Columbanus to the Gallic bishops, who considered that they themselves had a monopoly over the right to warn their congregations of the approach of the Last Judgment. But Columbanus's unflinching message set alight the hearts of scores, and later hundreds, of young men and women from the top ranks of the newly formed aristocracies of northern Gaul. Let us see how this happened.

Columbanus and the Monastic Life

We get closest to Columbanus if we read his *Instructiones*—the sermons that he wrote for his monks. Their authenticity has been verified and their distinctive tone has been brilliantly examined by Clare Stancliffe.[7] Reading them, we find ourselves at the ground zero of a mighty spiritual detonation.

Columbanus had read Cassian, but read him as he had never been read before. Unlike Cassian, Columbanus did not start from the monk examining his own soul in the quiet of a cell. Rather, he started from the immensity of God. This was not a God who could be approached with ease, through introspection or through contemplation of the sunny wonders of creation. For Columbanus, God was surrounded by deep silence.[8] He was as hidden as the depths that lurked beneath the surface of a chill, impassible ocean.[9] Yet this hidden God could be glimpsed in part by the pure of heart. *Ego sum Deus proximans et non Deus de longe* (Jer. 23:23): "I am a God Who comes near, and not a God who is far away."[10] For all His remoteness—Columbanus repeatedly insisted—He was *our* God: "He must yet be besought by us, often besought; ever must we cling to God, to the deep, vast, hidden, lofty and almighty God."[11] Distant though God might be, it was still possible, in this life, to take down the fire of His love from above the stars and to place it in one's own heart: "Would that I had the tinder to foster, feed, and keep alight that fire unceasingly, to nourish that flame, which knows no quenching and knows all increase!"[12]

And what was that tinder? It was a monastic regime that has long bruised the modern sensibility and from which the non-

Irish followers of Columbanus later retreated.[13] What we have to understand is why so harsh a therapy was thought necessary by Columbanus. It was because he was very much an adherent, through his reading of Faustus of Riez and Cassian, of the "Gallic consensus."[14] Human beings were tragically weak, but they had, at least, the remnant of a healthy will with which to wrestle with the horrendous, sinful, other will that had attached itself to them like "an insatiable and rabid leech."[15] They were free to fight back. They did so by opting for a regime of shared suffering that pushed its participants to the breaking point. This was the only way to shatter the power of the evil will. In the words of a follower of Columbanus, the life of a monk was a life of total surrender: "Let him not do as he wishes, let him eat what he is bidden, keep only so much as he is given, pay in the full account of his allotted work-load, be subject to the commands of one whom he does not wish to serve. Let him come weary to his bed and sleep walking, let him be forced to rise while his sleep is not yet finished . . . Let him fear the superior of his community as he would a lord."[16] This was a life that resembled that of slaves and of dependent serfs, whose labor on the growing domains of northern Francia had been notably intensified at just this time.

A regime that apparently allowed, for instance, only two and a half hours of sleep, followed by hours of chanting in wintertime, before dawn, in an unheated church, has rightly appalled its modern commentators. Such a regime was "a testimony both to [Columbanus's] own character, and to the toughness of his converts."[17]

It is, indeed, the "the toughness of his converts," and not Columbanus himself, who present the greatest mystery to the historian. What did these converts get in return? Put very briefly: They got the fire of God in their hearts through lighting, first, within themselves, the "fire of obedience."[18] Columbanus and his successors urged their monks and nuns to believe that the one fire led to the other. The inner fire of the love of God could only begin to burn once the total dismantling and reconstruction of the *persona* of young aristocrats (men and women alike) had taken place. The abandonment of personal freedom and unflinching obedience to a superior were the essence of the monastic life, for they were the only way to light the inner fire of the love of God.

Obedience was not an end in itself: It was the hard way toward building a heaven on earth. Obedience was to lead to transparency and love. Columbanus and many of his successors envisaged monasteries and convents as enclosed oases of grace and openness. Monasteries and convents were to be places of carefully orchestrated movements. They were to be filled with the sound of voices modulated by chanting. Day-to-day life was to be conducted through gentle, uncontentious interchanges. They were to be institutions held together through innumerable acts of mutual service and prompt obedience.

Columbanus and his followers were convinced that this beauty could be achieved. But it could be achieved only through pulverizing the hard, class-bound wills of the monks and nuns. To shed the proud will was the hardest work of all: "Admittedly, this training may seem hard to hard men, namely that a man should always hang on the mouth of an other."[19]

Furthermore, a new means toward achieving monastic perfection had recently been found. Columbanus brought with him to Gaul the Irish and British practice of regular confession, followed by "tariffed," that is, by minutely calibrated, penance for each sin. In the long run, this led to an "epoch-making acceptance" in Gaul of a new religious practice developed in what had hitherto been a marginal Christian region.[20]

We should not exaggerate the immediate impact of the new forms of confession and penance outside the convents and monasteries of Columbanus and his admirers. In Ireland and elsewhere, regular confession was a form of "elective piety."[21] It was never imposed on the church at large, as would happen in the High Middle Ages and in modern Catholicism. It was an elite practice, largely reserved for those with a religious vocation—for monks and nuns or for future monks and nuns.

But the role of frequent confession in grinding down the wills of proud men and women in the monasteries of Columbanus was crucial. Three times a day, in many convents, every nun would confess her sins of thought and action. She would receive absolution and a measured penance from the mouth of one of her fellows.[22] The long and anxious lucubrations of the desert hermits upon their varied and tenacious temptations (as Columbanus would have read in the works of Cassian) were rendered manageable by the practice of confession. Temptations were, as it were, "miniaturized." They were broken down into a series of clearly envisioned scenarios, each of which could be verbalized, spoken of to a fellow monk or nun, and then dealt with through a measured penance. It was a system that brought the gift of quick closure and the ease of a "purified" heart to an environment where monks and nuns were stretched to their limits in all other matters.

Not surprisingly, there were rebellions and breakouts in Columbanian monasteries and convents.[23] But these places were
also scenes of rare moments of serenity, achieved through the
pursuit of seemingly little things that highlighted the difference
between the quiet of the monastery or of the convent and the
strident world of an all-too-confident lay elite outside its sheltered spaces. The rules of Columbanus and his successors were
masterpieces of what modern sociologists call "emotion man-
agement."[24] But they did a lot more than control the behavior
of monks and nuns, they deliberately turned upside down the
codes of the elites from which they were recruited. They pro-
moted silence and self-effacement. They punished gossip and
every "grand word."[25] This was no small thing, for high talk and
taking down one's rivals by malicious tales had been the characteristic trait of great bishops, and of the swaggering courtiers,
warlords, and great landowners of the Frankish kingdom.[26]

In a manner not unlike that of the upper-class monastic converts of fifth-century Provence, the values and behavior patterns
of a proud and newly formed aristocracy were met by pointed
ascetic inversion. To pass from "the world" to a monastery or
convent of the Columbanian tradition was to pass from a ca-
cophony of proud words to a quiet pool of measured speech and
low-key, rhythmic movements. The monastic rules ensured that
polite petitions would be met, day in and day out, by peaceable
answers. This was the case even on so charged an issue as the
distribution of food to half-starving fellow monks and nuns.
Thus, the nun in charge of the cellar (the food supply) should
always answer: "with mild words and without any roughness in
response, so that the sweetness of her heart may be revealed by
the answering of her voice."[27]

These pointed inversions of the codes of the new aristocracy radiated outside the convents and monasteries. Long before he became a monk, the pious Wandregisil (later Saint Wandrille) was prepared to ruin his cloth-of-gold robe by helping to push a peasant's wagon out of deep mud in front of the royal palace— to the great amusement of his fellow courtiers. (One should add, though, that his mud-caked robe was miraculously dry-cleaned by angels before he entered the royal presence.) In the convent of Nivelles, Gertrude (the aunt of the ancestor of Charlemagne, no less) was buried with a bleak simplicity that was a rebuke to the magnificent grave goods of her worldly peers. These dramatic acts of role inversion may well have been particularly significant among the newly formed aristocracies of eastern Francia, where the social stratification of the nobility (shown by dress and by treasure-filled burials) had been most blatant.[28]

Monasteries, Convents, and Donors in Seventh-Century Francia

When studying the impact of Columbanus's message on Frankish society at large, it is important to have a sense of the passing of the generations. An entire generation after the death of Columbanus had passed when Jonas of Susa (a Burgundian monk from Bobbio, equally at home on either side of the Alps) wrote the classic *Vita Columbani* from 639 to 643. By that time things had changed in Gaul: Two crucial developments had occurred.

One development took place among a small but influential group at the very top of Frankish society. In the 630s, the monastic values of openness, mutual respect, and the absence of proud boasting, produced by the grinding routines of the

Columbanian monasteries, spilled out into the lay world. A monastic ethos helped to create a code of upper-class decorum among courtiers, bureaucrats, and bishops in the northern Frankish kingdom. This was especially the case among the golden youth at the court of Dagobert I (629–634)—the "Merovingian VIPs" of the next generation. These young men were brought together from many different regions, with differing family traditions. Some came from the still "Roman" southwest, and others from the Frankish north. The adoption of a common code of behavior among them was part of the homogenization of the Merovingian kingdom.[29]

This was a para-monastic code. For the very first time, we are dealing with a code of upper-class decorum that did not draw only on ancient, "worldly" wisdom associated with classical rhetoric and with Roman law. Although these elements were still present at the Merovingian court, they were now blended with pious habits taken from the Christian monastery. In these select circles, something like a *courtoisie*—a code of refined behavior suited to a royal court—flourished.

This half-ascetic, courtly lifestyle had one great advantage. It enabled royal servants to switch careers with greater ease. Bureaucrats could become bishops or heads of monasteries without seeming any longer to pass from one irrevocably different world to another. Courtiers influenced in this way by monastic practices were a solemn lot. Ceremonious and scrupulous, they invariably addressed each other as *peccator*—as "fellow sinners." They helped to create an ideology of consensual rule in an orderly and responsible polity—as if the Frankish kingdom itself were a great monastery. The seriousness of this endeavor has come to be appreciated as a result of the innovative work of Anne-Marie Helvétius and Jamie Kreiner.[30] This new view of the ruling class of the Frankish kingdom of the seventh century has come as a surprise to most scholars, who had tended to regard the later Merovingians and their followers as no more than unreconstructed thugs.

The other development was more widespread. It affected Frankish upper-class society as a whole. Monasteries and convents came to be viewed as holy institutions in themselves. Here we are dealing with a significant change. Columbanus had been a typical holy man of late antiquity—a vivid outsider who impinged dramatically on the society around him. But by the time that Jonas wrote his *Life of Columbanus,* this charismatic image of Columbanus had been eclipsed by a strong sense of group holiness. It was not the individual holy monk or nun who mattered. It was the amazing, clockwork-like life of the monks and nuns, unanimously devoted to long prayers, that held the attention of an ever-wider circle of lay patrons.[31]

Let us now look at these monastic settlements through the eyes of their patrons. These lay patrons did not wish to take on the bitter lifestyle of monks and nuns. Rather, they wished to bridge the chasm between the sacred and the profane through gifts. As is the case in many societies where an elite of ascetic virtuosos coexisted with large groups of wealthy laypersons, it was through gifts that the two, incommensurable worlds were thought to be joined.[32]

Such gifts should not be seen as cold transactions. Rather, they created a symbiotic relationship between the holy monasteries and convents and their lay supporters. This close relationship represented a high point in the mystical exchange of wealth for prayer that we first saw in the parable of the elm and the vine of the prophet Hermas in 140 AD. However, it had become an exchange in which the poor were absent. Monks and nuns replaced the poor as the intercessors par excellence.

Gifts also drew boundaries. They created a sort of "buffer zone" between the lifestyle of a laity that remained impenitently profane (and that now included warriors, with blood on their hands, as a militarized upper class replaced the civilian elites of Roman times) and monasteries and convents that radiated a raw sacrality.[33] This sense of the incommensurable otherness and the absolute worth of chosen monasteries and convents was best communicated by equally off-scale gifts.

These gifts amounted to much more than financial support. For many noble families, a convent or a monastery formed "the heart of its symbolic power." Many of these monasteries and convents were founded on family land. The presence of convents filled with upper-class nuns, in particular, rendered palpable the honor of great clans. The heads of these clans showed, by their foundations, that they could dispose of large tracts of land. They also advertised the fact that, as noblemen and royal servants, they could place even their own daughters in sites in the open countryside, with nothing to protect them from violence but a holy wall and the reputation of their kin.[34] By the end of the seventh century, many convents had endowments of up to 20,000 hectares of some of the richest and most intensely worked farmland in Europe.[35]

These monasteries and convents were seen as powerhouses of prayer. The disciplined ranks within them prayed constantly for the peace of the kingdom. But, more important still, they prayed for the souls of their founders and donors.[36] In this sense, the foundation of so many monasteries and convents in Gaul, and the massive endowments that many of them received, marked the grand finale of centuries of intercessory prayer. It was also an age that glutted its imagination on the notion of a mystical transfer of treasure from earth to heaven. To found a great monastery was to set commonsense ideas of wealth on their head, with stupendous imagined results. In the words of one wealthy courtier: "I cede . . . small things for great, earthly things for things celestial, what is on earth for what abides forever."[37]

As we saw in Chapter 5, donations were made, first and foremost, for the *remedium*—for the healing and protection—of the soul in the other world. It is not surprising, therefore, that monasteries founded to pray for the souls of their founders in the other world should generate vivid stories about that other world. These stories concentrated on the manner in which the soul entered the other world at the moment of death. Thus, when Jonas came to write the second book of his *Life of Columbanus*, a large section was devoted to glimpses of the other world among the nuns of the convent of Faremoutiers (near Meaux, on the edge of the valley of the Marne).

What was novel in these vivid stories was that the glimpses of the afterlife that they recorded did not take the form of visions or mighty dreams. They all took place at the deathbeds of ordinary nuns. It is as if, at the moment of death, a veil was pulled aside, and the array of angelic and demonic forces, which Salvian had already imagined (two hundred years before) at the deathbeds of the rich, stood there, to be seen by all.

But the message of Jonas, unlike that of Salvian, was optimistic: It was possible for good nuns to face, without danger, the threatening world beyond the grave. Duly prepared, and protected by the prayers of entire establishments of monks and nuns, even good lay patrons might hope to do the same. What mattered was to die well. In the well-chosen words of Jamie Kreiner, for Jonas and others "death is a time of deliberate conclusion."[38] One could not be too careful about the manner in which one reached that conclusion before one passed into the other world.

What Jonas stressed about the deaths of the nuns of Faremoutiers was that death itself was no more than one stage in the penitential life of the convent. It was a last summing up of the self. Sisetrudis was the first nun to die at Faremoutiers. It was a death for which she was prepared. It was revealed to her that she had forty days in which to prepare "for the journey," but on the thirty-seventh day she fell for a short time into a coma. She seemed to have died. Coming to herself, she told the gathered nuns what had happened: Two youths had carried her through the empty air. Then she was subjected to "many investigations"—*multis discussionibus*. We should note this word: *discussio* still retained strong juridical and fiscal overtones, as if the sifting of the soul of Sisetrudis was a tax audit.[39] No sooner was Sisetrudis placed among the angels than she was ordered to return to life. She had not yet qualified for the "presence" of Christ because her full forty days of preparation through penance had not been fulfilled. On the fortieth day, the entire convent gathered round her bed to pray for her passing, and the angels returned. Sisetrudis was now ready to go: "I come from here, my lords, I come."[40] This model death, wrote Jonas, was "the first exhortation for the convent which the Lord wished to show."[41]

It is revealing that none of the subsequent deaths that Jonas reports were straightforward triumphal entries into heaven. The soul of each nun passed through some form of testing that made good the omissions in their life in the convent. Thus, Gibitrudis, also, was taken up to heaven and sent back again: "Return, for you have not [yet] left the world."[42]

Gibitrudis had not yet "left the world" because she was still burdened by one sin. She had failed to forgive three nuns, despite the fact that every day she had prayed "Forgive us our sins, as we forgive those who sin against us."[43] What for Augustine had been the permanent, irresoluble (and somewhat ill-focused) lament of the sinner in general had become, in Faremoutiers, yet one more relentlessly precise occasion for confessing a particular sin, followed by the merciful release of absolution in return for a specific penance. Having done her penance by forgiving her fellow nuns, Gibitrudis was free to enter heaven.

Such stories implied that only souls that had already died to every sin could pass safely, through natural death, into the life of heaven. In a manner reminiscent of the *Book of the Dead* in ancient Egypt, each departing soul had to be "screened." The soul of every nun in Faremoutiers was examined minutely by guardians of the other world so as to make sure that no taint of the impurity of sin clung to it when it entered the stainless land of life. In the words of Jan Assmann, speaking of the Egyptian *Book of the Dead:* "For this reason, the threshold could never be high enough, the boundary could never be secure

enough, and the character of the guardians could never be terrifying enough."[44]

Not all nuns were spared that terror. Rebellious nuns died
badly. The doors of their bedrooms were torn open, and black
shades assembled at their bedside. Voices seemed to summon
them by name into the beyond.[45]

Some nuns only scraped by. The "worldly" mother of a saintly
child received no more than "forgiveness"—*venia*—but not before she had been "terrified by the sight of terrible demons."[46]
The passing of this more worldly lady was reassuring to the average layperson: "For what she could not achieve through her
own merits, she gained through the intercession of her daughter."[47]
Lay donors and admirers of Faremoutiers could hope for the
same for themselves.

These tales from a noble convent in the lush valley of the
Marne hint at a more general change. For persons of an earlier
generation, *venia*—"forgiveness"—could only be gained at the
feet of great male saints as they lay in their splendid tombs on
the outskirts of the ancient cities of Gaul. Now this most precious of all gifts—the gift of God's forgiveness—had moved to
different regions and lay in the hands of different persons. Forgiveness was now achieved not only through the intercession of
the ancient dead, but through the prayers of living saints—
noblewomen massed in convents that radiated a collective holiness. Furthermore, these convents were notionally as remote
from the busy life of the cities as if on a moon station. They were
rural institutions, placed in the fields and forests of northern and
eastern Gaul. Not one of them had existed when Gregory of
Tours laid down his pen in 591.

Journeys of the Soul: Fursa and Barontus

For the lay nobility, as well as for monks and nuns, the monasteries and convents of seventh-century Francia acted as antechambers to the afterlife. Reports began to appear of "journeys of the soul" connected with near-death experiences. These described in circumstantial detail the perils of the soul in the afterlife. The first of these to be published and widely circulated was provided by Fursa (or Fursey), an Irishman who finally settled in Gaul, having passed through East Anglia. He died at Lagny (near Noyon) in 650. The second appeared in 679, and was the account of a voyage to the gates of paradise and back by Barontus, a monk of the monastery of Saint-Peter at Longoretum (now Saint-Cyran, to the west of Bourges).[48] Nothing quite like them had appeared before.

The protagonists and the forms of these two visions could not have been more different from each other. The *Vision of Fursa* was set in distant Ireland and presented as a validation of Fursa's future career as a preacher of repentance. He claimed to have seen what no man had seen—and it was truly frightening. When he spoke of the vision in later years, he would sweat with fear in the icy chill of an East Anglian winter.[49] Barontus, by contrast, was an almost comic character. A late convert to the monastic life, he was the typical Frankish nobleman of his time—not a mindless man of violence (as we often imagine) but a former government official, and a much-married man, with far too many mistresses on his conscience.[50] We meet him floating over the fields in real space (at a rate of precisely twelve miles an hour!), looking down on a landscape dotted with familiar monasteries.

He even saw the monks of one of these monasteries, gathered for prayer below him, summoned by the sound of their monastery's bell. All the while he was being kicked in the rear by importunate demons. He was very much one of the *non valde boni*—the "not altogether goods"—of his age. He needed all the prayer he could get.[51]

Yet both near-death visions summed up the hopes and fears of their age. They were a new genre. Unlike the great visions of late antiquity, they were not "cosmic" journeys: They did not describe an ascent to a starry realm. Nor did they take the seer directly to the throne of God. In these visions, God was strangely absent. He was veiled in impenetrable splendor. What mattered was the fate of a particular soul at the hands of awe-inspiring intermediate powers—of angels and demons—who guarded the threshold of heaven, keeping sinners away from that place of utter perfection. The fate of the soul was determined by precise, personal sins that had not yet been purged by penance in the land of the living. Furthermore, in both visions, it was the demons that spoke with the voice of the monastic penitential system at its most rigorous. They stood for a principle of terrible transparency. Poor Barontus was simply overwhelmed by how much the demons seemed to know about him: "And they went over all the sins that I had committed from infancy onwards, including those which I had totally forgotten."[52]

Barontus was no saint. Fursa, by contrast, stood at the beginning of his missionary career when he experienced his vision.[53] He had to show that he had been fully "purged" of sin before he could undertake his public role as a preacher of repentance. The demons tested him in a merciless manner. Like spiritual guides in the strict Irish tradition, they reached down to the very roots of his actions. They pointed out that he had failed to forgive his enemies from the bottom of his heart.[54] He had not become "as a little child."[55] He had colluded with sinners by failing to rebuke them.[56]

Faced by this barrage of accusations, the angels who accompanied Fursa protested that the demons could have him only if he had committed *principalia crimina*—"top sins." They could not have him for mere minor sins.[57] This was not the view of the demons: "Every sin which is not purged on earth must be revenged in heaven . . . Here is no place for repentance."[58]

Nor could Fursa hope to benefit from some hidden reserve of divine mercy. The demons lived in an unbearably well-lit world: "*Quid enim hic occultum?* (What is there here that can be hidden?)"[59]

What were the sins for which both Barontus and Fursa were summoned to face punishment? Unlike so many late antique visions of the sufferings of souls in hell, their sins had nothing to do with sex. Money was what mattered. Barontus had held back twelve gold pieces for his own use when he entered the monastery. He was told by none other than Saint Peter to give one coin every month, sealed and blessed by a priest, into the hand of a poor man. With this solemn ritual, the primal Christian gesture of almsgiving for the expiation of the soul was delineated with crystalline clarity.[60]

For Fursa it was far worse. He was accused of having received gifts from sinners whose penance he had not investigated to make sure that their repentance had been sincere.[61] Gifts from the sinful were a constant issue at this time. They were dangerous.

Jonas records how a glass of wine given to Columbanus by the sinful King Theuderic exploded in his hand.[62] The vision of Fursa was written down in a monastery founded by a patron with a tainted reputation—by the increasingly unpopular mayor of the palace, Erchinoald, the top power broker of the Merovingian kingdom. In such an environment, the purity of gifts to monks was no small matter.[63]

For Fursa it was, quite literally, a burning issue. On his way back to earth he passed a bank of flame. Suddenly a demon emerged from the flame carrying a burning man, whom he threw at Fursa. The scorching body brushed against his jaw and shoulder. It was a man to whom Fursa had given inadequate penance in exchange for the gift of a cloak. The demons cried, "Do not push away what you once received."[64] From then onward the face of Fursa bore a livid scar. The horrible, searing embrace, jaw to jaw, of monk and donor summed up the deepest anxieties of this great age of pious giving.

Souls, Sin, and the Universe

And with this we can end. It is widely agreed that the seventh century constitutes a watershed in the history of Western Christianity. Watersheds, however, are often rather flat and featureless places. This is even more the case in religious history than it is in geography. The low-profile continuities of Christian thought and practice that link the third to the seventh centuries—the ancient world to the Middle Ages—are as significant as are the well-known turning points—such as the flowering of a new monastic culture and the emergence of the new genre of the "voyage of the soul."

What seems, at first sight, to be startlingly new and exotic often proves to be yet another mutation of a long-established species. There is very little in the dramatic debates between angels and demons in the visions of Fursa and of Barontus that Augustine had not considered (if with far greater hesitation) in his capacious works. What we take to be an irreversible change is frequently no more than a change of viewing point, as the spotlight of our evidence shifts to illuminate other aspects of the same continuum.[65] Yet we can still sense a change in the gradient. By 650, religion and society in Gaul had begun on a slope that would end with great monasteries, regular confession, the emergence of purgatory, and the great *Divina Commedia* of Dante Alighieri.

However, we must be careful to preserve a sense of historical perspective. We have followed the story of the Christian soul from a very ancient world, among the tombs of third-century Rome, to the threshold of the Middle Ages. By 650 AD, large monasteries had already begun to appear, founded so as to offer intercessory prayer for the souls of their founders; the outlines of a notion of purgatory were clearly visible; penance through confession had begun to be practiced. But, in the course of this momentous journey, we might fail to notice what has slipped out of view. Too great an emphasis on the future of Western Christianity can lead us to neglect what had been left behind. So, let us not look to the medieval future, but say good-bye to the ancient past.

To conclude: What did Western Christianity leave behind in these centuries? I would suggest that what was left behind was almost too big to be seen: the erosion and final replacement of the mystique of the ancient cosmos by a Christian model of the universe dominated by the notion of sin, punishment, and reward.

In order to understand this, it is best to go back to the late classical period and to a masterwork of synthesis, the *Afterlife in Roman Paganism* of Franz Cumont. Cumont conjures up, with rare serenity, the thrill of the ancient vision of the universe. Here was a world where what you saw was what you eventually might hope to get. It was a supremely manageable world: "When men raised their eyes to the constellations of the firmament, they thought they perceived its end. The depths of the sky were not for them unfathomable."[66]

The material universe was not only a clearly delimited world, it was coherent and carefully graded. There was a clear up and a clear down. Top souls reached top places as if by some law of moral physics. The souls of the blessed arrived at the Milky Way. In this manner, the moral structure of the other world coincided exactly with its physical structure. The souls of the good were on top, among the imperishable stars. Flawed souls, by contrast, lingered in the dank world beneath the moon.

This view was by no means limited to pagans. We need only read the funerary inscriptions of the Christian aristocracy of Rome and of their descendants, the upper-class bishops of Gaul, to appreciate this. Their souls, also, were declared to be lodged among or even beyond the stars as firmly as were the souls of any of their pagan peers and ancestors.[67] As we have seen, for Sulpicius Severus it was natural to think of the soul of Saint Martin vanishing from sight into the stars.

This image of the cosmos had already begun to weaken in Christian circles even in the third century. No matter how hard the poets who composed the tombstones for the Christian great might try, paradise—a Near-Eastern garden replete with God's blessing—could never be quite the same as the Milky Way. Circa 200 AD, Tertullian already knew this: "Shall we have to sleep high up in the ether along with Plato and the boy-chasing Worthies [of Greece]?"[68]

Tertullian had gotten the point. The Milky Way was not for the anonymous. It was for Worthies. Its heavy clusters validated the fame achieved on earth by acclaimed leaders of society. As Cumont reminds us, in such a worldview people only got as much immortality they had striven for—or were granted—on earth: "Immortality, as we [modern persons] conceive it, follows on the very nature of the soul . . . It is generally supposed to be absolute, eternal, universal. For the ancients, on the other hand, immortality was no more than conditional: it might not be perpetual and it might not belong to all men."[69]

Only the great remained great forever. Given a widespread belief in the transmigration of souls, the great might even come back again, after many centuries, to take up their role as rulers on earth. As we saw in Chapter 3, this view was supported by the famous description of the encounter of Aeneas with the souls of great Romans about to plunge back into their bodies in Book 6 of the *Aeneid*.[70] As Augustine pointed out in a sermon, this incident was widely known from representations in the theater. It had become part of a folk-classicism that reached far beyond literate circles.[71] The great returned from heaven so as to be great yet again on earth. In such a view, cosmos and social stratification co-inhered.

It is this intensely hierarchical image of the cosmos that slowly but surely waned in the back of Christian minds. We need only follow Augustine's pen, as he answered so many questions concerning death and the other world, to appreciate the extent to which, consciously or unconsciously, a chasm had opened up in his imagination between himself and the ancient majesty of the cosmos. He turned his back on the order of the cosmos that had graded even the nature of souls. To him, all souls were equal, because all souls were immortal. And all souls, also, were the souls of potential saints or sinners on their way to heaven or to hell.

The notion of eternal punishment, as Augustine and others proposed it, might seem grim to us. But at least it posited something indestructible to punish in each human person. Immortality was not "precarious and conditional."[72] No soul vanished into thin air to join the vast majority of inglorious spirits who had no place in the Milky Way. Right down to his defense of traditional commemorative practices against the upper-class *nouvelle vague* of burial beside the saints, Augustine upheld a democracy of souls. The low-profile nature of so many tombs found on the pavements of basilicas in Africa and Italy shows that there were many who thought as he did. To have been a *fidelis*, a baptized Christian privileged to enjoy proximity to the Eucharist both in this life and in the next (through the offerings of one's loved ones) was enough.

In this way, Christian debates about the care of the dead imperceptibly flattened the ancient cosmos. There were no privileged spaces, mapped by some spiritual topography onto the vast and high-pitched frame of the universe. Souls were no longer distributed throughout the cosmos along a vertical axis—up and down—according to some law of "moral physics," but according to their conformity with the will of God. The only hierarchy that mattered was no longer the great staircase that rose majestically from the base earth to the glory of the stars. It was, rather, the tripartite hierarchy created by the human will alone. This was a hierarchy made up of the *valde boni*, the *valde mali*, and the ever-interesting "Middle Way" of the *non valdes*—the "not altogether good" and the "not altogether bad"—on whom so much energy of thought and ritual action came to be lavished in Christian circles.

This was a silent revolution. No one thinker was responsible for it. But the changed imaginative status of the universe represented a profound shifting of tectonic plates in the ancient worldview. By the seventh century, the implications of this imaginative revolution were clear. The visions of Fursa and Barontus occurred in a world that no ancient person—at least, no ancient person committed to the agreed collective representation of the universe current among the educated—would have recognized. There were no stars. Instead, the voyage of each soul was determined by its sins and merits alone. And these sins and merits were not (as was often the case in the ancient world) horrendous crimes or deeds of great glory. They were the humble conglomerate of an entire life, built up like a coral reef by a deposit of thoughts and deeds so complex and so deeply rooted in the particularities of a given life, that (as in the case of the poor Barontus) they escaped the full consciousness even of those who had committed them. This implied a remarkably "thick" view of the human person. It was a view that had been fostered through the circumstantiality associated with the new practices of confession. In the words of Claude Carozzi, the *Vision of Barontus* was

"a first sketch of the awareness of the self on the part of the individual in Western Europe."[73]

At the time, visions of the voyage of the soul mainly concerned those engaged in the sheltered life of monasteries and
convents. In order to understand the waning of the cosmos in a
less specialized (though still privileged) environment, we should
turn to our Christian tombstones. Up to the middle of the sixth
century (and beyond, in the case of northern Italy), the stones
of southern Gaul, Mediterranean Spain, and Italy maintained
a proud cosmic language with which to talk of the good and
the great. The living spoke through florid memorial inscriptions
that insisted that the dead were as securely lodged in a star-filled
heaven as any of the Worthies of pagan Rome had been. Bishops,
clergymen, monks, nuns, and laypersons: All had gone upward
to the stars. Compared with the exquisite inscriptions of the
fourth century, these marble plaques were often covered in
clumsy Latin letters. But their messages showed a world still
bathed in the late, late sunlight of a very ancient view of the
world.[74]

Then, for a crucial generation, the ancient tombstones fell
silent. Carved epitaphs vanished for a moment. When they revived, we hear a very different voice. No longer do we hear the
voice of the living, praising the dead. Instead, we hear a voice
from the grave. Gradually, region by region (from Ireland to
Rome), we begin to hear the dead themselves asking for the
prayers of the living: *oroit do*—"a prayer for" in Ireland, *orate pro*
in Latin.[75] One of the first examples comes from seventh-century
Gothic Septimania (in what is now the French side of the Pyr-
enees). Crudely carved along the frame of a great stone, deco-

rated with three large, protective crosses, it is the dead man who speaks: "In the name of Christ, all men pray for Trasemir."[76] When the bond between the living and the dead, constantly cemented by the rituals of the church, became a cosmos of its own—a subject of deep preoccupation, the stuff of visions, and the object of the regular prayers and donations of millions—then we can say, around the year 650 AD, that the ancient world truly died in Western Europe.

Notes

INTRODUCTION

1. Julian of Toledo, *Prognosticon futuri saeculi*, ed. J. N. Hillgarth, *Corpus Christianorum* 115 (Turnholt: Brepols, 1976).

2. R. Collins, *Early Medieval Spain: Unity and Diversity, 400–1000* (London: Macmillan, 1983), 78.

3. C. Carozzi, *Le voyage de l'âme dans l'au-delà dans la littérature latine (ve–xiiie siècle)*, Collection de l'École française de Rome 189 (Rome: Palais Farnèse, 1994), 95.

4. Notably Cyprian's *de mortalitate* in *Prognosticon* 1.14–16, 28–34; and his *ad Fortunatum* in *Prognosticon* 2.36, 74.

5. Cyprian, *de mortalitate* 3, ed. W. Hartel, *Corpus Scriptorum Ecclesiasticorum Latinorum* 3 (Vienna: Gerold, 1868), 298.

6. Cyprian, *ad Fortunatum* 13, 347; and Julian, *Prognosticon* 2.37, 74, citing Augustine, *City of God* 20.9.

7. See E. Gonzalez, *The Fate of the Dead in Early Third Century Africa*, Studien und Texte zu Antike und Christentum 83 (Tübingen: Mohr Siebeck, 2014), 69–71.

8. É. Rebillard, *Christians and Their Many Identities in Late Antiquity, North Africa, 200–450 CE* (Ithaca, NY: Cornell University Press, 2012), 34–55.

9. Tertullian, *de anima* 55.5, ed. J. H. Waszink, *Corpus Christianorum* 1 (Turnholt: Brepols, 1954), 863.

10. G. W. Bowersock, *Martyrdom and Rome* (Cambridge: Cambridge University Press, 1995), 41–74.

11. Marcus Aurelius, *Meditations* 11.3, ed. C. Haines, *Marcus Aurelius Antoninus*, Loeb Classical Library (Cambridge, MA: Harvard University Press, 1961), 294. See R. B. Rutherford, *The Meditations of Marcus Aurelius: A Study* (Oxford: Clarendon Press, 1989), 188.

12. F. Dölger, "Gladiatorenblut und Märtyrerblut," *Vorträge der Bibliothek Warburg* 1 (1923–1924), 196–214.

13. Lucian, *Peregrinus*, 11–14 and 35, ed. A. M. Harmon, *Lucian* 5, Loeb Classical Library (Cambridge, MA: Harvard University Press, 1972), 12–16 and 38–40; see J. König, "The Cynic and Christian Lives of Peregrinus," in *The Limits of Ancient Biography*, ed. B. McGing and J. Mossman (Swansea: Classical Press of Wales, 2006), 227–254.

14. See esp. A. Stuiber, *Refrigerium interim: Die Vorstellungen vom Zwischenzustand und die frühchristliche Grabeskunst,* Theophaneia 11 (Bonn: P. Hanstein, 1957); and C. E. Hill, *Regnum Caelorum: Patterns of Millennial Thought in Early Christianity* (Grand Rapids, MI: Eerdmans, 2001). Readers should know that Gonzalez, *Fate of the Dead,* 186–195, treats the opinion of Tertullian on the interim nature of the afterlife of nonmartyrs as only one opinion among others—and one that was in competition with other views that would eventually prevail.

15. F. Cumont, *The Afterlife in Roman Paganism* (New Haven, CT: Yale University Press, 1922), 193–213; and H. Wrede, *Consecratio in formam deorum: Vergöttlichte Privatpersonen in der römischen Kaiserzeit* (Mainz: von Zabern, 1981).

16. Tertullian, *de resurrectione mortuorum* 34.10, ed. J. Borleffs, *Corpus Christianorum* 2 (Turnhout: Brepols, 1954), 966.

17. Cyprian, *Epistula* 6.4, ed. W. Hartel, *Corpus Scriptorum Ecclesiasticorum Latinorum* 3 (Vienna: Tempsky, 1871), 484; A. Alföldi, *Die monarchische Repräsentation im römischen Kaiserreiche* (Darmstadt: Wissenschaftliche Buchgesellschaft, 1970), 41.

18. Irenaeus, *Adversus Haereses* 5.32.1, ed. W. Harvey, *Sancti Irenaei adversus haereses* 2 (Cambridge: Cambridge University Press, 1857), 413. See Stuiber, *Refrigerium interim,* 43–74; H. Finé, *Die Terminologie der Jenseits-*

vorstellungen bei Tertullian, Theophaneia 12 (Bonn: P. Hanstein, 1958), 150–196. In invoking the notion of *refrigerium interim* to explain all aspects of the art of the Christian catacombs, Stuiber overreached. For a more nuanced view, see D. Hofmann, "'Der, Ort der Erfrischung': *Refrigerium* in der frühchristlichen Literatur und Grabkultur," in *Topographie des Jenseits: Studien zur Geschichte des Todes in Kaiserzeit und Spätantike,* ed. W. Ameling, Altertumswissenschaftliches Kolloquium 21 (Stuttgart: F. Steiner, 2011), 103–122.

19. Gonzalez, *Fate of the Dead,* 130–139, links this change to the upward pressure of popular beliefs in immortality shared with pagans, in what has been called by Ramsay MacMullen the "Second Church." See R. MacMullen, *The Second Church: Popular Christianity A.D. 200–400* (Atlanta, GA: Society of Biblical Literature, 2009), 104–105. I am less certain that these beliefs had a "popular" origin.

20. Julian, *Prognosticon,* pref., 12.

21. Julian, *Prognosticon* 18, 36.

22. Julian, *Prognosticon* 1.18, 36.

23. Julian, *Prognosticon* 2.19, 55–56.

24. Notably, B. E. Daley, *The Hope of the Early Church: A Handbook of Patristic Eschatology* (Cambridge: Cambridge University Press, 1991; 2nd ed., Grand Rapids, MI: Eerdmans, 2010).

25. Carozzi, *Le voyage de l'âme,* 43–61.

26. P. Fouracre, "Eternal Light and Earthly Needs: Practical Aspects of the Development of Frankish Immunities," in *Property and Power in the Early Middle Ages,* ed. W. Davies and P. Fouracre (Cambridge: Cambridge University Press, 1995), 53–81.

27. Defensor of Ligugé, *Liber Scintillarum* 49.9, ed. H. M. Rochais, *Corpus Christianorum* 117 (Turnhout: Brepols, 1957), 166.

28. *Testamentum Leodegarii,* ed. B. Krusch, W. Gundlach, and L. Traube, *Corpus Christianorum* 117 (Turnhout: Brepols, 1957), 513.

29. W. John, "Formale Beziehungen der privaten Schenkungsurkunde Italiens und des Frankenreiches und die Wirksamkeit der Formulare," *Archiv für Urkundenforschung* 14 (1935): 1–104. I am particularly grateful to Professor Helmut Reimitz for his help in the delicate matter of assessing the authenticity of some of the earliest Merovingian charters of donation.

30. S. Liebermann, "Some Aspects of the Afterlife in Early Rabbinic Judaism," in *Harry Austryn Wolfson Jubilee Volume* (Jerusalem: Magnes Press, 1965), 495–532; J. Smith and Y. Haddad, *The Islamic Understanding of Death and Resurrection* (Albany, NY: SUNY Press, 1981; new ed., 2001); L. Halevi, *Muhammad's Grave: Death Rituals and the Making of Islamic Society* (New York: Columbia University Press, 2007), 226–233; M. Dal Santo, *Debating the Saints' Cult in the Age of Gregory the Great* (Oxford: Oxford University Press, 2012), 237–320.

Chapter 1   MEMORY OF THE DEAD IN EARLY CHRISTIANITY

1. Matt. 19:21; cf. Mark 10:21 and Luke 18:22.

2. Luke 12:33.

3. Peah 15b, 63–75, trans. M. Schwab, *Le Talmud de Jérusalem* (Paris: Maisonneuve, 1972), 2:7; and G. A. Wewers, *Pea/Ackerecke* in *Übersetzung des Talmud Yerushalmi* (Tübingen: Mohr-Siebeck, 1986), 2:2, 10–11.

4. Cyprian, *de zelo et livore* 16, ed. W. Hartel, *Corpus Scriptorum Ecclesiasticorum Latinorum* 3 (Vienna: Gerold, 1868), 431.

5. Luke 16:19.

6. Gregory, *Dialogues* 4.38.1, ed. A. de Vogüé, *Grégoire le Grand: Dialogues*, Sources chrétiennes 265 (Paris: Le Cerf, 1980), 136; trans. O. J. Zimmermann, *Saint Gregory the Great: Dialogues*, Fathers of the Church 39 (New York: Fathers of the Church, 1959), 241.

7. Gregory, *Dialogues* 4.37.15, ed. A. de Vogüé, 134; trans. Zimmermann, 241.

8. G. Anderson, *Charity: The Place of the Poor in the Biblical Tradition* (New Haven, CT: Yale University Press, 2013), 123–135.

9. K. Koch, "Der Schatz im Himmel," in *Leben angesichts des Todes: Beiträge zum theologischen Problem des Todes. Helmut Thielecke zum 60. Geburtstag* (Tübingen: Mohr, 1968), 47–60, at 52.

10. E. Diehl, *Inscriptiones Latinae Christianae Veteres* (henceforward *ILCV*) (Dublin: Weidmann, 1970), no.1067, of 449 AD.

11. J. Guyon and M. Heijmans, eds., *D'un monde à l'autre: Naissance d'une Chrétienté en Provence, ive—vie siècles* (Arles: Musée d'Arles antique, 2001), 87.

12. E. Urbach, "Treasure Above," in *Hommages à Georges Vajda: Études d'histoire et pensée juives*, eds. G. Nahon and C. Touati (Louvain: Peeters, 1980), 117–124, at 118 and 124.

13. J. Parry, "*The Gift*, the Indian Gift and the 'Indian Gift,'" *Man*, n.s. 21 (1986): 453–473, at 466; and M. Bloch and J. Parry, "Introduction," in *Money and the Morality of Exchange*, ed. M. Bloch and J. Parry (Cambridge University Press, 1989), 1–32, at 2. See my remarks in P. Brown, *"Through the Eye of a Needle:" Wealth, the Fall of Rome, and the Making of Christianity in the West, 350–550 AD* (Princeton, NJ: Princeton University Press, 2012), 84–85; and "'Treasure in Heaven:' The Implications of an Image," *Cristianesimo nella storia* 33 (2012): 377–396.

14. M. Hénaff, *The Price of Truth: Gift, Money, and Philosophy*, trans. J.-L. Morhonge and A.-M. Feenberg-Dibon (Stanford, CA: Stanford University Press, 2010).

15. D. C. Ullucci, *The Christian Rejection of Animal Sacrifice* (Oxford: Oxford University Press, 2012), 65–118.

16. J. Lakoff and M. Johnson, *Metaphors We Live By* (Chicago: Chicago University Press, 1980).

17. Anderson, *Charity*, 170.

18. Gal. 2:10; see D. Georgi, *Remembering the Poor: The History of the Pauline Collection for Jerusalem* (Nashville, TN: Abingdon Press, 1992); and D. J. Downs, *The Offering of the Gentiles: Paul's Collection for Jerusalem and Its Chronological, Cultural and Cultic Context* (Tübingen: Mohr Siebeck, 2008).

19. Hermas, *The Shepherd*, Similitude 2.52, ed. R. Joly, *Hermas: Le Pasteur*, Sources chrétiennes 53 bis (Paris: Le Cerf, 1968), 214–218; trans. J. B. Lightfoot, *The Apostolic Fathers* (Grand Rapids, MI: Eerdmans, 1956), 201. See C. Osiek, *Rich and Poor in the Shepherd of Hermas: An Exegetical-Social Analysis*, Catholic Biblical Quarterly Monograph Series 15 (Washington, DC: Catholic Biblical Association of America, 1983), 25.

20. Hullin 92a, Babylonian Talmud, trans. E. Cashdan (London: Soncino Press, 1948), 516.

21. P. Brown, *Poverty and Leadership in the Later Roman Empire*, Menahem Stern Jerusalem Lectures (Hanover, NH: University Press of New England, 2002), 24–26; and Brown, "*Through the Eye of a Needle*," 36–39. The best-known early Christian community in the West was that of

Carthage. It has been studied in an exemplary manner by G. Schöllgen in *Ecclesia Sordida? Zur Frage der sozialen Schichtung frühchristlicher Gemeinden am Beispiel Karthagos zur Zeit Tertullians, Jahrbuch für Antike und Christentum* Ergänzungsband 12 (Münster: Aschendorff, 1984), 155–269, 286–294, and 299–311.

22. Anderson, *Charity,* 70–82.

23. R. Krautheimer, *Rome: Profile of a City, 312–1308* (Princeton, NJ: Princeton University Press, 1980), 16, esp. fig.16.

24. On this theme I owe most to Steffen Diefenbach's *Römische Erinnerungsräume: Heiligenmemoria und kollektive Identitäten im Rom des 3. bis 5. Jahrhunderts n.Chr.,* Millennium Studien 11 (Berlin: de Gruyter, 2007), 38–62, esp. 43–55.

25. *Passio Perpetuae* 8.4, ed. H. Musurillo, *The Acts of the Christian Martyrs* (Oxford: Clarendon Press, 1972), 116.

26. *Inscriptiones Christianae Vrbis Romae* (henceforward *ICVR*), n.s. 5, ed. A. Ferrua (Vatican: Pontificium Institutum Archaeologiae Christianae, 1971), nos. 12907–13096, 89–40.

27. Diefenbach, *Römische Erinnerungsräume,* 16.

28. *ICVR,* n.s. 5, no. 12936, 14; and 12954, 17.

29. *ICVR,* n.s. 6, ed. A. Ferrua (Vatican: Pontificium Institutum Archaeologiae Christianae, 1975), nos. 16547 and 16548, from the catacomb of Saints Marcellinus and Peter.

30. *ILCV,* no. 2315—San Callisto.

31. K. Argetsinger, "Birthday Rituals: Friends and Patrons in Roman Poetry and Cult," *Classical Antiquity* 23 (1992): 175–193.

32. *ICVR,* n.s. 5, no. 12933, 14.

33. C. Rapp, "'For Next to God, You Are My Salvation': Reflections on the Rise of the Holy Man in Late Antiquity," in *The Cult of the Saints in Late Antiquity and the Early Middle Ages: Essays on the Contribution of Peter Brown,* ed. J. Howard-Johnston and P. A. Hayward (Oxford: Oxford University Press, 1999), 63–81, at 66–67. See also Anderson, *Charity,* 136–148.

34. Augustine, *de civitate Dei* 21.27.186, ed. B. Dombart and A. Kalb, *Corpus Christianorum* 48 (Turnhout: Brepols, 1955), 804, citing Virgil, *Aeneid* 6.664; trans. H. Bettenson, *Concerning the City of God against the Pagans* (Harmondsworth: Penguin, 1972), 1020.

35. Tertullian, *Apologeticum* 39.2, ed. E. Dekkers, *Corpus Christianorum* 1 (Turnhout: Brepolis, 1954), 150

36. *ICVR*, n.s. 5, no. 2959, 18.

37. See esp. J. Bodel, "From *Columbaria* to Catacombs: Collective Burial in Pagan and Christian Rome," in *Texts and Artifacts in Context: Studies in Roman, Jewish and Christian Burials*, ed. L. Brink and D. Green (Berlin: de Gruyter, 2008); and Brown, *"Through the Eye of a Needle,"* 47–49. On bucolic themes in Christian funerary art, see F. Bisconti, "Primi passi di un'arte cristiana: I processi di definizione e l'evoluzione dei significati," *Antiquité Tardive* 19 (2011): 35–46, esp. 39–40.

38. A. Dworkin, *Intercourse* (New York: Free Press, 1987), 128.

39. E. Bruck, *Über römisches Recht im Rahmen der Kulturgeschichte* (Berlin: Springer, 1954), 71.

40. For example, the mausoleum of Vincentius, former prefect of the city, is described in A. Bertolino, "'In area Callisti': contributo alla topografia di Roma tardoantica," *Rivista di archeologia cristiana* 70 (1994): 181–190.

41. *ICVR*, n.s. 5, no. 13273, 69.

42. P. Brown, *The Cult of the Saints: Its Rise and Function in Latin Christianity* (Chicago: Chicago University Press, 1981, rpt. with Intro., 2014), 62–63; J. G. Deckers, "Von Denker zum Diener: Bemerkungen zu den Folgen der konstantinischen Wende im Spiegel der Sarkophagplastik," in *Innovation in der Spätantike*, ed. B. Brenk (Wiesbaden: Reichert, 1996), 137–172.

43. *ILCV*, no. 3433.5.

44. *ILCV*, no. 3446.4. On Proiecta, see Brown, *"Through the Eye of a Needle,"* 205–206 and 252. This development is well studied by P. Courcelle, "Quelques symbols funéraires du néoplatonisme latin," *Revue des etudes anciennes* 46 (1944): 65–93 and J. Fontaine, "Les images virgiliennes de l'ascension céleste dans la poésie latine chrétienne," *Jenseitsvorstellungen in Antike und Christentum. Gedenkschrift für A. Stuiber,* Jahrbuch für Antike und Christentum: Ergänzungsband 9 (Münster: Aschendorff, 1982): 55–67.

45. M. Handley, *Death, Society and Culture: Inscriptions and Epitaphs in Gaul and Spain, AD 300–750,* BAR International Series (Oxford: Oxbow, 2003), 35–39, at 39.

46. P. Brown, "The Diffusion of Manichaeism in the Roman Empire," *Journal of Roman Studies* 59 (1969): 92–103, reprinted in *Religion and Society in the Age of Saint Augustine* (London: Faber, 1972), 94–118. On the Syriac elements in Manichaeism, the best treatment remains F. C. Burkitt, *The Religion of the Manichees* (Cambridge: Cambridge University Press, 1925), 71–86, 92–99, and 111–119.

47. *Coptic Documentary Texts from Kellis*, ed. I. Gardner, A. Alcock and W. P. Funk (Oxford: Oxbow, 1999), 79; N. J. Baker-Brian, *Manichaeism: An Ancient Faith Rediscovered* (Edinburgh: T. and T. Clark, 2011), 54.

48. I. Gardner and S. N. C. Lieu, "From Narmouthis (Medinat Madi) to Kellis (Ismant al-Kharab)," *Journal of Roman Studies* 86 (1996): 146–169. Much of this material has been translated in I. Gardner and S. N. C. Lieu, *Manichaean Texts from the Roman Empire* (Cambridge: Cambridge University Press, 2004).

49. S. G. Richter, *Die Aufstiegspsalmen des Herakleides. Untersuchungen zum Seelenaufstieg und zur Seelenmesse bei den Manichäern* (Wiesbaden: O. Harrassowitz, 1997), 61–67.

50. W. P. Funk, "The Reconstruction of the Manichaean *Kephalaia*," in *Emerging from Darkness,* ed. P. Mirecki and J. Be Duhn (Leiden: Brill, 1997), 143–159; and T. Pettipiece, *Pentadic Redaction of the Manichaean Kephalaia* (Leiden: Brill, 2009).

51. P. Brown, "Alms and the Afterlife: A Manichaean View of an Early Christian Practice," in *East and West: Essays in Ancient History Presented to Glen W. Bowersock,* ed. T. Corey Brennan and Harriet I. Flower (Cambridge, MA: Dept. of Classics, Harvard University, 2008), 145–158.

52. *Kephalaion* 115, ed. A. Böhlig, *Kephalaia: Teil I. Zweite Hälfte: Lieferung* 11/12 (Stuttgart: Kohlhammer, 1966), 270.26–30; trans. I. Gardner, *The Kephalaia of the Master* (Leiden: Brill, 1995), 276.

53. *Kephalaion* 115, ed. Böhlig, 271.10–12; trans. Gardner, 277.

54. *Kephalaion* 144, ed. W.-P. Funk, *Kephalaia: Teil I. Zweite Hälfte. Lieferung* 13/14 (Stuttgart: Kohlhammer, 1999), 347.5.

55. *Kephalaion* 115, ed. Böhlig, 277.21; trans. Gardner, 282.

56. *Kephalaion* 115, ed. Böhlig, 280.12; trans. Gardner, 283–284.

57. *Kephalaion 87, On Alms,* ed. H. Ibscher, *Kephalaia: Teil I. Zweite Hälfte. Lieferung* 1–10 (Stuttgart: Kohlhammer, 1940), 217.16–20; trans. Gardner, 225.

58. *The Kellis Agricultural Account Book*, ed. R. S. Bagnall (Oxford: Oxbow, 1997), 82–84.

59. *P. Kell. Copt.* 21.51–56, in *Coptic Documentary Texts from Kellis*, 188–189.

60. Laurentius, 8, *Prosopographie chrétienne du Bas Empire 2: Italie*, ed. C. Pietri and L. Pietri (Rome: École française de Rome, 2000), 2:1236. His brother Dulcitius was active in Africa and also plied Augustine with questions: Dulcitius, 2, *Prosopographie chrétienne du Bas-Empire 1: Afrique*, ed. A. Mandouze (Paris: CNRS, 1982), 330–333.

61. Augustine, *Sermon* 172.2.2; *Kephalaion* 144, ed. Funk, 346. 22–26.

62. *Kephalaion* 92, ed. Ibscher, 235.2–11; trans. Gardner, 241–242.

63. Augustine, *Enchiridion* 29.110; trans. B. Harbert, *The Works of Saint Augustine: A Translation for the 21st Century* (Hyde Park, NY: New City Press, 2005), 336–337.

64. P. A. Février, "La mort chrétienne," in *Segni e riti nella chiesa alto medioevale*, Settiimane di Studi 33 (Spoleto: Centro di Studi sull'Alto Medioevo, 1987), 881–942, at 932.

Chapter 2   VISIONS, BURIAL, AND MEMORY

IN THE AFRICA OF SAINT AUGUSTINE

1. *[New] Letter* 23A.4, *Lettres 1*–29**, Bibliothèque augustinienne: Oeuvres de Saint Augustin 46B (Paris: Études Augustiniennes, 1987), 378 and commentary on 532–547. In this chapter, references to the works of Augustine will be cited by their conventional titles and without author name. Only in certain cases will I cite a modern edition.

2. B. Shaw, "The Cultural Meaning of Death. Age and Gender in the Roman Family," in *The Family in Italy from Antiquity to the Present*, ed. D. Kertzer and R. P. Saller (New Haven, CT: Yale University Press, 1991), 66–90, at 67.

3. J. Dresken-Weiland, *Sarkophagbestattungen des 4.–6. Jahrhunderts im Westen des römischen Reiches*, *Römische Quartalschrift* Supplementband 55 (Rome: Herder, 2003), 14.

4. U. Volp, *Tod und Ritual in den christlichen Gemeinden der Antike*, Supplements to *Vigiliae Christianae* (Leiden: Brill, 2002), 112.

5. S. T. Stevens, "Commemorating the Dead in the Communal Cemeteries of Carthage," in *Commemorating the Dead: Texts and Artifacts in Context. Studies in Roman, Jewish and Christian Burials*, ed. L. Brink and D. Green (Berlin: de Gruyter, 2008), 70–103, at 86 and 94.

6. See esp. L. Dossey, *Peasant and Empire in Christian North Africa* (Berkeley: University of California, 2010), 149–162.

7. Augustine, *de civitate Dei* 21.2.187, ed. B. Dombart and A. Kolb, *Corpus Christianorum* 48 (Turnhout: Brepols, 1955), 804; trans. H. Bettenson, *Concerning the City of God against the Pagans* (Harmondsworth: Pelican Books, 1972), 1020.

8. G. Elliot, *Middlemarch*, cited by G. Halsall, *Barbarian Migrations and the Roman West, 376–568* (Cambridge: Cambridge University Press, 2007), 518.

9. On Uzalis, see T. Ghalia, "Le site d'Uzalis: Recherches récentes en archéologie et en épigraphie," in *Les miracles de saint Étienne*, ed. J. Meyers, *Hagiologia* 5 (Turnholt: Brepols, 2006), 81–87.

10. *Letter* 158.1–2, ed. A. Goldbacher, *Corpus Scriptorum Ecclesiasticorum Latinorum* (Vienna: Tempsky, 1904), 488–490.

11. *Letter* 158.3, ed. Goldbacher, 490.

12. M. Dulaey, *Le rêve dans la vie et la pensée de saint Augustin* (Paris: Études augustiniennes, 1973), 217–223.

13. *Letter* 158.10, ed. Goldbacher, 495–496.

14. *Passio Perpetuae* 11.8, ed. H. Musurillo, *The Acts of the Christian Martyrs* (Oxford: Clarendon Press, 1972), 120.

15. *Passio Perpetuae* 12.6, 120. On this gaming table and others see H. Dessau, *Inscriptiones Latinae Selectae* 8626a (Berling: Weidmann, 1892), 2: 964 and H.-G. Horn, Si per me misit, nil nisi vota feret. Ein römischer Spielturm aus Froitzheim, *Bonner Jahrbücher* 189 (1989): 139–160, at p. 158.

16. T. Mathews, *The Clash of Gods: A Reinterpretation of Early Christian Art* (Princeton, NJ: Princeton University Press, 1993; 2nd. rev. and exp. ed., 1999). For my review, see P. Brown, *Art Bulletin* 77 (1995): 499–502. Looking back, I would now say that Mathews was too concerned to prove that the image of Christ was *not* modeled on that of an emperor. What may have mattered was the ambiguity of the image—it could be of an emperor or it could be of some other beloved and authoritative figure. The

interplay of multiple visual associations gave force to the image. Images of Epicurus had played on a similar ambiguity: see B. Frischer, *The Sculpted Word: Epicureanism and Philosophical Recruitment in Ancient Greece* (Berkeley: University of California Press, 1982).

17. See J. Matthews, *The Roman Empire of Ammianus Marcellinus* (London: Duckworth, 1989): The ritual of being allowed to "adore" (by kissing) the hem of the emperor's purple robe acted as "a demarcation, acted out before one's eyes, of those imperial supporters entitled to a place in the emperor's presence" (246). See also W. T. Avery, "The *Adoratio Purpurae* and the Importance of Imperial Purple in the Fourth Century of the Christian Era," *Memoirs of the American Academy in Rome* 17 (1940): 66–80.

18. E. Diehl, *Inscriptiones Latinae Christianae Veteres* [henceforth *ILCV*] (Dublin: Weidmann, 1970), no. 63b, 28–29.

19. Virgil, *Aeneid* 4.79, ed. R. Mynors, *P. Vergili Maronis opera* (Oxford: Clarendon Press, 1969), 178.

20. *Letter* 158.7, ed. Goldbacher, 493. Cf. *Acts of the Council of Chalcedon.* Session 3. 64, ed. J. D. Mansi, *Sacrorum Conciliorum Amplissima et Nova Collectio* (Florence, 1761; rpt. Paris: H. Welter, 1901), 6: 1033 B; trans. R. M. Prince and M. Gaddis, *The Acts of the Council of Chalcedon* (Liverpool: Liverpool University Press, 2005), 2: 63. I think that the accusation that the patriarch Dioscoros of Alexandria had blocked the reception of imperial *laurata* (the Greek loanword from the Latin *laureata*) in Alexandria referred not to imperial images, but to documents accompanied by wreaths in the manner of imperial images.

21. *Letter* 158.9, ed. Goldbacher, 494–495.

22. *Letter* 158.4, ed. Goldbacher, 491. See esp. V. Zangara, *Exeuntes de corpore. Discussioni sulle apparizioni dei morti in epoca agostiniana* (Florence: Olschki, 1990).

23. *Letter* 158.7, ed. Goldbacher, 493.

24. *de Genesi ad litteram* 12.18.39, ed. J. Zycha, *Corpus Scriptorum Ecclesiasticorum Latinorum* 28 (Vienna: Tempsky, 1904), 406.

25. *Letter* 159.5, ed. Goldbacher, 502.

26. *Letter* 159.2, ed. Goldbacher, 499. This was already the case for Augustine in 390: *Letter* 7.2.

27. *Letter* 158.5, 6, and 11, ed. Goldbacher, 491–492 and 496.

28. Dulaey, *Le rêve*, 77.

29. W. Baltes, "Platonisches Gedankengut im Brief des Evodius an Augustin (*Ep.* 158)," *Vigiliae Christianae* 40 (1986): 251–260.

30. G. Smith, "Physics and Metaphysics," *The Oxford Handbook to Late Antiquity*, ed. Scott Johnson (Oxford: Oxford University Press, 2012), 513–561 at 539.

31. *Letter* 159.1, ed. Goldbacher, 498.

32. Tertullian, *de anima* 47.2, ed. J. H. Waszink, *Corpus Christianorum* 2 (Turnhout: Brepols, 1954), 853.

33. W. H. C. Frend, *The Donatist Church* (Oxford: Clarendon Press, 1952), 79, note 7 and 105, note 4. See, in general, J. Amat, *Songes et visions: L'au delà dans la littérature latine tardive* (Paris: Études Augustiniennes, 1985), 25–158.

34. B. Shaw, *Sacred Violence: African Christianity and Sectarian Hatred in the Age of Augustine* (Cambridge: Cambridge University Press, 2011); and P. Brown, *"Through the Eye of a Needle": Wealth, the Fall of Rome, and the Making of Christianity in the West, 350–550 AD* (Princeton, NJ: Princeton University Press, 2012), 328–336.

35. See esp. B. Kriegbaum, *Kirche der Traditoren oder Kirche der Märtyrer? Die Vorgeschichte des Donatismus* (Innsbruck: Tyrolia, 1986).

36. *Epistola ad catholicos de unitate ecclesiae* 19.49, ed. M. Petschenig, *Corpus Scriptorum Ecclesiasticorum Latinorum* 52 (Vienna: Tempsky, 1908), 296.

37. *Council of Carthage* (401), canon. 83, ed. C. Munier, *Corpus Christianorum* 149 (Turnholt: Brepols, 1974), 204–205.

38. Shaw, *Sacred Violence*, 721–770; on Donatist dreams see Dulaey, *Le rêve*, 41.

39. *de cura pro mortuis gerenda* 12.14, ed. J. Zycha, *Corpus Scriptorum Ecclesiasticorum Latinorum* 41 (Vienna: Tempsky, 1900), 643; see Dulaey, *Le rêve*, 205–210.

40. A. Besançon, *The Forbidden Image: An Intellectual History of Iconoclasm*, trans. J. M. Todd (Chicago: University of Chicago Press, 2000), 18.

41. Cynegius, *Prosopographie chrétienne du Bas-Empire 2: Italie*, ed. C. Pietri and L. Pietri (Rome: École française de Rome, 1999), 512; and Y. Duval, "Flora était-elle africaine?," *Revue des etudes augustiniennes* 34 (1988): 70–77.

42. *ILCV*, no. 3482.7.

43. Brown, *"Through the Eye of a Needle,"* 224–240.

44. P. Brown, *The Cult of the Saints: Its Rise and Function in Latin Christianity* (Chicago: Chicago University Press, 1981), 34–38. See also *"Through the Eye of a Needle,"* 281–282, on the criticism of the cult of the saints by Vigilantius, who may have been provoked by the splendid buildings of Paulinus.

45. P. Rose, *Augustine and the Relations between the Living and the Dead: Discourse-Linguistic Commentary on the de cura pro mortuis gerenda* (Amsterdam; Vrije Universiteit, 2011), 154–259 and 283–297.

46. *de cura pro mortuis gerenda* 4.6 and 18.22.

47. Y. Duval and J.-Ch. Picard, ed., *L'inhumation privilegiée du ive au viiie siècle en Occident* (Paris: de Boccard, 1986).

48. Maximus of Turin, *Sermon* 12.2, ed. A. Mutzenbecher, *Corpus Christianorum* 23 (Turnhout: Brepols, 1962), 42.

49. Y. Duval, *Auprès des saints corps et âme: L'inhumation "ad sanctos" dans la chrétienté d'Orient et d'Occident du iiie au viie siècle* (Paris: Études Augustiniennes, 1988).

50. H. Kotila, *Memoria mortuorum: Commemoration of the Dead in Augustine,* Studia Ephermeridis Augustinianum 38 (Rome: Institutum Patristicum Augustinianum, 1992). See M. A. Handley, *Death, Society and Culture: Inscriptions and Epitaphs in Gaul and Spain, AD 300–750,* British Archaeological Reports, International Series 1135 (Oxford: Oxbow, 2003), 17: "Certain formulae are more common in Africa than elsewhere. In particular, *fidelis* [baptized] *in pace* and *memoria* are very common."

51. A. M. Yasin, *Saints and Churches: Spaces in the Late Antique Mediterranean: Architecture, Cult and Community* (Cambridge: Cambridge University Press, 2009), 71–91 and 221.

52. *Confessions* 9.13.35–37, ed. P. Knöll, *Corpus Scriptorum Ecclesiasticorum Latinorum* 33 (Vienna: Tempsky, 1906), 224–226.

53. *Confessions* 9.13.37, ed. Knöll, 225; see J. J. O'Donnell, *Augustine: Confessions. Commentary* (Oxford: Clarendon Press, 1992), 3:148.

54. *Confessions* 9.11.28 and 9.13.36, ed. Knöll, 219 and 224–225.

55. *Confessions* 9.13.34, ed. Knöll, 223.

56. *Confessions* 9.13.36, ed. Knöll, 224–225.

57. *Confessions* 7.21.27, ed. Knöll, 225, is the only other time. Significantly, it is when Augustine is speaking of the false attempts of the pagan Platonists to reach heaven.

58. Brown, *"Through the Eye of a Needle,"* 361–362.

Chapter 3   ALMSGIVING, EXPIATION, AND THE OTHER WORLD

1. P. Brown, *"Through the Eye of a Needle": Wealth, the Fall of Rome, and the Making of Christianity in the West, 350–550 AD* (Princeton, NJ: Princeton University Press, 2012), 61–68.

2. P. Veyne, *Le pain et le cirque* (Paris: Le Seuil, 1976), 44–183, trans. B. Pierce, *Bread and Circuses* (London: Allen Lane Penguin, 1990), 16–69; E. Patlagean, *Pauvreté économique et pauvreté sociale à Byzance: 4e–7e siècles* (Paris: Mouton, 1977), 17–35, 181–196, and 423–432. See P. Brown, *Poverty and Leadership in the Later Roman Empire,* The Menahem Stern Jerusalem Lectures (Hanover, NH: University Press of New England, 2002), 6–16, for a survey of the issue.

3. See esp. R. Finn, *Almsgiving in the Later Roman Empire: Christian Promotion and Practice, 313–450* (Oxford: Oxford University Press, 2006).

4. Brown, *Poverty and Leadership,* 29–44.

5. Brown, *Poverty and Leadership,* 74–80.

6. I. Schiller, D. Weber, and C. Weidmann, "Sechs neue Augustinuspredigten: Teil 2 mit Edition dreier Sermones zum Thema Almosen," *Wiener Studien* 122 (2009): 171–213.

7. Brown, *"Through the Eye of a Needle,"* 66–68.

8. *Erfurt Sermon* 4.6, ed. I. Schiller, D. Weber and C. Weidmann, "Sechs neue Augustinuspredigten: Teil 2 mit Edition dreier Sermones zum Thema Almosen," *Wiener Studien* 122 (2009): 211.

9. Brown, *"Through the Eye of a Needle,"* 347–358. See also R. Lim, "Augustine and Roman Public Spectacles," in *A Companion to Augustine,* ed. M. Vessey (Oxford: Wiley-Blackwell, 2012), 138–151.

10. *Enarrationes in psalmos* 149.10, ed. E. Dekkers, and J. Fraipont, *Corpus Christianorum* 40 (Turnhout: Brepols, 1956), 1462–1463.

11. J. Maxwell, *Christianization and Communication in Late Antiquity: John Chrysostom and His Congregation at Antioch* (Cambridge: Cambridge University Press, 2008), 125 and 147.

12. *Sermon* 9.21, ed. C. Lambot, *Corpus Christianorum* 41 (Turnhout: Brepols, 1961), 148–151.

13. See C. Wickham, *Framing the Early Middle Ages: Europe and the Mediterranean, 400–800* (Oxford University Press, 2005), 708–712. G. Génelle, *La vie économique et sociale dans l'Afrique romaine tardive d'après les sermons de saint Augustin* (Lille: Atelier National de Réproduction des Thèses, 2005) shows the extent to which Augustine drew on commercial imagery in his preaching.

14. *Sermon* 86.10.11 and 177.10, *Patrologia Latina* 38: 582 and 959.

15. R. Sorabji, *Emotion and Peace of Mind: From Stoic Agitation to Christian Temptation* (Oxford: Oxford University Press, 2000), 165.

16. *Sermon* 60.6.7, *Patrologia Latina* 38: 405–406.

17. *Sermon,* 86.9.11, *Patrologia Latina* 38: 582.

18. J. P. Oleson, *Greek and Roman Mechanical Water-Lifting Devices: The History of a Technology,* Phoenix Supplementary Volume 16 (Toronto: University of Toronto Press, 1984).

19. *Enarrationes in psalmos* 38.12, ed. E. Dekkers and J. Fraipont, *Corpus Christianorum* 38 (Turnhout: Brepols, 1956), 413–415.

20. *Erfurt Sermons* 2.1 and 3.2, ed. Schiller, Weber and Weidmann, 10 and 17; *Enarrationes in psalmos* 121.11.

21. Brown, *"Through the Eye of a Needle,"* 16, on the games of Symmachus in Rome. In 445, Bishop Rusticus of Narbonne rebuilt the cathedral of Narbonne through donations that amounted to 2,500 *solidi:* H. I. Marrou, "Le dossier épigraphique de l'évêque Rusticus de Narbonne," *Rivista di archeologia cristiana* 3–4 (1970): 331–347.

22. Brown, *"Through the Eye of a Needle,"* 287–288.

23. Gerontius, *Life of Melania* 16, Greek ver. ed. D. Gorce, *Vie de Sainte Mélanie,* Sources chrétiennes 90 (Paris: Le Cerf, 1962), trans. E. A. Clark, *Life of Melania the Younger* (New York: Edwin Mellen, 1984), 39.

24. Matt. 19:24.

25. Gerontius, *Life of Melania* 21, Gorce, 172, trans. Clark, 44.

26. Gerontius, *Life of Melania* 20, Gorce, 170, trans. Clark, 43.

27. Brown, *"Through the Eye of a Needle,"* 308–321.

28. Pseudo-Pelagius, *de divitiis* 12.2, ed. A. Kessler, *Reichtumskritik und Pelagianismus: Die pelagianische Diatribe de divitiis,* Paradosis 43 (Fribourg-en-Suisse: Universitätsverlag, 1999), 292: trans. B. R. Rees,

228   NOTES TO PAGES 96–99

The Letters of Pelagius and His Followers (Woodbridge: Boydell Press, 1991), 194.

29. Augustine, *Letter* 156 and 159.4.23, ed. Goldbacher, 448 and 472–473; see also *Letter* 157.4.23.

30. Dan. 4.27.

31. *Mekilta Israel,* trans. J. Lauterbach, *Mekilta de-Rabbi Ishmael* (Philadelphia: Jewish Publication Society, 1935), 3:86–87.

32. G. Anderson, *Sin: A History* (New Haven, CT: Yale University Press, 2009), 9 and 135; see also G. Anderson, *Charity: The Place of the Poor in the Biblical Tradition* (New Haven, CT: Yale University Press, 2013), 114–116.

33. *Wisdom of Ben Sirach [Ecclesiasticus]* 3:30, *The New English Bible with Apocrypha* (Oxford: Oxford University Press, 1961), 116.

34. Prov. 19:17. See Anderson, *Sin,* 12; and M. Hénaff, *The Price of Truth: Gift, Money, and Philosophy,* trans. J.-L. Morhonge and A.-M. Feenberg-Dibon (Stanford, CA: Stanford University Press, 2010), 93. It was precisely the manner in which commerce in general and interest in particular might "give rise to unthinkable unlimitedness" that made Aristotle so hostile to usury.

35. Anderson, *Sin,* 106.

36. Anderson, *Sin,* 108. The book grew over time. A seventh-century vision speaks of Satan as carrying "a volume of enormous size and unbearable weight" containing the deeds and thoughts of each person: Bede, *Ecclesiastical History* 5.13, ed. B. Colgrave and R. A. B. Mynors (Oxford: Oxford University Press, 1969), 500.

37. Anderson, *Sin,* 131; *Charity,* 29.

38. É. Rebillard, *In hora mortis: Évolution de la pastorale de la mort aux ive et ve siècles dans l'Occident latin,* Bibliothèque de l'École française d'Athènes et de Rome 282 (Rome: Palais Farnèse, 1994), 148–167.

39. *Enarrationes in psalmos* 103; *Sermon* 3.18, ed. Dekkers and Fraipont, *Corpus Christianorum* 40, 1515–1516.

40. Matt. 6:12.

41. This was conclusively shown by A.-M. La Bonnardière, "Les commentaires simultanés de Mat.6.12 et 1 Jo.1.18 dans l'oeuvre de saint Augustin," *Revue des études augustiniennes* 1 (1955): 129–147.

42. *Enarrationes in psalmos* 140.18, ed. Dekkers and Fraipont, *Corpus Christianorum* 40, 2038–2039.

43. *Sermon* 58.9.10, *Patrologia Latina* 38:398; and *Enarrationes in psalmos* 43.8.

44. *Sermon* 56.7.11, *Patrologia Latina* 38:381–382.

45. *Sermon* 9.11.17, ed. Lambot, 141–142.

46. *Enarrationes in psalmos* 52.9, ed. Dekkers and Fraipont, *Corpus Christianorum* 38, 644; *Tractatus in Johannem* 50.6, ed. R. Willems, *Corpus Christianorum* 36 (Turnhout: Brepols, 1954), 435.

47. *De perfectione iustitiae* 20.43, ed. C. Urba and J. Zycha, *Corpus Scriptorum Ecclesiasticorum Latinorum* 42 (Vienna: Tempsky, 1902), 46.

48. *Sermon* 9.11.17, ed. Lambot, 141–142. See also, among many passages, *de fide et operibus* 16.27, ed. J. Zycha, *Corpus Scriptorum Ecclesiasticorum Latinorum* 41 (Vienna: Tempsky, 1900), 69–72 (which Augustine later copied out in his answer to one of the questions posed by Dulcitius: *Quaestiones ad Dulcitium* 1.6, ed. A. Mutzenbecher, *Corpus Christianorum* 44A [Turnhout: Brepols, 1975], 260–263) and the classic statement in *de civitate Dei* 21.26.40–66, ed. B. Dombart and A. Kalb, *Corpus Christianorum* 48 (Turnhout: Brepols, 1955), 797.

49. Possidius, *Life of Augustine* 24.4, ed. M. Pellegrino, *Vita di Santo Agostino* (Alba: Edizioni Paoline, 1955), 126.

50. E. Diehl, *Inscriptiones Latinae Christianae Veteres* (Dublin: Weidmann 1970), no. 1915.

51. Jerome, *Dialogus contra Pelagianos* 1.28: *Patrologia Latina* 23:520C–522C.

52. Jerome, *In Isaiam* 18.66.24: *Patrologia Latina* 24:676B–678B.

53. B. Daley, *The Hope of the Early Church: A Handbook of Patristic Eschatology* (Cambridge: Cambridge University Press, 1991), 104.

54. *contra duas epistulas Pelagianorum* 3.5.14. One should add that the thought of Pelagius himself on sinners in the church was considerably more nuanced—but that of his followers was not. See A. Thier, *Kirche bei Pelagius,* Patristische Texte und Studien 50 (Berling: de Gruyter, 1999).

55. Augustine, *New Letter* 4*.3, Bibliothèque augustinienne 46B, 112. For a full commentary on the background of this letter, see 430–442.

56. Augustine, *New Letter* 4*.4, 114.

57. C. Carozzi, *Le voyage de l'âme dans l'au-delà dans la littérature latine (ve–xiiie siècle)*, Collection de l'École française de Rome 189 (Rome: Palais Farnèse, 1994), 23.

58. *de civitate Dei* 21.26.105–113, 798.

59. *de civitate Dei* 10.30.29–55, 307–308; and 12.21.56–112, 378–379, with *Sermons* 240.4, and 241.4.4–7.7.

60. A. Smith, *Porphyry's Place in the Neoplatonic Tradition: A Study of Post-Plotinian Neoplatonism* (The Hague: M. Nijhoff, 1974), 67.

61. Virgil, *Aeneid* 6.721, ed. R. Mynors, *P. Vergili Maronis opera* (Oxford: Clarendon Press, 1969), 249. See esp. A. Settaioli, *La vicenda dell'anima nel commento di Servio su Virgilio* (Frankfurt am Main: Peter Lang, 1995).

62. For a similar "presence" of Manichaeism as a body of ideas and questions to which Augustine had to pay constant attention, see J. Be Duhn, *Augustine's Manichaean Dilemma 2: Making a "Catholic" Self* (Philadelphia: University of Pennsylvania Press, 2013).

63. See, recently, I. Moreira, *Heaven's Purge: Purgatory in Late Antiquity* (Oxford: Oxford University Press, 2010).

64. *Enarrationes in psalmos* 80.20.

65. P. Brown, "The Decline of the Empire of God: Amnesty, Penance and the Afterlife from Late Antiquity to the Middle Ages," in *Last Things: Death and the Apocalypse in the Middle Ages*, ed. C. W. Bynum and P. Freedman (Philadelphia: University of Pennsylvania Press, 2000), 41–59 at 47–50.

66. Prudentius, *Cathemerinon* 5.133–135, ed. and trans. H. J. Thomson, Loeb Classical Library (Cambridge, MA: Harvard University Press, 1869), 1:46.

67. *Visio Pauli* 44.2–4, ed. C. Carozzi, *Eschatologie et au-delà. Recherches sur l'Apocalypse de Paul* (Aix-en-Provence: Publications de l'Université de Provence, 1994), 250–252.

68. Brown, *Poverty and Leadership*, 81–91.

69. *de civitate Dei* 21.24.78–101, 790–791.

70. Daley, *Hope of the Early Church*, 132.

71. *Enchiridion* 29.112, trans. E. Evans, *Saint Augustine's Enchiridion* (London: S.P.C.K., 1953), 97–98.

72. Possidius, *Life of Augustine* 31.1–2.

Chapter 4   PENANCE AND THE OTHER WORLD IN GAUL

1. Salvian, *de gubernatione Dei* 8.12. 72, ed. G. Lagarrigue, *Salvien de Marseille: Oeuvres* 2, Sources chrétiennes 220 (Paris: Le Cerf, 1975), 408.

2. Brown, *"Through the Eye of a Needle": Wealth, the Fall of Rome, and the Making of Christianity in the West, 350–550 AD* (Princeton, NJ: Princeton University Press, 2012), 380–407.

3. Salvian, *de gubernatione Dei* 6.15, 416.

4. Salvian, *Letter* 1.5–6, ed. G. Lagarrigue, *Salvien de Marseille: Oeuvres* 1, Sources chrétiennes 176 (Paris: Le Cerf, 1971), 78.

5. Gennadius of Marseilles, *de viris illustribus* 68, ed. E. Richardson (Leipzig: Hinrichs, 1896), 84–85. All the works of Salvian are translated by J. F. O'Sullivan, *The Writings of Salvian the Presbyter*, Fathers of the Church 3 (New York: CIMA, 1947); and the *de gubernatione Dei* alone by E. M. Sanford, *The Government of God*, Columbia Records of Civilization (New York: Columbia University Press, 1930). On Salvian in general, see esp. D. Lambert, "The Uses of Decay: History in Salvian's *de gubernatione Dei*," *Augustinian Studies* 30 (1999): 115–130; R. Alciati, *Monaci, vescovi e scuola nella Gallia tardoantica* (Rome: Edizioni di Storia e Ltteratura, 2009), 83–101; Brown, *"Through the Eye of a Needle,"* 441–453; and P. Brown, "Salvian of Marseilles: Theology and Social Criticism in the Last Century of the Western Empire," (Dacre Lecture, Oxford University, 2010). See also D. Lambert, "Salvian and the Bacaudae," *Gallien in Spätantike und Frühmittelalter: Kulturgeschichte einer Region,* ed. S. Diefenbach and G. M. Müller, Millennium-Studien 43 (Berlin: de Gruyter, 2012), 255–278.

6. Salvian, *de gubernatione Dei* 7.3.14, ed. Lagarrigue, 438.

7. Salvian, *de gubernatione Dei* 7.2.8, ed. Lagarrigue, 434–436.

8. *Didache* 1, ed. J. B. Lightfoot, *The Apostolic Fathers* (Grand Rapids, MI: Baker, 1956), 123 cited in Augustine, *Enarrationes in psalmos* 102.12, ed. E. Dekkers and J. Fraipont, *Corpus Christianorum* 40 (Turnhout: Brepols 1956), 1462.

9. Salvian, *ad Ecclesiam* 3.13.57–58, ed. Lagarrigue, *Salvien de Marseille: Oeuvres* 1, Sources chrétiennes 176 (Paris: Le Cerf, 1971), 282–284.

10. Salvian, *ad Ecclesiam* 3.3.15, ed. Lagarrigue, 250.

11. Salvian, *ad Ecclesiam* 3.18.81, ed. Lagarrigue, 298.

12. I. Moreira, *Dreams, Visions and Spiritual Authority in Merovingian Gaul* (Ithaca, NY: Cornell University Press, 2002), 40. On Lérins in general, see S. Pricoco, *L'isola dei santi: Il cenobio di Lérins e le origini del monachesimo gallico* (Rome: Edizioni dell'Ateneo e Bizzarri, 1978); and A. de Vogüé, *Histoire littéraire du mouvement monastique* (Paris: Le Cerf, 2003), 7:58–180.

13. See, for example, Athanasius, *Life of Anthony* 66, Latin version ed. G.J.M. Bartelink, *Vita di Antonio*, Fondazione Lorenzo Valla (Rome: Mondadori, 1974), 128–130; Palladius, *Historia Lausiaca* 21.16–17, ed. G.J.M. Bartelink, *Palladio: La Storia Lausiaca*, Fondazione Lorenzo Valla (Rome: Mondadori, 1974), 116; *Bohairic Life of Pachomius* 88, trans. A. Veilleux *Pachomian Kononia* 1, Cistercian Studies 45 (Kalamazoo, MI: Cistercian Studies, 1980), 113–117. See also A. Recheis, *Engel, Tod und Seelenreise* (Rome: Edizioni di storia e letteratura, 1958), 169–184; and Carozzi, *Eschatologie et au-delà. Recherches sur l'Apocalypse de Paul* (Aix-en-Provence: Publications de l'Université de Provence, 1994), 81–92.

14. *Apophthegmata Patrum:* Ammonas 1: *Patrologia Graeca* 65:120A. Needless to say, this was not the only attitude of the desert monks to the Last Judgment. Some faced it with considerably more tranquility. But even those who felt more confident of God's mercy considered that meditation on "the river of fire, Tartarus and the outer darkness" was necessary for the monk. See *Apophthegmata Patrum:* Sisoes 19:397D–400A.

15. N. Constas, "'To Sleep, Perchance to Dream': The Middle State of Souls in Patristic and Byzantine Literature," in *Byzantine Eschatology: Views of Death and the Last Things, 8th to 15th Centuries*, Dumbarton Oaks Papers 55 (2001): 91–124, at 123.

16. M. Giorda, *Il regno di Dio in terra* (Rome: Edizioni di storia e letteratura, 2011), 43–67.

17. V. D. Sicard, *La liturgie de la mort dans l'église latine des origines à la réforme carolingienne*, Liturgiewissenschaftliche Quellen und Forschungen 63 (Münster: Aschendorff, 1978), 399.

18. Maximus of Turin, *Sermon* 12.2, ed. A. Mutzenbecher, *Corpus Christianorum* 23 (Turnhout: Brepols, 1962), 42.

19. *Recueil des inscriptions chrétiennes de la Gaule: Première Belgique*, ed. N. Gauthier (Paris: CNRS, 1975), no. 170, 426–430.

20. E. Diehl, *Inscriptiones Latinae Christianae Veteres* (Dublin: Weidmann, 1970), no. 1729.6.

21. See esp. S. J. Shoemaker, *Ancient Traditions of the Virgin Mary's Dormition and Assumption* (Oxford: Oxford University Press, 2004), 255 and 314–315. This earlier dating of the origin of the legend might modify the impression that a "new sense of insecurity and foreboding" in the face of death set in only after 400 AD, as is argued by Brian E. Daley in "'At the Hour of our Death': Mary's Dormition and Christian Dying in Late Patristic and Early Byzantine Literature," in *Byzantine Eschatology*, 71–89, at 74. But Daley's interpretation of the overall intention of the *Transitus Mariae* remains valid: It was circulated so as to reassure the dying that even the Virgin Mary had to pass through the terrors of death, and that she—like they—did so successfully.

22. *Transitus Mariae* 2 and 7, ed. M. Haibach-Reinisch, *Ein neue "Transitus Mariae" des Pseudo-Melito* (Rome: Bibliotheca Assumptionis Beatae Virginis Mariae, 1962), 67 and 75.

23. C. Vogel, *La discipline pénitentielle en Gaule des origines à la fin du septième siècle* (Paris: Letouzey et Ané, 1952), 157–158.

24. François Bonal, *Le temps chrétien* 3, 165 (1655), cited in H. Brémond, *Histoire du sentiment religieux en France, vol. 1: L'humanisme dévot* (Paris: Bloud et Gay, 1916), 404.

25. É. Rebillard, *In hora mortis: Évolution de la pastorale de la mort aux ive et ve siècles dans l'Occident latin*, Bibliothèque de l'École française d'Athènes et de Rome 282 (Rome: Palais Farnèse, 1994), 169–227; M. B. De Jong, "Transformations of Penance," in *Rituals of Power: From Late Antiquity to the Early Middle Ages*, ed. F. Theuws and J. L. Nelson (Leiden: Brill, 2000), 185–224; K. Uhalde, *Expectations of Justice in the Age of Augustine* (Philadephia: University of Pennsylvania Press, 2007), 105–134; and K. Uhalde "Juridical Administration in the Church and Pastoral Care in Late Antiquity," in *A New History of Penance*, ed. Abigail Firey (Leiden: Brill, 2008), 97–120.

26. *Vita Eutropii* 4, *Acta Sanctorum Mai. VI* (Paris: Victor Palmé, 1866), 693E.

27. I owe the term to P-G. Delage, "Le canon 13 de Sardique ou Les inquiétudes d'évêques d'origine modeste," in *Les Pères de l'Église et la voix des pauvres*, ed. P.-G. Delage (La Rochelle: Histoire et Culture,

2006), 55–74, at 73. For the tensions created by the emergence of monk-bishops from Lérins, see Brown,"*Through the Eye of a Needle*," 412–414 and 419–428.

28. Hilarius, *Vita Honorati* 17, ed. S. Cavallin, *Vitae Sanctorum Honorati et Hilarii episcoporum Arelatensium* (Lund: Gleerup, 1952), 54.

29. Hilarius, *Vita Honorati* 17, ed. Cavallin, 61.

30. Hilarius, *Vita Honorati* 28, ed. Cavallin, 69.

31. Julianus Pomerius, *de vita contemplativa* 2.9, *Patrologia Latina* 59:454A.

32. Juianus Pomerius, *de vita contemplativa* 2.9, 453C.

33. Honoratus of Marseilles, *Vita Hilarii* 16 and 18, ed. S. Cavallin, *Vitae Sanctorum Honorati et Hilarii* (Lund: Gleerup, 1952), 94–95 and 96.

34. See esp. R. Barcellona, *Fausto di Riez interprete del suo tempo: Un vescovo tardoantico dentro le crisi dell'impero* (Soveria Mannelli: Rubettino, 2006).

35. Faustus of Riez, *de gratia*, ed. A. Engelbrecht, *Corpus Scriptorum Ecclesiasticorum Latinorum* 21 (Vienna: Tempsky, 1891), 3–98; and *Letter* 1, 161–168.

36. Faustus of Riez, *Letter* 3, ed. Engelbrecht, 168–181.

37. Faustus of Riez, *Letters* 4–5, ed. Engelbrecht, 181–195, to Paulinus of Bordeaux; *Letter* 6, 195–200, to Felix.

38. Sidonius Apollinaris, *Carmen* 16.117, ed. and trans. W. B. Anderson, Loeb Classical Library (Cambridge, MA: Harvard University Press, 1956), 1: 252.

39. C. Leyser, "Semi-Pelagianism," in *Augustine through the Ages: An Encyclopedia*, ed. A. D. Fitzgerald (Grand Rapids, MI: Eerdmans, 1999), 761–766, at 764; Brown, *"Through the Eye of a Needle,"* 428–430.

40. Faustus of Riez, *de gratia*, prolog. 3, ed. Engelbrecht, 20.

41. Faustus of Riez, *de gratia* 1.10, ed. Engelbrecht, 35.

42. Gennadius of Marseilles, *de viris illustribus* 86.

43. Faustus of Riez, *Letter* 6, ed. Engelbrecht, 197.

44. Faustus of Riez, *Letter* 9, ed. Engelbrecht, 216.

45. Faustus of Riez, *Letter* 6, ed. Engelbrecht, 196.

46. Faustus of Riez, *Letter* 5, ed. Engelbrecht, 183. See D. J. Nodes, *"De subitanea paenitentia* in Letters of Faustus of Riez and Avitus of Vienne," *Recherches de théologie ancienne et médiévale* 55 (1988): 30–40.

47. Faustus of Riez, *Letter* 3, ed. Engelbrecht, 175, citing John Cassian, *Conferences* 7.13. For the extent of Faustus's dependence on Cassian, see esp. C. M. Kasper, *Theologie und Askese: die Spiritualität des Inselmönchtums von Lérins im 5. Jahrhundert* (Münster: Aschendorff, 1991), 139–145.

48. Faustus of Riez, *de spiritu sancto* 2, 1, ed. Engelbrecht, 132–133 and Cassian, *Conferences* 7.15.

49. Faustus of Riez, *Letter* 5, ed. Engelbrecht, 195.

50. See esp. E. L. Fortin, *Christianisme et culture philosophique au cinquième siècle: La querelle de l'âme humaine en Occident* (Paris: Études Augustiniennes, 1959); and M. Di Marco, *La polemica sull'anima tra [Fausto di Riez] e Claudiano Mamerto,* Studia Ephemeridis Augustinianum 51 (Rome: Institutum Pontificium Augustinianum, 1995).

51. Claudianus Mamertus, *de statu animae* 2.7 and 2.9, ed. A. Engelbrecht, *Corpus Scriptorum Ecclesiasticorum Latinorum* 11 (Vienna: Gerold, 1885), 128 and 133.

52. See esp. G. Smith, "Physics and Metaphysics," *The Oxford Handbook of Late Antiquity,* ed. S. Johnson (Oxford: Oxford University Press, 2012), 513–561, at 539, for the very real mental reservations of contemporary thinkers on the extreme "immaterialism" of Plotinus and Augustine.

53. Tertullian, *de anima* 7, ed. J. H. Waszink, *Corpus Christianorum* 2 (Turnhout: Brepols, 1954), 790. See P. Kitzler, *"Nihil enim anima si non corpus.* Tertullian und die Körperlichkeit der Seele," *Wiener Studien* 122 (2009): 145–169.

54. Faustus of Riez, *Letter* 3, ed. Engelbrecht, 177–178.

55. See esp. W. Klingshirn, *Caesarius of Arles: The Making of a Christian Community in Late Antique Gaul* (Cambridge: Cambridge University Press, 1994); R. A. Markus, *The End of Ancient Christianity* (Cambridge: Cambridge University Press, 1990), 202–208.

56. R. H. Weaver, *Divine Grace and Human Agency: A Study of the Semi-Pelagian Controversy* (Macon, GA: Mercer University Press, 1996); Leyser, "Semi-Pelagianism," 764–765.

57. *Vita Caesarii* 2.32, trans. W. Klingshirn, *Caesarius of Arles: Life, Testament, Letters* (Liverpool: Liverpool University Press, 1994), 58. See esp. Klingshirn, *Caesarius of Arles: The Making,* 146–170.

58. *Vita Caesarii* 1.27, trans. Klingshirn, 22.

59. *Vita Caesarii* 1.61, trans. Klingshirn, 41.

60. Klingshirn, *Caesarius of Arles*, 201–243.

61. L. K. Bailey, *Christianity's Quiet Success: The Eusebius Gallicanus Sermon Collection and the Power of the Church in Late Antique Gaul* (Notre Dame, IN: Notre Dame University Press, 2010), 96–104

62. *Vita Caesarii* 2.6, trans. Klingshirn, 46.

63. Patricius, *Confessio* 4.18, ed. L. Bieler, *Liber epistolarum sancti Patricii episcopi* (Dublin: Royal Irish Academy, 1993), 59. See T. O'Loughlin, *Discovering Saint Patrick* (Mahwah, NJ: Paulist Press, 2005), 81.

64. C. Carozzi, *Eschatologie et au-delà*, 11–12 ; L. Jiroušková, *Die Visio Pauli: Wege und Wandlungen einer orientalischen Apokryphe im lateinischen Mittelalter* (Leiden: Brill, 2006), 5–20; I. Moreira, *Heaven's Purge: Purgatory in Late Antiquity* (Oxford: Oxford University Press, 2012), 39–62.

65. Caesarius, *Sermo* 20, ed. G. Morin, *Corpus Christianorum* 103 (Turnhout: Brepols, 1953), 91–94; see B. Fischer, *"Impedimenta mundi faciunt eos miseros," Vigiliae Christianae* 5 (1951): 84–87.

66. *Visio Pauli* 4, ed. Carozzi, *Eschatologie et au-delà*, 188.

67. *Vitae Patrum Jurensium* 2 (93), ed. F. Martine, *Vies des Pères du Jura*, Sources chrétiennes 142 (Paris: Le Cerf, 1968), 338.

68. Brown, *"Through the Eye of a Needle,"* 392–406.

69. I have discussed this mistaken view and preferable alternatives to it in my preface to the Tenth Anniversary Revised Edition of *The Rise of Western Christendom: Triumph and Diversity, A.D. 200–1000* (Oxford: Wiley-Blackwelll, 2013), xxii–xxxiii.

70. C. Wickham, *Framing the Early Middle Ages: Europe and the Mediterranean, 400–800* (Oxford: Oxford University Press, 2005), 168–203 and 794–803; J. Banaji, "Aristocracies, Peasantries and the Framing of the Early Middle Ages," *Journal of Agrarian Change* 9 (2009): 59–91. See also R. Naismith, "Gold Coinage and Its Use in the Post-Roman West," *Speculum* 89 (2014): 273–306, at 289–300.

71. S. Esders, *Sacramentum fidelitatis: Treueid, Militärwesen und Formierung mittelalterlicher Staatlichkeit* (Berlin: de Gruyter, forthcoming). See also J. Kreiner, "About the Bishop: The Episcopal Entourage and the Economy of Government in Post-Roman Gaul," *Speculum* 86 (2011): 321–360.

72. Banaji, "Aristocracies," 64.

73. The situation is well described by B. Dumézil in *Les racines chrétiennes de l'Europe: Conversion et liberté dans les royaumes barbares, v^e–viiie siècle* (Paris: Fayard, 2005), 226.

74. *Praeceptum* of Childebert (511–558), ed. A. Boretius, *Capitularia Regum Francorum: Monumenta Germaniae Historica: Legum Sectio* 2.1 (Hannover: Hahn, 1883), 2.

75. *Edict* of Guntram (585), ed. Boretius, *Capitularia*, 11; trans. J. N. Hillgarth, *Christianity and Paganism, 350–750: The Conversion of Western Europe* (Philadelphia: University of Pennsylvania Press, 1986), 96.

76. R. Dworkin, *Justice in Robes* (Cambridge, MA: Harvard University Press, 2006), 5.

77. See esp. K. Ubl, *Inzestverbot und Gesetzgebung: Die Konstruktion eines Verbrechens (300–1100)*, Millennium-Studien 20 (Berlin: de Gruyter, 2008), 115–213.

Chapter 5 THE OTHER WORLD IN THIS WORLD

1. From a superabundant literature, see esp. I. N. Wood, *Gregory of Tours*, Headstart History Papers (Bangor: Headstart History, 1994); M. Heinzelmann, *Gregory of Tours: History and Society in the Sixth Century*, trans. C. Carroll (Cambridge: Cambridge University Press, 2001); and K. Mitchell and I. N. Wood, eds., *The World of Gregory of Tours* (Leiden: Brill, 2002).

2. For a criticism of this consensus and a statement of the case for a single time of composition after 585, see A. C. Murray, "Chronology and the Composition of the *Histories* of Gregory of Tours," *Journal of Late Antiquity* 1 (2008): 157–196.

3. Gregory of Tours, *Libri historiarum* [henceforth *Histories*] 10.31, ed. B. Krusch and W. Levison, *Monumenta Germaniae Historica: Scriptores Rerum Merowingicarum* 1:1 (Hannover: Hahn, 1937–1951), 535–536; trans. L. Thorpe, *Gregory of Tours: History of the Franks* (London: Penguin, 1974), 603. [Henceforth I shall cite the works of Gregory without mention of the author's name. I will cite the various books of the *Libri miraculorum* by their Latin titles].

4. I. Wood, *The Merovingian Kingdoms* (London: Longman, 1994), 89.

5. *Histories* 5.4, 199; trans. Thorpe, 258.

6. G. Halsall, "The Preface to Book V of Gregory's *Histories:* Its Form, Context and Significance," *English Historical Review* 122 (2007): 297–317, at 310.

7. *Histories* 5, "Preface," 193; trans. Thorpe, 253–254.

8. *Epistulae Austrasiacae* 9.1, ed. W. Gundlach, *Corpus Christianorum* 117 (Turnhout: Brepols, 1957), 424.

9. W. Goffart, *Narrators of Barbarian History (AD 550–800): Jordanes, Gregory of Tours, Bede and Paul the Deacon* (Princeton, NJ: Princeton University Press, 1988; 2nd ed., Notre Dame, IN: Notre Dame University Press, 2005), 117–119.

10. H. Reimitz, *Frankish Identity and Western Ethnicity* (Cambridge: Cambridge University Press, forthcoming).

11. *Histories* 4.51, 189–190; trans. Thorpe, 249.

12. On evidence for the circulation of versions of the *Visio Pauli* in Merovingian Gaul, see M. Heinzelmann, "L'hagiographie mérovingienne: Panorama des documents potentiels," *L'hagiographie mérovingienne à travers ses réécritures,* ed. M. Goulet, M. Heinzelmann, C. Veyrarel-Cosme, Beiheft der *Francia* 71 (Ostfildern: Thorbecke, 2010), 27–83, at 77, n. 223.

13. *Histories* 1, "Preface," 3; trans. Thorpe, 67.

14. R. Buchner (revising W. Giesebrecht), *Gregor von Tours: Zehn Bücher Geschichten* (Berlin: Rütten and Loening, 1955), 6; trans. Thorpe, *Gregory of Tours,* 67.

15. Salvian, *ad Ecclesiam* 2.12.59, ed. G. Lagarrigue, *Salvien de Marseille: Oeuvres* 1, Sources chrétiennes 176 (Paris: Le Cerf, 1971), 141. Cf. *Sortes Sangallenses* 33. R8: "*habebis spem fidei, sed de desperato*" ("from someone you did not expect"), in A. Dold, *Die Orakelsprüchn im St. Galler Palimpsestcodex 908, Österreichische Akademie der Wissenschaften: Sitzungsberichte* 225:4 (1948), 24 and note on 110.

16. Marculf, *Formulae* 2.3, trans. A. Rio, *The Formularies of Angers and Marculf: Two Merovingian Legal Handbooks* (Liverpool: Liverpool University Press, 2008), 184.

17. B. Dumézil, *Les racines chrétiennes de l'Europe. Conversion et liberté dans les royaumes barbares, v^e —viiie siècle* (Paris: Fayard, 2005), 375; on the "clericalization" of society as one of the ideals of Gregory, see Heinzelmann, *Gregory of Tours,* 176–181.

18. *Histories* 10.13, 496–500, trans. Thorpe, 560–566.

19. *Histories* 10.13, 498, trans. Thorpe, 563.

20. Theodoret of Cyrrhus, *Eranistes,* Dialogue 3 (260), ed. G. H. Ettlinger (Oxford: Clarendon Press, 1975), 214.27.

21. M. Dal Santo, *Debating Saints' Cults in the Age of Gregory the Great* (Cambridge: Cambridge University Press, 2012), 23–83 and 158.

22. Heinzelmann, "L'hagiographie mérovingienne," 31–32.

23. *De virtutibus sancti Martini* 3.1, ed. B. Krusch, *Gregorii episcopi Turonensis Miracula et Opera Minora: Scriptores Rerum Merowingicarum* 1:12 (Hannover: Hahn, 1885), 182; trans. R. Van Dam, *Saints and Their Miracles in Late Antique Gaul* (Princeton, NJ: Princeton University Press, 1993), 260.

24. *Histories* 10.29, 524 ; trans. Thorpe, 591.

25. *De virtutibus sancti Martini* 2.43 and 55, 175 and 178; trans. Van Dam, 251 and 255–256.

26. *Vita Patrum* 7.3, 238, trans. E. A. James, *Life of the Fathers* (Liverpool: Liverpool University Press, 1985), 62.

27. Sulpicius Severus, *Letter* 3.15–16, ed. J. Fontaine, *Sulpice Sévère: Vie de Saint Martin,* Sources chrétiennes 133 (Paris: Le Cerf, 1967), 342.

28. *De virtutibus sancti Martini* 1.4, 140; trans. Van Dam, 206.

29. *De gloria confessorum* 5, 501; trans. Van Dam, *Gregory of Tours: Glory of the Confessors* (Liverpool: Liverpool University Press, 1988), 22–23.

30. Augustine, *de civitate Dei* 21.17–27, ed. B. Dombart and A. Kalb, *Corpus Christianorum* 48 (Turnhout: Brepols, 1955), 783–805.

31. *De virtutibus sancti Martini* 2.60, 180; trans. Van Dam, 134.

32. *De gloria martyrum* 106, 111, trans. R. Van Dam, *Gregory of Tours: The Glory of the Martyrs* (Liverpool: Liverpool University Press, 1988), 134.

33. *pro remedio animae: Miracula sancti Juliani* 14, 120; trans. Van Dam, *Saints and Their Miracles,* 173; *Histories* 9.26, 445, trans. Thorpe, 513; and *Histories* 9.42, 472; trans. Thorpe, 536.

34. M. Weidemann, *Das Testament des Bischofs Bertram von Le Mans vom 27. März 616: Untersuchungen zu Besitz und Geschichte einer fränkischen Familie im 6. und 7. Jahrhundert,* Römisch-germanisches Zentralmuseum. Monographien 9 (Mainz: R. Habelt, 1986), 11; see also M. Borgolte, *"Felix est homo ille qui amicos bonos relinquit:* Zur sozialen Gestaltungskraft

letztwilliger Verfügungen am Beispiel Bischofs Bertram von Le Mans (616)," in *Festschrift für Berent Schwineköper*, ed. H. Maurer and H. Patze (Sigmaringen: J. Thorbecke, 1982), 5–18, at 7. See also I. N. Wood, "Entrusting Western Europe to the Church," in *Transactions of the Royal Historical Society* (forthcoming).

35. S. Diefenbach, "'Bischofsherrschaft': Zur Transformation der politischen Kultur im spätantiken und frühmittelalterlichen Gallien," in *Gallien in Spätantike und Frühmittelalter: Kulturgeschichte einer Region*, ed. S. Diefenbach and M. Müller, Millennium-Studien 43 (Berlin: de Gruyter, 2012), 91–149.

36. Diefenbach, "'Bischofsherrschaft,'" 113–115.

37. Brown, "*Through the Eye of a Needle*," 494–498.

38. M. Heinzelmann, *Bischofsherrschaften in Gallien: Zur Kontinuität römischer Führungsschichten vom 5. bis 7. Jahrhundert*, Beihefte der *Francia* 5 (Munich: Artemis Verlag, 1976).

39. S. Patzold, "Zur Sozialstruktur des Episkopats und zur Ausbildung bischöflicher Herrschaft in Gallien zwischen Spätantike und Frühmittelalter," in *Völker, Reiche und Namen im Frühmittelalter*, ed. M. Becher and S. Dick (Munich: W. Fink, 2010), 121–140.

40. *Histories* 8.6, 375; trans. Thorpe, 438. See Diefenbach, "'Bischofsherrschaft,'" 102.

41. *Miracula sancti Juliani* 17, 122; trans. Van Dam, *Saints and Their Miracles*, 176–177.

42. *Vita Patrum* 4.4, 226; trans. James, 46.

43. Brown, "*Through the Eye of a Needle*," 506–509.

44. For example, *Histories* 9.42, 472, trans. Thorpe, 536.

45. Borgolte, "*Felix est ille homo*," 13; T. Sternberg, *Orientalium more secutus: Räume und Institutionen der Caritas des 5. bis 7. Jahrhunderts in Gallien*, Jahrbuch für Antike und Christentum, Ergänzungsband 16 (Münster: Aschendorff, 1991), 126–135.

46. See esp. G. de Nie, *Views from a Many-Windowed Tower: Studies of Imagination in the Works of Gregory of Tours* (Amsterdam: Rodopi, 1987), 27–57.

47. *Histories* 5.34, 239–294; trans. Thorpe, 297.

48. See J. Baschet, *Les Justices de l'au delà: Les représentations de l'enfer en France et en Italie, xiie–xive siècle*, Bibliothèque de l'École française

d'Athènes et de Rome 279 (Paris: de Boccard, 1993), 146–163, on the special conditions at Conques at the time of the Peace of God.

49. See esp. G. de Nie, "History and Miracle: Gregory's Use of Metaphor," in *The World of Gregory of Tours*, 261–279. On the predecessors of Gregory, see G. de Nie, *Poetics of Wonder: Testimonies of the New Christian Miracles in the Late Antique Latin World* (Turnhout: Brepols, 2011), 431–486.

50. On paralysis: *De gloria confessorum* 73, 357; trans. Van Dam, 97; on fever: *de virtutibus sancti Martini* 4.37, 209; trans. Van Dam, 300. See also de Nie, *Poetics of Wonder*, 162–164; A. Rousselle, *Croire et guérir: La foi en Gaule dans l'antiquité tardive* (Paris: Fayard, 1990), 96–97 and 115.

51. *De virtutibus sancti Martini* 3, "Preface," 182 ; trans. Van Dam, 206.

52. *De virtutibus sancti Martini* 4, "Preface," 199; trans. Van Dam, 285.

53. de Nie, *Views from a Many-Windowed Tower*, 161.

54. *De gloria confessorum* 93, 357; trans. Van Dam, 97.

55. Diefenbach, "'Bischofsherrschaft,'" 127, note 153, referring to the classic study of F. Graus, "Die Gewalt bei den Anfängen des Feudalismus und die 'Gefangenenbefreiungen' der merowingischen Hagiographie," in *Jahrbuch für Wirtschaftsgeschichte 1961*, 61–156.

56. *De virtutibus sancti Martini* 1.23, 150; trans. Van Dam, 219.

57. *Histories* 4.49, 186; trans. Thorpe, 246; *De virtutibus sancti Martini* 2.7, 161; trans. Van Dam, 232.

58. *De virtutibus sancti Martini* 1.23, 150; trans. Van Dam, 219.

59. *Histories* 5, "Preface," 194, trans. Thorpe, 245.

EPILOGUE

1. D. Bullough, "The Career of Columbanus," in *Columbanus: Studies in the Latin Writings*, ed. M. Lapidge, Studies in Celtic History (Woodbridge: Boydell, 1997), 1–28; P. Brown, *The Rise of Western Christendom: Triumph and Diversity, A.D. 200–1000*, 10th anniv. rev. ed. (Oxford: Wiley-Blackwell, 2013), 248–252. See also T. Leso, "Columbanus in Europe: The Evidence of the *Epistulae*," *Early Medieval Europe* 21 (2013): 358–389, esp. 363–368.

2. See the exhaustive study of Y. Fox, "Columbanian Monasticism and Frankish Aristocracy: Power and Religion in Merovingian Gaul" (PhD diss., Open University of Israel). I owe access to this dissertation

and to that of A. O'Hara (at note 13) to the kindness of Professor Helmut Reimitz.

3. E. James, "Archaeology and the Merovingian Monastery," in *Columbanus and Merovingian Monasticism,* ed. H. B. Clarke and M. Brennan, BAR International Series 113 (Oxford: Oxbow, 1981), 33–55.

4. Columbanus, *Instructiones* 2.1, ed. G. S. M. Walker, *Sancti Columbani Opera,* Scriptores Latini Hiberniae 2 (Dublin: Dublin Institute for Advanced Studies, 1970), 68.8. For the survival of the *Letters* of Faustus in southwest Gaul in a "literary cum family circle" that looked back to friends of the friends of Sidonius Apollinaris, see R. W. Mathisen, "The *Codex Sangallensis* and the Transmission of the Classical Tradition," *International Journal of the Classical Tradition* 5 (1998): 163–194, at 173.

5. Walker, *Sancti Columbani Opera,* lxxxi.

6. Columbanus, *Epistulae* 2.2, ed. Walker, 12.23.

7. C. Stancliffe, "The Thirteen Sermons Attributed to Columbanus and the Question of Their Authorship," in Lapidge, *Columbanus,* 93–202.

8. Columbanus, *Instructiones* 2.1, ed. Walker, 66.23.

9. Columbanus, *Instructiones* 1.4, ed. Walker, 64.4.

10. Columbanus, *Instructiones* 1.3, ed. Walker, 62.20.

11. Columbanus, *Instructiones* 1.5, ed. Walker, 66.11.

12. Columbanus, *Instructiones* 12.2, ed. Walker, 114.1.

13. C. Stancliffe, "Jonas' *Life of Columbanus and His Disciples,*" in *Studies in Irish Hagiography: Saints and Scholars,* ed. J. Carey, M. Herbert, and P. Ó Riain (Dublin: Four Courts Press, 2001), 189–220, at 205–219. See also A. O'Hara, "Jonas of Bobbio and the *Vita Columbani:* Saints and Community in the Seventh Century" (PhD diss., University of St. Andrew's, 2009).

14. Stancliffe, "The Thirteen Sermons," 114–115 and 138–141.

15. Columbanus, *Instructiones* 7.1, ed. Walker, 90.4.

16. Columbanus, *Regula Monachorum* 10, ed. Walker, 140.22. It is not certain that this section was written by Columbanus, but it condenses forcefully his extreme valuation of obedience.

17. J. Stephenson, "The Monastic Rules of Columbanus," in Lapidge, *Columbanus,* 203–216, at 210. See also C. Stancliffe, "Columbanus' Monasticism and the Sources of his Inspiration: From Basil to the Master?," in

Tome: Studies in Medieval Celtic History and Law in Honour of Thomas Charles-Edwards, ed. F. Edmonds and P. Russell, Studies in Celtic History (Woodbridge: Boydell, 2011), 17–28.

18. Jonas, *Vita Columbani* 1.2, ed. B. Krusch, *Monumenta Germaniae Historica: Scriptorum Rerum Merovingicarum* 4 (Hannover: Hahn, 1902), 78.8.

19. Columbanus, *Regula Monachorum* 9, ed. Walker, 138.6.

20. Bullough, "The Career of Columbanus," 8; see also T. M. Charles-Edwards, "The Penitential of Columbanus," in Lapidge, *Columbanus*, 217–239. In general, see Brown, *Rise of Western Christendom*, 241–246.

21. C. Etchingham, *Church Order in Ireland, A.D. 650–1000* (Maynooth: Department of Old and Middle Irish, St. Patrick's College, 1999), 291–318.

22. G. Muschiol, *Famula Dei: Zur Liturgie in merovingischen Frauenklöstern* (Münster: Ashendorff, 1994), 222–263.

23. See, for example, Jonas, *Vita Columbani* 2.19, ed. Krusch, 140; trans. J. A. McNamara and J. E. Halborg, *Sainted Women of the Dark Ages* (Durham, NC: Duke University Press, 1992), 171–173.

24. A. Diem, "Van liefde, vrees en zwijgen. Emoties en 'emotioneel beleid' in vroegmiddeleuwse Kloosters," *Groniek. Historisch Tijdschrift* 173 (2006): 409–429, at 410.

25. Columbanus, *Regula Monachorum* 5, ed. Walker, 128.9.

26. P. Brown, "Relics and Social Status in the Age of Gregory of Tours," in *Society and the Holy in Late Antiquity* (Berkeley: University of California Press, 1982), 222–250, at 243–245.

27. *Regula cuiusdam patris ad virgines*, 4.11 and 19, *Patrologia Latina* 88:1057D.

28. *Life of Wandregisil* 7; B. Effros, "Symbolic Expressions of Sanctity: Gertrude of Nivelles in the Context of Merovingian Mortuary Custom," *Viator* 27 (1996): 1–10.

29. A.-M. Helvétius, "Hagiographie et formation politique des aristocrates dans le monde franc (vii\u1d49—viii\u1d49 siècle)," *Historiographie, idéologie et politique au Moyen Âge*, ed. E. Bozóky, Hagiologia 8 (Turnhout: Brepols, 2012), 59–80. For a description of one such circle of "Romans" in southwest Gaul, see R. W. Mathisen, "Desiderius of Cahors: Last of the Romans," in *Gallien in Spätantike und Frühmittelalter. Kulturgeschichte einer Region,*

ed. S. Diefenbach and G. M. Müller, Millennium-Studien 43 (Berlin: de Gruyter, 2012), 455–469; and B. Rosenwein, *Emotional Communities in the Early Middle Ages* (Ithaca, NY: Cornell University Press, 2006), 130–142, esp. n. 39 on 139.

30. See J. Kreiner, "About the Bishop: The Episcopal Entourage and the Economy of Government in Post-Roman Gaul," *Speculum* 86 (2011): 321–360; and Kreiner, *The Social Life of Historiography in the Merovingian Kingdom* (Cambridge: Cambridge University Press, 2014).

31. A. Diem, "Monks, Kings, and the Transformation of Sanctity: Jonas of Bobbio and the End of the Holy Man," *Speculum* 82 (2007): 521–559.

32. I. Silber, *Virtuosity, Charisma and Social Order: A Comparative Study of Theravada Buddhism and Medieval Catholicism* (Cambridge: Cambridge University Press, 1995), 254.

33. Ibid.

34. R. Le Jan, "Convents, Violence and Competition in Seventh-Century Francia," in *Topographies of Power in the Early Middle Ages*, ed. M. De Jong and F. Theuws, with C. Van Rijn (Leiden: Brill, 2001), 243–270, at 262.

35. Brown, *Rise of Western Christendom*, 255.

36. Brown, *Rise of Western Christendom*, 228–231 and 255; Muschiol, *Famula Dei*, 179–191.

37. *Vita Eligii: Carta Cessionis* 3, ed. Krusch, *Monumenta Germaniae Historica*, 747.10 (donated to the monastery of Solignac, near Limoges).

38. J. Kreiner, "Autopsies and Philosophies of a Merovingian Life: Death, Responsibility, Salvation," *Journal of Early Christian Studies* 22 (2014): 113–152, at 120.

39. Jonas, *Vita Columbani* 2.11, ed. Krusch, 131.1: trans. McNamara and Halborg, 162. See the entries on *discussio* in the *Theodosian Code* and the *Novellae*, in O. Gradenwitz, *Heidelberger Index zum Theodosianus* (Berlin: Weidmann, 1925), 64; and *Ergänzungsband* (Berlin: Weidmann, 1929), 21.

40. Jonas, *Vita Columbani* 2.11, ed. Krusch, 131.1; trans. McNamara and Halborg, 162.

41. Jonas, *Vita Columbani* 2.11, ed. Krusch, 131.10; trans. McNamara and Halborg, 163.

42. Jonas, *Vita Columbani* 2.12, ed. Krusch, 132.20; trans. McNamara and Halborg, 164.

43. Jonas, *Vita Columbani* 2.12, ed. Krusch, 132.23; trans. McNamara and Halborg, 164.

44. J. Assmann, *Death and Salvation in Ancient Egypt* (Ithaca, NY: Cornell University Press, 2005), 149.

45. Jonas, *Vita Columbani* 2.19, ed. Krusch, 140.1; trans. McNamara and Halborg, 172.

46. Jonas, *Vita Columbani* 2.15, ed. Krusch, 135.18; trans. McNamara and Halborg, 167.

47. Jonas, *Vita Columbani* 2.15, ed. Krusch, 135.19; trans. McNamara and Halborg, 167.

48. See esp. C. Carozzi, *Le voyage de l'âme dans l'au-delà d'après la littérature latine (v^e—xiiie siècle)*, Collection de l'École française de Rome 189 (Rome: Palais Farnèse, 1994), 99–138 (on Fursa) and 139–186 (on Barontus). The two visions are edited with an Italian translation by M. P. Ciccarese, *Visioni dell'Aldilà in Occidente* (Florence: Nardini, 1987), 184–275. See also Y. Hen, "The Structure and Aims of the *Visio Baronti*," *Journal of Theological Studies* 47 (1996): 477–497; J. J. Contreni, "'Building Mansions in Heaven': The *Visio Baronti*, the Archangel Raphael, and a Carolingian King," *Speculum* 78 (2003): 673–706; I. Moreira, *Dreams, Visions and Spiritual Authority in Merovingian Gaul* (Ithaca, NY: Cornell University Press, 2000), 155–167; and I. Moreira, *Heaven's Purge: Purgatory in Late Antiquity* (Oxford: Oxford University Press, 2010), 113–145.

49. Bede, *Ecclesiastical History* 3.19, ed. B. Colgrave and R. A. B. Mynors (Oxford: Oxford University Press, 1969), 194.

50. *Visio Baronti* 12, ed. W. Levison, *Monumenta Germaniae Historica: Scriptores Rerum Merovingicarum* 5 (Hanover: Hahn, 1910), 388.10; trans. J. N. Hillgarth, *Christianity and Paganism: The Conversion of Western Europe, 350–750* (Philadelphia: University of Pennsylvania Press, 1986), 199. See Carozzi, *Le voyage de l'âme*, 141–145.

51. *Visio Baronti* 4 and 5, 380.20 and 381.7; trans. Hillgarth, 196–197.

52. *Visio Baronti* 12, 386.13; trans. Hillgarth, 199.

53. *Visio Fursei* 15.19 and 17.3, ed. Carozzi, *Le voyage de l'âme*, 691 and 692.

54. *Visio Fursei* 7.3, ed. Carozzi, 682.

55. *Visio Fursei* 7.10, ed. Carozzi, 681.

56. *Visio Fursei* 6.10, ed. Carozzi, 681.

57. *Visio Fursei* 7.2, ed. Carozzi, 682.

58. *Visio Fursei* 9.8 and 9.14, ed. Carozzi, 684.

59. *Visio Fursei* 9.14, ed. Carozzi, 684.

60. *Visio Baronti* 13, 388.12; trans. Hillgarth, 200.

61. *Visio Fursei* 9.7, ed. Carozzi, 684.

62. Jonas, *Vita Columbani* 1.19, ed. Krusch, 87.24. Note that both the vision of Fursa and the *Vita Columbani* cite *Ecclesiasticus* 34:23: *Munera impiorum reprobat Altissimus.*

63. Carozzi, *Le voyage de l'âme*, 100–102.

64. *Visio Fursei* 16.3, ed. Carozzi, 691.

65. This has been brilliantly demonstrated by I. N. Wood, "A Prelude to Columbanus: The Monastic Achievement in the Burgundian Territories," in Clarke and Brennan, *Columbanus and Merovingian Monasticism*, 3–32. An entire world of monastic foundations in Burgundy had already existed before Columbanus, but was not mentioned in our principal sources, such as Gregory of Tours.

66. F. Cumont, *Afterlife in Roman Paganism* (New Haven, CT: Yale University Press, 1922), 29.

67. J. Fontaine, "Les images virgiliennes de l'ascension céleste dans la poésie latine chrétienne," *Jenseitsvorstellungen in Antike und Christentum. Gedenkschrift für A. Stuiber*, Jahrbuch für Antike und Christentum: Ergänzungsband 9 (Münster: Aschendorff, 1982), 55–67. See, in general, R. Lattimore, *Themes in Greek and Latin Epitaphs* (Urbana: University of Illinois Press, 1962).

68. Tertullian, *de anima* 55, ed. J. H. Waszink, *Corpus Christianorum* 2 (Turnhout: Brepols, 1954), 862.

69. Cumont, *Afterlife*, 110.

70. See esp. S. MacCormack, *Shadows of Poetry: Virgil in the Mind of Augustine* (Berkeley: University of California Press, 1998), 111.

71. Augustine, *Sermon* 241.5.5, ed. *Patrologia Latina* 38:1136.

72. Cumont, *Afterlife*, 128.

73. Carozzi, *Le voyage de l'âme*, 638.

74. G. Sanders, "La perennité du message épigraphique: De la communauté chrétienne élitaire du Bas-Empire au corps professionnel de Bo-

logne," in *La terza età dell'epigrafia*, ed. A. Donati (Faenza: Fratelli Lega, 1988), 349–414, at 364.

75. Innumerable examples of *oroit do* are collected in R. A. S. Macalister, *Corpus Inscriptionum Insularum Celticarum* 2 (Dublin: Stationary Office, 1949); see also Sanders, "La perennité du message épigraphique," 385–401. For Italy, see for instance, P. Rugo, *Le iscrizioni dei secoli vi-vii-viii in Italia* (Cittadella: Bertoncello, 1975), vol. 2, no.142, 97; vol. 3 (1976), no. 28, 33 and no. 64, 53; vol. 4 (1978), no. 108, 85.

76. G. Ripoll López and I. Velázquez Soriano, "El epitafio de Trasemirus (Mandourle, Villeséque de Corbières, Aude)," *Espacio, Tiempo y Forma* 3 (1990): 273–287.

Acknowledgments

THIS BOOK IS based on lectures I delivered at the Institut für die Wissenschaften vom Menschen—the Institute for Human Sciences—in Vienna in October 2012. I look back with particular pleasure to this contact with a truly remarkable institution. My only sorrow is that I was deprived, through his illness, of the opportunity to meet its director, the late Krzyztof Michalski, whose guiding spirit was ever present in the width, the variety, and the rare commitment to serious issues that characterized the Institute. The warmth of the welcome given me by Cornelia Klinger, Klaus Nellen, and Eva Forgacs, as by other fellows and associates of the Institute, still lingers with me, as does the care with which Mary Nicklas made our journey and stay in Vienna both easy and memorable for us.

I also appreciate the zest of so many friends and colleagues (all of them long-term heroes and heroines)—Bernhard Palme,

Walter Pohl, Herwig Wolfram, Claudia Rapp, and Helmut Reimitz. Altogether, the visit gave meaning to the old Latin adage: *Ubi amici, ibi patria*—"where there are friends, there is my homeland." No adage could be more appropriate to an Institute and to a city that have long fostered the joining in friendship of so many *patriae*.

While turning these lectures into a book, I was singularly fortunate to be able to benefit constantly from the advice and criticism of Helmut Reimitz and of Jamie Kreiner. I am also particularly grateful to the anonymous readers of my manuscript. The book has emerged changed for the better on many crucial points as a result of their generous and pertinent comments.

But I owe most of all to my wife, Betsy. She has accompanied me, both in reality and in the imagination, on the many journeys that went into the making of this book. Under her alert eyes the book itself became, I trust, ever more clear, accessible, and tightly argued. It is to her that the book is dedicated.

Index